Architecture
of Middle Georgia
THE OCONEE AREA

Architecture
of Middle Georgia

THE OCONEE AREA

John Linley

University of Georgia Press

Library of Congress Catalog Card Number:
72–188569
International Standard Book Number:
0–8203–0295–3

The University of Georgia Press, Athens 30601

Dedicated to the Garden Club of Georgia which in its concern for the environment has through the years fought pollution and blight and has supported the conservation of natural resources, the restoration of beauty where it has been destroyed, the preservation of beauty where it still exists, and the creation of new forms of beauty that derive from ever-changing conditions.

The original study for this book was
sponsored by the
Oconee Area Planning and Development Commission
in cooperation with
The Institute of Community and Area Development
and the School of Environmental Design
University of Georgia

This pictorial history of the Oconee Area
is published with the hope that
it will serve as a graphic record of its past
and as such may be of help in planning its future.

Contents

Acknowledgments

This book represents the combined work of several institutions and organizations, and of many individuals. The Oconee Area Planning and Development Commission with the Institute of Community and Area Development of the University of Georgia and the School of Environmental Design of the University of Georgia were the initiating and constant sustainers of the project. The Georgia Historical Commission and the Garden Club of Georgia have encouraged its publication.

The idea for the work was originated and promoted by J. MacDonald Wray when he was executive director of the Oconee Area Planning and Development Commission, and was further fostered by his successor Eugene P. Nuss. J. W. Fanning, Vice President for Services at the University of Georgia, and Ernest E. Melvin, Director of the Institute of Community and Area Development, gave their vigorous and unceasing support. H. B. Owens, Dean of the School of Environmental Design of the University of Georgia, lent books from his personal library, arranged work loads to permit the writer to have maximum time to devote to the book, and rallied support for its publication. Mrs. Mary G. Jewett, Executive Secretary of the Georgia Historical Commission, and William R. Mitchell, Jr., Director of the Georgia Historical Commission, were particularly helpful. Mrs. James T. Anderson's endorsement and enthusiasm assured the vital support of the Garden Club of Georgia when she was president of that organization.

James C. Bonner of the Department of History and Social Science of the Georgia College at Milledgeville guided the writer to places of outstanding historical architectural significance, and furnished much of the data for the work.

Most of the photography is by Kenneth Kay or Robbie Hattaway; such are indicated by the initials of the photographer. Of those taken by the writer, many were developed by Robbie Hattaway or Kirk Prouty. These are indicated by the initials JL and RH or JL and KP.

Interested citizens of the Oconee Area spent many hours gathering data for the various buildings; other citizens graciously permitted the writer to measure and photograph their houses. Such contributions of time, work, and cooperation have been too numerous to list, but special acknowledgment must be made of the work and time contributed by Mrs. E. W. Allen, Sr., Joseph Branch, Mrs. Clay Chester, Mrs. W. I. Dixon, Murray Hall, Miss Louise Irwin, Mrs. E. M. Lancaster, Joseph T. Maddox, Mrs. G. B. Moore, Jr., Mrs. L.

Terrell Moore, Harvey J. Powell, Mrs. George Rives, W. Oscar Shivers, and Mrs. Hunter Strickland.

I wish to express my personal appreciation to the above; also to Robert J. Hill, who proposed that I be chosen to carry out this work, to Mrs. William Tate and John W. Bonner, Jr., for invaluable help in locating source materials, to Mrs. W. A. Glenn for patiently and capably seeing that the manuscript was typed and retyped through many changes, and to John C. Waters and Robert S. Gamble for their helpful criticism.

And, my belated thanks to Professor Jean Labatut, who long ago taught me to search for ageless principles which are basic to all good architecture.

Preface

This book was written with many objectives. Among these were the desires that a permanent record be made of the outstanding architecture of the area and that the attention of the citizens of this area be directed to their unique architectural heritage, with the hope of utilizing and thus saving the best architectural examples. Such an objective study of past and present architecture should be of help in the future planning of buildings and communities.

Because architecture is an all-encompassing art, a study in depth of the architecture of a community results in an atlas of that community, so this book has likewise become an atlas of the Oconee Area and includes information from the reports of studies conducted by the Oconee Area Planning and Development Commission. For the benefit of the architectural scholar, and for those who might be designing comparable buildings, dimensions of architectural features of some of the antebellum buildings have been included, usually at least one example of each development in style. Orientation of the antebellum buildings was included where it seemed significant.

The procedure for selecting the buildings to be included, and for obtaining data may be of interest. Dr. J. C. Bonner, an authority on Georgia history, listed the buildings and places which he felt were of architectural or historical significance, and located them on county maps. He also went with me to each county seat to search out local historians for further guidance. Forms requesting suggestions regarding buildings of architectural or historical significance were distributed by individuals or by clubs in communities throughout the area. With the information thus assembled, I drove to the places listed, occasionally finding other noteworthy buildings along the way. Despite this procedure, some examples of outstanding architecture were missed completely. The Sam Hollis house near Sparta, the Woodlief S. Parks and James Gilchrist houses (the latter formerly known as the B. E. Gooch place), both out of Eatonton, were among those which were discovered too late for inclusion, as was the country home of Flannery O'Connor, an old plantation located a few miles from her other home in Milledgeville.

Most of the information regarding dates, architects, and owners was assembled by interested citizens in the various communities. In Baldwin County, such data had previously been collected for most of the historic buildings, and was usually complete. In other counties, such data was rare, and there were gaps in the lists of the former owners of many of the buildings. Once started, interest in such research seemed to grow, and new information concerning the history of the buildings continued to come in; doubtless more will be forthcoming after publication of the book.

The architectural data was noted on the site. Dimensions were usually easily obtainable, though there were some difficulties. To find the diameter of round columns, a kind of caliper was improvised by using two framing squares. An extensible fishing pole served as a ruler to measure the height of tall columns. Columns on the old Governor's Mansion were so high the pole would not reach to the top, and for that reason their precise height could not be determined.

With more than two hundred houses scattered over an area of nearly three thousand miles, it was impossible to arrange a schedule to get inside every house. Residents who were at home were, in general, most gracious. Refusing southern hospitality in order to get on with the work was more of a problem than noncooperation, though the latter occasionally occurred—once or twice with belligerence.

The older houses presented a constantly varying pattern of use: some were deserted; some were occupied by tenants; some were in the process of being restored; a surprising number were kept up by owners who lived elsewhere, but who returned for occasional visits. The majority were in fair to excellent shape and were occupied by appreciative owners, some of whom were making real sacrifices to maintain the old houses. Many of the plantations were still operating, were obviously well run and apparently profitable. At one particularly pleasant farmhouse, a diesel-powered Mercedes was casually parked in a lean-to wagon shed. The explanation was that the owners spent a good part of every year in Europe, and the diesel fuel engine was an advantage there.

Unlike the houses they lived in, the owners could not be typed. All seemed individualistic, and most were delightful. Meeting the residents, studying the houses, travelling throughout the length and breadth of the Oconee Area was a sometimes frustrating, frequently enjoyable, and always rewarding experience.

It is doubtful that any two people would agree entirely about the architectural value of a large group of buildings of various ages and styles. In other places, however, it has been found that much valuable architecture has been saved by being evaluated. In Charleston, South Carolina, the buildings were divided into five groups: Nationally Important, Valuable to the City, Valuable, Notable, and Worthy of Mention. Following their guide, the writer has, with trepidation, divided those in the Oconee Area into the five groups: Nationally Important, Valuable to the Area, Valuable, Notable, and Worthy of Mention. Modern (post-1900) and recently remodeled work shown is not evaluated, since a greater lapse of time is necessary for a reasonably unbiased judgment.

The effigies known as the Rock Eagle Mounds could not be designated within the listed categories because they are of more than national importance.

This book was compiled over a period of several years and most of the information was obtained in 1968. Where changes have since occurred, they have been noted. Where they were known, dates, names of architects, names of original owners, interim owners, and present owners of the houses illustrated are given. There are omissions, and doubtless some inaccuracies, for which the writer apologizes.

John W. Linley, A.I.A.
January 1972

Introduction

For a publication entitled *Architecture of Middle Georgia: The Oconee Area* much is included that does not seem to apply to buildings, and many of the buildings illustrated are of a type not usually associated with the word "architecture."

Good architecture, however, is governed to a great degree by climate and topography, by natural resources, local industries, and native mores. For this reason, a resume of these factors is an integral part of this study, and more emphasis is placed on the viable aspects of architecture which derive from such factors than is placed on stylistic detail.

Buildings from periods such as late Victorian and early twentieth century, periods usually scoffed at, are included. It is often easy to admire the styles of the distant past but difficult to appreciate those of the immediate past. This has always been true and is reflected in the old saying that "we admire the styles of our grandfather's day, while abhorring those of our father's." We note with regret the folly of our forebears who neglected the architecture of their fathers even as we disdain the architecture of our immediate predecessors. Examples of the recent past have been included with the hope that this will lead to an appreciation of work done in an era both too near and too far away to be rightly appreciated today.

1. *The Old Capitol*, Milledgeville
   Map no. 4-1
   Photo taken about 1936 by Eberhart Studios

1. The Land That Is Oconee

The Oconee Area is in central Georgia,[1] and like the state itself, is bisected by the "fall line." In prehistoric times, the Atlantic Ocean extended to this irregular line. In a modified way the geography of the Oconee Area is a microcosm of the geography of the state. The northwestern counties are Piedmont: rolling hills and plateaus (2), sometimes forested, sometimes planted, and sometimes flaunting the rich colors of red clay subsoil. Below the fall line stretch both plains and sandhills, pastures, croplands, pine forests, and occasional areas where trees with long gray moss are reflected in dark clear waters typical of the "low country" swamps (3).

One Oconee Area county, Jasper, is bordered on the west by the Ocmulgee River, while every other county is bordered in part by the Oconee River. Downstream the two rivers merge and form the Altamaha River. There was a time when these rivers were the highways to central Georgia. Now of little use for transportation, their value to the economy and well-being of the area is greater than ever. Cities and industry are dependent upon such water supplies, and Lake Sinclair a few miles north of Milledgeville is a good example of how these rivers are serving the community.

CLIMATE

The climate of the Oconee Area may be characterized as humid and temperate but warmer than average, and much warmer during the occasional "hot spells" which occur more often in the southeastern portion of the area than in those sections above the fall line. Specific climatic data for each county is included in the chapters related to those counties.

The connection between climate and architecture is most apparent in the early architecture, particularly that of the houses built just before the Civil War. Such characteristics as separate buildings for the kitchen, large porches, open hallways, high ceilings, oversize windows and doors, louvered blinds, lattice sun screens, and a preference for white or light colors were developed in part, at least, for their cooling effect. The practice of leaving the space under the house open for the wind to blow through, and the conscious orientation and arrangement of rooms for summer breezes and winter sun are further indications of the influence of climate on antebellum architecture.

It is interesting to note that these almost forgotten aspects of early southern architecture have been forcibly brought to the attention of modern designers who have the responsibil-

2. *Uplands,* Jasper County
JL & KP

3. *Dark Waters and Spanish Moss near Ball's Ferry,* Washington County
JL & KP

ity of keeping air conditioning costs down, and that the better architects today are concerned with sun and wind control as were their antebellum predecessors.

TOPOGRAPHY, EARTH, AND MINERALS

Within the Oconee Area there is a diversity of geological features. The northern one-third of the Oconee Area, including Jasper, Putnam, and portions of Hancock and Baldwin counties, is considered part of the Georgia Piedmont. Its broadly rolling surface has developed through repeated and long continued wearing away of exposed crystalline rocks. At its southern margin the Piedmont merges with the Coastal Plain. This zone of contact between ancient crystalline rocks and younger sands and clays is called the fall line, after the waterfalls and rapids often found where streams drop from the more resistant Piedmont to the more easily eroded Coastal Plain.

Most of Washington County, southwest Wilkinson County, and all of Johnson County are in the Coastal Plain proper. This region is characterized by gently rolling hills, broad rounded summits, and overall comparative smoothness. The soils are sands and sandy loams which are white to gray in color with sandy to sandy clay subsoils. The color of the subsoil varies from the white of kaolin to gray, yellow, and pink. Gold has been found in the Oconee Area, as have semiprecious stones, and there are legends of ancient Spanish silver mines in nearby counties. It is the more mundane minerals, however, which have been of importance in shaping the economy and the architecture of the area.

Most of the brick used in pre-Civil War days was manufactured within the area, usually near the building site and of local earth, so that variations occurred because of the variation in the clays as well as in the method of manufacture. In the southern part of Jasper County much of the old brick is tan to cream in color instead of the usual range from brown to dark red. Brick, tile, and pipe are still being manufactured in Baldwin County.

Lime for mortar and plaster was formerly obtained from lime sinks existing in the area. Remains of prehistoric fossils have been found in and near the lime sinks. Deposits of phosphate also have been found. Local granite has been used continuously since before the Civil War. In important buildings such as the Masonic Hall in Milledgeville, granite was frequently used from the footing to floor level, being more frost resistant than brick. It was also used extensively for lintels and for steps, and in some instances for all exterior walls. Granite quarries in Hancock County are still producing both

4. *Maypop Bloom*
   JL & RH

blocks and crushed stone, and are world famous as a source of rare pink granite. Blue chalk, bauxite, and fuller's earth were formerly mined in the Oconee Area. Feldspar is mined at an open pit operation in Jasper County, fireclay is mined in Wilkinson County, and chalk is mined in Washington County. Economically overshadowing these operations is the kaolin mining and processing industry of Washington and Wilkinson counties.

Flora and fauna

Most of the land in the Oconee Area was once densely forested, with pines predominating in the Coastal Plain and hardwoods in the Piedmont. The great naturalist, William Bartram, who travelled through the region in 1775, left a detailed description of the flora and fauna of that time in his book *Travels*. Since then the forests have been cleared and the land cultivated. Now the cycle is being completed with the reestablishment of a predominant forest cover, this time mostly pine in the Piedmont as well as in the Coastal Plain. Moist bottomlands throughout the area contain a variety of hardwoods, including black and tupelo gum, cypress, ash, maple and bottomland oaks.

As is true of most of the eastern part of the United States, spring is heralded in the Oconee Area by budding deciduous trees and by the pale reds, greens, and yellows of maple blossoms. Pink wisps of the redbud, then the dogwood contrast with the dark evergreens. Scattered throughout the area is the Carolina jessamine, an evergreen vine with masses of yellow flowers that have the scent of violets. In late spring the honeysuckle begins its long season of blooming. Along the rivers and in undisturbed woods rare wild flowers grow. Roadside flowers abound in summer. Daisies and Queen Anne's lace, little white asters and brilliant purple verbena, black-eyed susans and the orange butterfly weed are common throughout the area. Common also is the moon vine with large white morning glory-like blooms, and the trumpet vine with yellow, orange, or red trumpet-shaped flowers. Wild plums and blackberries thrive in the abandoned fields.

A favorite with children is the maypop (4), whose bloom is known as the passion flower and which has the botanical name of *passiflora incarnata*. It is a small vine which spreads over the ground, and has spectacular bluish-purple flowers with globular yellow centers. The fringe of colored filaments inside the petals has been compared to the crown of thorns, while other parts of the bloom have been considered emblematic of implements of the crucifixion, thus the name "passion flower." Children tie the fringe-like petals down as

5. *Muscadine Vine*
   RH

6. *Cherokee Rose*
   JL & RH

7. *Kudzu*
JL & KP

8. *Bitterweed*
JL & KP

they do hollyhock blossoms, to make "maypop ladies" with long fringed, Hawaiian skirts. The fruit, or maypop, is ovoid and dark green until ripe. It pops delightfully when thrown against the hard earth, thus the name "maypop." It has a bittersweet taste when ripe which adults dislike but loyal children profess to enjoy.

Fall color comes to the Oconee Area with goldenrod and autumn foliage, and comes with special brilliance to the swamps and lowlands of the Coastal Plain. Muscadines (5) and scuppernongs, the most delicious of the wild grapes, ripen in September. They are native only to the Southeast, and have a wild, woodsy flavor that is different from but reminiscent of the crushed leaf buds of the hickory tree, or of pine needles warmed by the sun. They are much used for making wine, but their unique fragrance and flavor is lost in the process.

The predominance of evergreens lends life to the woods and swamps even during winter. Besides the pines, cedars, magnolias, laurels, and live oaks, there is the American holly with its red berries, and that loveliest of parasites, the mistletoe, with ivory-colored, translucent berries like clusters of pearls. In contrast to the evergreens, are tawny fields of broomsedge, a tall grass that ripples in the breeze and seems to store and reflect the light and warmth of the winter sun.

Some of the plants which are now a familiar part of the Oconee landscape are not native. The Cherokee Rose (6), whose Indian name sounds so American and which is the state flower of Georgia, is said to be an import from China. Long escaped from cultivation, it thrives particularly in the old fields and along the roads of Jasper County. The soft pink or mauve trees which in summer blend into the landscape of plantations and farms are crape myrtles in bloom, another import. Newer colors ranging from pure white to garish pink have been developed. The sculpturesque beauty of its trunk when allowed to grow naturally, and the brilliance of its autumn foliage are less publicized qualities.

A more questionable import is kudzu (7), a rampant vine which has been planted extensively both as cattle food and to stop soil erosion. Where allowed to grow unchecked, it has spread to cover trees, forests, and even houses. Its rich foliage is gorgeous in summer, but menacing as it spreads across the landscape. Another questionable import is the bitterweed [*helenium amarum*] (8), supposed to have been imported for medicinal purpose for cattle. Its odor is spicy and acrid. Dairy cattle seem to have a particular fondness for the plant, a weed which imparts an unpleasant flavor to milk. Like wild onions, another import, it is a bane to farmers. Few weeds are so persistent, and despite the low regard in which it is held, few flowers are so brilliant. And to the unprejudiced eye, few scenes are so radiant as a field of golden bitterweed.

Early reports indicate that there were once buffalo, bears, panthers, and wolves in the Oconee Area. Deer and wild turkeys were plentiful, and game was an important source of food and revenue. As the land was increasingly put into agricultural production the large game disappeared, and by 1920 rabbits, squirrels, doves, and partridges were about all that was left for the hunter. Since that time, the trend has reversed. Much of the land has been withdrawn from cultivation, and much has been set aside as natural forest or wildlife refuge. Numerous ponds and lakes have been built. The Georgia Game and Fish Commission has restocked game and fish and protected them. Foxes, both red and gray, are numerous. The otter, the racoon, and the beaver again flourish along the streams and rivers of the area. Wild ducks and geese are seen in increasing numbers and the wild turkey is seen in remote areas. Deer have increased until they are a recognized menace on the highways in some sections. The snakes seem to have remained throughout, and they include poisonous moccasins and rattlesnakes.

Some of the fauna are peculiar to the Southeast or the eastern part of the United States. The o'possum, a lumbering rodent-like marsupial which can hang by its tail like a monkey, has become adapted to cities as well as to the woods and is found throughout the area. It is an edible animal, but there is a diversity of opinion as to its desirability. Buzzards are a part of the southern scene, whether devouring a dead animal as drawn by Audubon, or perched like ghouls on the branches of a dead tree, or soaring lazily and gracefully through the sky.

Amazing to westerners and delightful to all is the lightning bug, a flying bug that literally has a taillight. On warm summer nights particularly in low and damp places, hundreds of their tiny lights can be seen twinkling a few feet above the ground.

AGRICULTURE

Cotton was the major crop and considered the foundation of the antebellum economy of the Oconee Area, but it was other agricultural products which made the area practically self-sustaining, at least so far as necessities were concerned. Even in the towns and villages, most households had their own vegetable gardens, chickens, and a cow or so. The plantations produced food, fuel, clothing, quilts, coverlets, and the simpler items of furniture; also soap, whiskey, wine, gamecocks, and world-famous racehorses. Considering the

9. *Pine Tree*
   JL & RH

10. *Ancient Oak Tree at Tomkins Tavern*
    KK

11. *Silos and Barn, Taylor Farm,* Washington County
    Map no. 13-1
    JL & RH

12. *New Pine Forest,* Johnson County
    JL & RH

total value of all the other agricultural products of that time, the importance of cotton to the antebellum economy may have been exaggerated.

From the years following the Civil War up through the 1920s there was an increasing tendency on the part of the farmers to grow as much cotton as possible, frequently at the expense of other farm products. The depression and five-cent cotton proved that it was impossible for the Oconee Area farmer to make a dependable living on cotton alone, but the age of specialization was too far developed to turn back to diversified farming. Instead many farmers and plantation owners began specializing in agricultural products other than cotton. Actually a few individuals had specialized in dairy (11) and various agricultural products other than cotton many years before, but it was not until depression days that there was a real trend in that direction. By 1964, dairying was of major importance, while cattle contributed about 25 percent of the income from agriculture in the Oconee Area.

Other major agricultural products include peaches, pecans, corn, soybeans, small grain, and, almost incidentally, cotton. Of these, soybeans seem to hold most promise for the future, though there is a possibility that with mechanization, cotton will make a comeback.

Commercial forest land (12) now occupies more than three-fourths of the area. In 1949, 75 percent of the area was in farms, indicating a complete reversal in a span of a little more than fifteen years. During that same time, the number of farms dropped dramatically, but the average size of those remaining increased, a possible, and distressing, indication that only large farms can survive today.

INDUSTRY

A study of the construction methods employed in the early architecture of the Oconee Area indicates the aggregate importance of the many small local and home industries of that time. Logs, framing, and lumber were usually cut, dried, and milled near the site of construction. Brick was made locally, and lime for mortar and for plaster was obtained within the area. Notched joints and handmade pegs held the timbers in place, and where nails were used, they were frequently made by a local smith. So also were the fine old H and L and strap hinges. It has often been noted that the early buildings had a harmonious unity of design with each other and with the landscape. The almost exclusive use of local materials was a contributing factor to this harmony.

Industries in the area were not confined to the building

trades. On the plantations, food was preserved, whiskey distilled, yarn spun, and cloth woven. Fancy soaps might be imported, but in those pre-detergent days soap for washing clothes, dishes, and kitchen floors was made at home. The list of plantation and home industries would be long, and when the total cost of importing such products is considered, the importance of these small industries to the economy of the area is obvious. In addition there were a number of independent industries. Of these, a few gristmills and cotton gins survive to this day.

The trend toward mass production began even before the Civil War. A publication of 1855 lists three large textile mills in the area: the Milledgeville Manufacturing Company, the Hancock Manufacturing Company, and the Eatonton Cotton Factory.[2] The three mills had a combined total of 9,572 spindles and 189 looms. The mill in Milledgeville was housed in a brick building four stories high; in the Sparta mill the engine was a hundred horsepower (this for forty-five hundred spindles, one hundred looms); and the Eatonton mill was notable for its attention to the instruction of the operators' children.

The Civil War and its aftermath seem to have dealt a death blow to the plantation industries, and not until the middle of the twentieth century were there enough large-scale industries in the area to compensate for their loss and to start the trend toward a more balanced economy. Two manufacturing industries predominate throughout the Oconee Area today. These are the industries producing lumber and wood products, and those producing textiles and textile products or apparel. Ranking economically with the wood and textile industries are the kaolin mining and processing operations (13) in Washington and Wilkinson counties. Both counties rank in the top ten in the state in mineral production. Smaller industries manufacture or process metals, chemicals, printing, foods, and other goods.

TRANSPORTATION AND COMMERCE

The history of the old towns in the Oconee Area reveals both the changing and changeless nature of the demands of transportation and commerce. The site of Milledgeville was well known long before its founding because of its proximity to Rock Landing at the junction of several Indian trails and the Oconee River. Sandersville grew around the site of an old Indian trading post, important in its day because it was located at the intersection of two major Indian trails.

The rivers have lost their importance as transportation routes, but both the railroads and the highways follow the

13. *The Freeport Kaolin Manufacturing Company*
Gordon, Wilkinson County
Map no. 15-2
JL & KP

14. *The St. Stephens Episcopal Church,* Milledgeville
    Valuable to Area
    Map no. 4-2
    RH

15. *The Red Level Methodist Church,* Wilkinson County
    Circa 1848, Notable
    Map no. 15-3
    JL & RH

general routes of the old Indian trails. In the days before the automobile and hard-surfaced roads, staples were generally supplied by stores scattered throughout the area. Some of these carried a large variety of goods, goods that varied from groceries and clothes to hardware and coffins. With a few exceptions, easier access to towns doomed the old general store. Now the stores in the towns are in turn faced with competition from large cities which no longer seem distant. Attempts to meet this competition have too often been made with gaudy storefronts and flashy signs.

A more thoughtful approach has been taken by the successful banks in the area. Their new buildings are noteworthy not only because of their harmonious modern facades, but also because of the careful attention given to service and parking facilities so that these are an integral part of a pleasant landscape. If the merchants can work out parking and service facilities as did the banks, and at the same time restore and enhance the inherent beauty of the old towns so that they again become delightful places in which to linger, the trend toward shopping in the larger cities might be reversed.

CHURCHES

In old Oconee Town near Rock Landing and the present town of Milledgeville, a Spanish mission called San Francisco de Oconee was established and a church built in 1680.[3] This was doubtless the first Christian church in the area. When William Bartram encamped at Rock Landing in 1775, he noted that the Indians had evacuated "the old Oconee town" about sixty years before. Most of the early church buildings in the towns have been replaced or remodeled, though St. Stephens Episcopal Church in Milledgeville, and Union Church in Irwinton are antebellum. Union Church, built to be used jointly by the Presbyterians, Baptists, and Methodists, has recently been restored after years of nonuse. A photograph and description of the building is included in the section on Wilkinson County.

St. Stephens Episcopal Church (14) was built in 1843 in what is now called the Carpenter Gothic style, that is, Gothic forms translated into simple wood construction which local carpenters could erect. The exterior has been changed somewhat, but like so many of the churches built in this style, its simple lines based on Gothic impressions still have a strong appeal. The interior which was originally finished in plaster was much damaged by Union troops, and after the war the mutilated walls and ceilings were covered with beaded boards of a type that used to be designated simply as "ceiling." The boards have darkened with age, and the interior is obviously more somber than originally planned. It is likely that it is also more impressive because the subdued light and the wood finish give the interior a quality of richness and warmth that would be difficult to achieve in plaster.

There are several antebellum church buildings still standing in the rural areas. These were built for small congregations, and were frequently severely simple in design. Red Level Methodist Church in Wilkinson County (15) is typical, its architectural appeal deriving solely from good proportions and simple lines. It was built about 1848, but the only stylistic clues are the entrance door with the two vertical panels so typical of the Greek Revival and the vigorous Greek Revival moldings. The pulpit appears to be original, as does the delicate Communion rail.

Red Level Methodist Church

ARCHITECTURAL DATA

DIMENSIONS	Width 36′, length 50′, ceiling height 14′ 6″
DOORS	3′ by 7′, 2 vertical panels
WINDOWS	18-light with 14″ wide by 16″ panes
PICKETS FOR	
ALTAR RAIL	⅝″ face by ⅞″, 4″ on center
	The main entrance doors and the pulpit are on the same end of the church, which end is aligned with the highway and faces northeast. There is no gallery.

Older than Red Level Methodist Church and similar, except that it has a porch, is Concord Methodist Church in Putnam County (16). The porch with its four slender wood posts and clapboard gable does not seem to be based on classic precedent. Instead it provides logical protection from the weather where it is most needed, and its form derives directly from sound principles of wood construction. Since the classic portico evolved in the same manner, it is not surprising that there should be an affinity between them.

Such was the case with Mt. Zion Presbyterian (later Methodist) Church, in Hancock County (17). The plan with its end portico with two entrance doors is similar to that of Concord Methodist Church. Instead of verge boards flat against the siding, the porch gable has a projecting eave, which is returned as a horizontal member at the base of the gable (or pediment to use the classic term) and thus forms the cornice of the entablature below.

The columns are square, and proclaim their wood construction, but they are much heavier than those at Concord

16. *The Concord Methodist Church,* Putnam County
Valuable to Area
Map no. 11-3
JL & KP

17. *The Mt. Zion Presbyterian (later Methodist) Church,* Hancock County
Valuable
Map no. 5-1
JL & KP

18. *The Tennille Methodist Church,* Washington County
    Built 1945. W.E. Dunwoody, A.I.A., Architect
    Map no. 13-2
    RH

19. *The Sacred Heart Catholic Church,* Milledgeville
    Valuable
    Map no. 4-3
    RH

Church and much heavier than required for structural support. Instead their dimensions were made to conform with the classic dimensions of stone columns. The kinship of the architecture of this church with that of Concord Church is obvious, and its differences, though minor, label the architecture of Mt. Zion Church as Greek Revival.

Mt. Zion Church

ARCHITECTURAL DATA

DIMENSIONS	Width 52′, length 66′ plus 8′ porch (total 74′), ceiling height 16′ 10″
COLUMNS	14¼″ square untapered, 14′ 8″ high including base and cap
DOORS	47″ wide by 8″ high
WINDOWS	Twelve 12″ wide by 18″ panes per sash, 24-light, 4-lights wide

The pews, pulpit, and wide floor boards all appear original. No gallery. The entrance, evidently aligned with an old road, faces south.

The classic tradition has continued into the twentieth century, and is well exemplified by the Tennille Methodist Church in Tennille (18). Built in 1945 to replace an older church which was destroyed by fire, it was designed by the architect W. E. Dunwoody, Jr., of Macon, Georgia. Following the breakdown of the plantation system, postwar churches were generally built within the towns and villages of the area.

The main part of the Sacred Heart Catholic Church in Milledgeville (19) was built in 1874, utilizing material from a demolished hotel. The Gothic-arched clear glass windows are said to have been salvaged from the hotel, that style window having been used there to harmonize with the Gothic architecture of the old State House.

An outstanding example of late Victorian architecture is Bethlehem Baptist Church in Warthen (20). The powerful roof lines are repeated and accentuated by the triangular pediments over the windows and doors. The towers, like those of medieval churches, appear to be deliberately non-symmetrical, despite the symmetrical layout of the interior. The church was established in 1790, and the present building erected in 1890. Like most antebellum church congregations, the one at Bethlehem Church was composed of both white and Negro communicants, and the minutes of the postwar years frequently mention requests being granted to Negro members to transfer to the newer all-Negro churches.

Many denominations are represented in the Oconee Area, and they include: Episcopal, Baptist, Latter Day Saints,

Methodist, Presbyterian, and Roman Catholic. Because of their sheer numbers, only a few of the twentieth-century church buildings have been included in this study. Examples of several are included in the section devoted to individual counties.

EDUCATION

In antebellum days and throughout much of the nineteenth century, schools in the Oconee Area were generally of two types, the so-called old field schools for lower grades, and academies with boarding facilities for the upper grades. In the village of Jewell in Hancock County, there still stands in a good state of preservation one of the old schools (21), probably built in the 1880s. It is two-story, but with a single classroom downstairs, and a meeting hall upstairs. Inside are some of the original benches, and still in place are the blackboards (wooden boards painted black), the raised platform, and the stove for heating the room. In the vestibule winding stairs of quaint and ingenious design lead to the second story (22).

The old academies were exclusively for male students or exclusively for female students, preparing them for their different roles in life. With the growth of towns and villages, the academies were gradually replaced by public schools. These have improved through the years so that today modern plant facilities exist in each county to provide education through the high school level to all children (23).

The Oconee Area is presently the home of two institutions of higher learning, the Georgia College at Milledgeville and the Georgia Military College. The Georgia College was founded in 1889 as a college for women, with the formidable name of the Georgia Female Normal and Industrial College. Being a woman's college, it freely asserted its right to change its name, first to Georgia State College for Women, then to the Woman's College of Georgia, then to Georgia College for Women. Having become coeducational, the name was again changed in 1967, this time to Georgia College at Milledgeville. Today it is a fast growing college with seven dormitories and a faculty numbering well over one hundred.

The college buildings facing Hancock Street present an unusually fine architectural composition. Built at various times, and some of them remodeled to conform, all are of red brick with columned porticoes and porches. There is variety in the size and the shape of the buildings and in the size, type, and arrangement of the columns. The virtue of its classic architecture is that the repetition of the columns in varied forms sets up a powerful rhythm, at once accentuating the

20. *The Bethlehem Baptist Church,* Warthen, Washington County
Valuable
Map no. 13-3
JL & RH

21. *Old School Building,* Jewell, Hancock County
Valuable to Area
Map no. 5-2
RH

22. *Stairway,* Old School Building, Jewell, Hancock County
Map no. 5-2
RH

23. *The Wilkinson County High School,* near Irwinton
Built 1954. Webb and Company, Architects
Map no. 15-4
JL & RH

unity and the variety of the ensemble (24). In front of these buildings is a magnificent tree-shaded lawn stretching to Hancock Street.

The Georgia Military College likewise boasts a beautiful tree-shaded campus and, in addition, the historic buildings that once formed the state capitol. It is a junior military college and preparatory school which was established in 1879. The interior of the old State House was destroyed by fire, and rebuilt to conform to the needs of the school. The exterior walls were repaired and painted, but otherwise unchanged. The beautiful gates were built soon after the Civil War, but the original part of the State House was built in 1807, designed by the architects Smart and Lane. This might well be the oldest Gothic Revival public building in the United States, and is classified as nationally important. Another interesting campus building is the new Georgia Military College Field House (25), completely modern in design, yet acknowledging with its narrow pointed windows, the Gothic architecture of the grand old State House.

SPECIAL INSTITUTIONS

Since Milledgeville was once the capitol of Georgia, a number of state institutions were located in its vicinity. Many of these were transferred to Atlanta after it became the capitol city. Among those transferred was the state penitentiary, which was at one time located on the square which is now the site of the Georgia College at Milledgeville. According to an 1855 description, the outer walls were of brick and enclosed 2½ acres. They averaged 20′ in height, and were 2½′ thick. The prison proper was a three-story granite building 200′ long by 30′ wide. There was a one-story octagon-shaped workshop; also a two-story building in which were apartments for the sick, for female convicts, etc. Both the latter buildings were of brick.

The Milledgeville State Hospital has remained, and the antebellum architecture of the Powell building (26) still dominates the expanded plant. The architects for the great domed building with its Greek Revival portico were probably Scholl and Fay. The main portion, which has been classified as valuable to the area, was built in 1856, but the wings are a later addition. With over twelve thousand patients, and four thousand employees, the Central State Hospital is today one of the largest of its kind in the United States. The Youth Development Center, also located in Baldwin County and operated by the State of Georgia, provides a rehabilitation program for males between the ages of fourteen and seventeen who have broken the laws of the state. Another state-owned facility is the Rock Eagle 4-H Club Center located in Putnam County. The Center, developed around the prehistoric Rock Eagle effigy, serves as a unique educational, recreational complex with facilities that can shelter, feed, and assemble more than one thousand people.

The Oconee Area includes a number of historic courthouses and other public buildings. Among these is the Mary Vinson Memorial Library building (27) which, with its arches, quoins, balustrades, and studied proportions, all based on classic precedent is an unusually fine example of Classic Revival architecture. Complementing these older public buildings are modern health facilities which include a county public health unit for each Oconee county, three publicly owned hospitals, and a private clinic in Wilkinson County. Two counties, Putnam and Hancock, have construction underway for new county hospitals.

SOCIAL AND RECREATIONAL ASPECTS

Insofar as the writer knows, no history has been published dealing primarily with recreation in the antebellum South. We know from the diaries of travelling clergymen that in the very early days drinking, brawling, and fighting along with other sinful revels were not uncommon. From scattered accounts we know that games similar to baseball and football were played, while ladies' diaries mention walking for pleasure, horseback riding, boating, picnicking, barbecues, and balls. Then as now hunting and fishing were favorite sports, and many a southern belle boasted of her marksmanship with a rifle.

24. *The Georgia College at Milledgeville,* Parks Hall (1911), Atkins Hall (1896), Terrell Hall (1907), Bell Hall (1928)
    Map no. 4-4
    RH

25. *Field House, Georgia Military College,* Milledgeville
    Built 1954. Robert and Company, Associates, Architects.
    Map no. 4-5
    RH

On a larger scale were the horse races and tournaments, the latter possibly inspired by Scott's novels and conducted with pageantry. These were especially popular with the students at the male academies and featured displays of horsemanship for the particular edification of female spectators. The Marquis de Lafayette visited the area in 1825 and was feted with a grand ball and supper at the State House, and a barbecue on the grounds. There were theatrical productions in the area at least as early as 1825, and behind modern store-fronts, parts of an antebellum opera house still exist in Milledgeville. Politics and county fairs, circuses and medicine shows added their share of entertainments.

Judging from the number of buildings which were spared from the torch of Sherman's army because of Masonic affiliations, Freemasonry must have been a powerful force both in the Oconee Area, and among the officers of the Union Army. The antebellum Masonic building in Sandersville was spared by the invading army, but accidentally burned in 1921. It was a graceful building in the form of a tetra-prostyle Greek temple with brick walls and round brick columns of the Ionic order. The Masonic building in Milledgeville (28, 29), which is classified of national importance, was designed by John Marler (also spelled Marlor), and built between 1832 and 1834. The fine workmanship and exquisite detail suggest an earlier era. As in Vignola's entablature for the Farnese Palace, console type brackets were used instead of the more traditional type adornments of the frieze and cornice. Unlike those of the Farnese Palace, the brackets vary in size, some extending below the architrave thus forming a rhythmic pattern which accentuates the principal architectural features of the building.

The ironwork of the exterior is particularly fine, and the

26. *The Powell Building, State Hospital*, Milledgeville
    Built 1856. Scholl and May, Architects.
    Valuable to Area
    Map no. 4-7
    RH

27. *The Mary Vinson Memorial Library*, Milledgeville
    Built 1911 for U.S. Post Office. John Knox Taylor, Supervising
        Architect.
    Map no. 4-8
    JL & RH

28. *The Masonic Building*, Milledgeville
    Of National Importance
    Map no. 4-9

29. *Stairway*, Masonic Building
    RH & KP

Masonic emblem is incorporated into the design of the brackets supporting the balcony. Inside, there is a magnificent circular stairway that spirals to the third floor, where the architectural treatment and delicately carved woodwork again suggest the restrained elegance of the late Georgian or early Federal period.

The Oconee Area still has open space and forests, rivers and lakes. Hiking and other outdoor sports can be a part of the daily life of all residents of the Area, and for the many who live near the lakes or who don't mind travelling a few miles, there is also fishing, swimming, and boating. The Oconee National Forest, located in Jasper and Putnam Counties, includes over fifty thousand acres. Among the game provided by these forest areas are deer, rabbit, quail, dove, racoon, fox, gray squirrel, and some wild turkey. Two major lakes in the Oconee Area are Lake Sinclair and Lake Jackson (30). Lake Sinclair, covering more than fifteen thousand acres provides fishing and facilities for boating, water skiing, and swimming. Lake Jackson, A 4,750-acre impoundment, borders Jasper County and likewise provides fishing and boating facilities. Throughout the area, small parks and recreational facilities have been and are being developed.

Of particular interest is a pond in Washington County which was created as a result of kaolin mining operations and has been taken over by the public (31). Though it is to be hoped that most of the mined areas will eventually be reforested, this one, and doubtless some others, offers opportunities for development into a unique park. The desert-like area with multicolored soils and strange man-made hills and valleys, is all the more fascinating because it lies in the midst of a verdant countryside, a kind of oasis in reverse. In the hands of an imaginative designer who could exploit the un-

usual characteristics of the site, and who could design facilities in keeping with the fanciful landscape, a truly great park could be developed.

POPULATION AND STATISTICS[4]

The seven counties making up the Oconee Area had a combined population of 94,320 in 1970. The number was 143 larger than the 1960 total, a small gain but significant in that it reverses a continual loss in population, a losing trend that started shortly after the Civil War.

In 1970 nearly half of the area's total population was non-white, overwhelmingly Negro. During the preceding decade there had been a gain (2,773) in the white population and a loss (1,273) in the nonwhite population.

30. *Lake Jackson,* Jasper County
    Map no. 7-1
    RH

31. *Abandoned Kaolin Mine,* Washington County
    Map no. 13-4
    KK

32. *Rock Eagle Effigy*, Putnam County
Of International Importance
Map no. 11-4
RH

Rock Eagle Effigies
Copied from measured drawings in vertical file labeled "Rock Eagle,"
Georgia Room, University of Georgia Library; copy and composition by
Kenneth Paolini

2. The First Georgians

There were strange and mighty monuments in Georgia long before Columbus's time. De Soto, in search of treasure and the rewards of exploration, noted them. The Indians of that time knew only legends of the long-vanished race which had erected them.

Two hundred years later, but still before the Revolutionary War, William Bartram, the naturalist, tried to solve the riddle of their origin, but ended by writing: "The Cherokees themselves are as ignorant as we are, by what people or for what purpose they were raised; they have various stories concerning them, the best of which amount to no more than conjecture, and leave us entirely in the dark; but they have a tradition in common with the other nations of Indians, that they found them in much the same condition as they now appear when their forefathers arrived from the West and possessed themselves of the country, after vanquishing the nations of red men who then inhabited it, who themselves found them when they took possession of the country, the former possessors delivering the same story concerning them. . . ."[1]

Shortly after the Civil War, Charles C. Jones, Jr., made a thorough study of the ancient Indian monuments, particularly of those in Georgia, and published his findings under the title *Antiquities of the Southern Indians, Particularly of the Georgia Tribes*[2] in 1873. The mounds in the Valley of Little Shoulder Bone Creek, about nine miles from Sparta, were measured and drawings of them included in his book. A copy of these drawings is reproduced in this study. Jones noted with regret the deterioration of these monuments, many of which had formerly been much higher and more precise in outline. Deterioration and some destruction have doubtless continued.

The study convinced him that the whole area around Sparta had at one time been densely populated by a nation whose living habits were completely different from those of the nomadic Indians of more modern times. The moats, canals, reservoirs, and the sheer magnitude of the task of constructing the mounds all point to a nation whose mode of life was stable. The discovery of stone images in the vicinity further indicates the differences, as neither the Creeks nor the Cherokees were idol worshipers.

Almost as baffling is Jones's failure to mention the much older monuments in Putnam County, the great "rock eagle" at the Rock Eagle 4-H Club, and the similar monument a few miles away at the headwaters of Little Shoulder Bone Creek.

Indian Mounds and Monuments
Copied from plate 2 (opposite p. 144) of *Antiquities of the Southern Indians* by C. C. Jones (New York: D. Appleton, 1873)

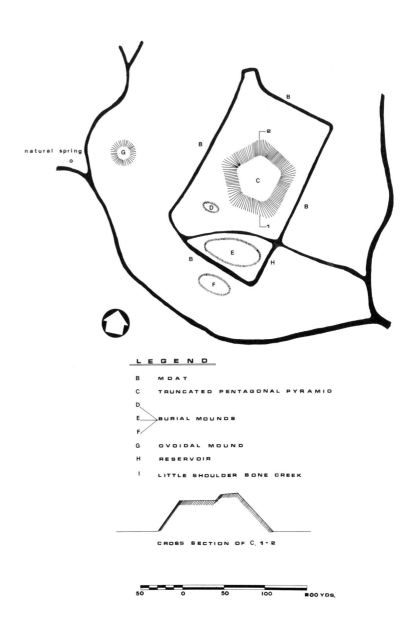

LEGEND

B   MOAT

C   TRUNCATED PENTAGONAL PYRAMID

D

E   BURIAL MOUNDS

F

G   OVOIDAL MOUND

H   RESERVOIR

I   LITTLE SHOULDER BONE CREEK

CROSS SECTION OF C, 1-2

50   0   50   100   200 YDS.

Evidently they were not entirely unknown, because shortly thereafter he made measurements and drawings of both mounds, with descriptions for the Smithsonian Institute.[3] This appears to be the first written description of them, and woefully little data are available even today.

Herein lies a further mystery. Did the fact that these gigantic mounds were made in the form of an eagle escape modern notice until the measured drawings were made? Once the form has been viewed from an airplane or from the tower built for the purpose, the outline is clear and can be traced on the ground, but so tremendous are these mounds, that it is only from above that their true shape can be appreciated.

A photograph of the mound at Rock Eagle Camp (32) and drawings of both effigies are included. It will be noted that the two eagles do not face in the same direction. The dimension from head to tail of each is the same (102′) but the wingspread of the one at Rock Eagle is 120′ while that at Little Shoulder Bone Creek measures 132′ from wing tip to wing tip; also the latter is a fatter bird.

Research by Dr. A. L. Kelly of the University of Georgia revealed that the mound at Rock Eagle was underlaid by alternating layers of humus and soil mixed, red clay, and yellow clay, the latter of a type not found in the vicinity. Aboveground the mounds are composed wholly of quartz rock and boulders, ranging from baseball size to boulders which would require several men to move.

There are mounds in Ohio and in Wisconsin built in the shape of serpents and other fauna, but this (Rock Eagle) one was declared the most perfect effigy mound in America today by Dr. Stirling, chief of the Bureau of Ethnology.[4] The two in Georgia are the only known North American effigies constructed of stone.[5]

As impressive as the effigies themselves is the mystery: Who built these ancient monuments? When? Why? Why were they built so that they could only be viewed from above or from the heavens? Was the effigy at Rock Eagle originally encircled with stones as is the one near Oconee River? Could these encircling stones be astrological in character as are those at Stonehenge? Does the stylized figure represent a true eagle? or, as has been suggested, a vulture?

As with much primitive architecture, this image has an all-powerful simplicity that seems close to some modern art and architecture. Its scale is that of today's immense water tanks, of our modern stadiums and coliseums built for thousands. Such modern structures, built for man in the aggre-

gate rather than for individuals, are closely akin in scale and in spirit to the pyramids, to the sphinx, and to the Rock Eagles.

Impressive mounds and monuments of the prehistoric Indians remain throughout the Oconee Area: only the more outstanding or better documented ones have been described here. Of the later tribes, little in the way of architecture remains. De Soto and early explorers have left vivid descriptions of their villages and of the people. These were the Indians of romance, Indians whose pride was in courage and valor, not material things. Describing all the buildings of a typical village is beyond the scope of this study, but the following paragraph from *Antiquities of the Southern Indians* is too interesting to omit: "Perhaps the most minute and satisfactory description of the dwellings of the Southern Indians is that presented by Mr. Lawson. [Lawson (Surveyor-General), *History of Carolina etc.* London, 1714. Page 176.] Referring more particularly to the Carolina tribes, he writes: 'These Savages live in Wigwams or Cabins built of bark, which are made round like an Oven, to prevent any Damage by hard Gales of Wind. They make the Fire in the middle of the House, and have a Hole at the Top of the Roof right above the Fire, to let out the Smoke. These Dwellings are as hot as Stoves, where the Indians sleep and sweat all Night. The Floors thereof are never paved nor swept, so that they have always a loose Earth on them. They are often troubled with a multitude of Fleas, especially near the Places where they dress their Deer-Skins, because that Hair harbors them; yet I have never felt any ill, unsavory Smell in their Cabins, whereas, should we live in our Houses, as they do, we should be poison'd with our own Nastiness; which confirms these Indians to be, as they really are, some of the sweetest People in the World.' "[6]

There was a variety of types of buildings, none of which were built to survive the intervening centuries. Where they were of logs, most accounts mention that the logs were set upright. It was probably not until after the European settlers set the example that the Indians began building the type log cabins that are seen in the Cherokee, North Carolina Reservation today, cabins similar to those of eighteenth- and early nineteenth-century pioneers.

Though the Indians had a profound effect on the lives and mores (it was the Indians who introduced the white Georgians to hominy grits) of the settlers, little or none of this influence is apparent in the later architecture. Occasionally a unique type of bird house made for the purple martins is seen in the area. It consists of an upright pole with cross arms from which the gourds are suspended (33). I have read or heard that such martin houses were a feature of many Indian villages, and that the custom of erecting them originated with the Indians. I have not found the supporting data for this.

Other than tribal-owned land, the Indians' possessions and buildings were generally of little material value. More than wealth or "treasures on earth" they seemed to have valued freedom from wealth. They gloried in spiritual possessions: courage, valor, loyalty and honor. And they admired wisdom and bodily strength and beauty.

The Oconee Area was opened to settlement by three different Indian land cessions, the first part in 1790, another in 1802, and the last in 1804, all obtained by treaties with the Creek Indians. Whether by treaty as in the Oconee Area, by brotherly love as in Pennsylvania, or by forced expulsion as in West Georgia, the net result was much the same: the Europeans and Americans acquired the land eventually forcing the Indians to retreat to ever-dwindling areas or "reservations." In the Oconee Area, only their mementos remain—a few practices that were adapted by the settlers, the ancient monuments, thousands of artifacts and trinkets, and the poignant legends of a noble race. Also the music of their names—Oconee, Ogeechee, Ohoopee, Ocmulgee.

33. *Gourds and Plastic Bottles for Martin Houses,* Johnson County
    JL & RH

42. *The Harrison-Walker-Brown House*, Washington County
KK

3. Early Settlers and Indigenous Architecture

A Spanish mission was established for the Indians at "Old Oconee Town" in 1680. This town was at Rock Landing near Milledgeville. When William Bartram encamped there in 1775, he noted that the Indians had deserted the town sixty years earlier. This old Spanish mission, referred to as "San Francisco de Oconee" in the *History of Baldwin County* by Mrs. A. M. G. Cook,[1] was probably the first building erected in the area by others than the Indians.

In *Antiquities of the Southern Indians*[2] substantial evidence is given that the Spaniards were operating gold mines in the North Georgia mountains during the seventeenth century. The same source describes a circular earth work upon the headwaters of the Great Ogeechee River five miles from Sparta. The fortification was known locally as the Spanish Fort; and at the time (1873) was thought to have been an entrenched camp of De Soto, but no satisfactory proof of the legend could be established. It was noted, however, that Bartram in his "Travels" had mentioned the remains of fortresses in the vicinity of Silver Bluff (near Augusta) which were supposed to be abandoned camps of Spaniards who had formerly fixed themselves at that place in the hope of finding silver. It is known that De Soto passed near or through the area, and legends of Spanish settlements are numerous. Part of the foundation of the Gilmore home near Sandersville is said to have been originally the foundation of an ancient Spanish hacienda.

It would be an interesting project for a scholar to study these remains and to explore the records and legends in order to see to what extent the Spaniards settled in the area. Other than the above-mentioned foundation which determined the proportions of three very lovely rooms of the Gilmore plantation house, the Spanish explorers and colonists seem to have had no influence on the architecture of the Oconee Area.

As in colonial times the first settlers of the Oconee Area frequently brought with them the building methods and styles which were used in the areas whence these settlers originated. And, as in colonial times, such building methods and styles might be considered outdated and old-fashioned in older, more established areas. Thus the Oconee Area has houses such as the Jordan-Pierson house and Old Dominion which have characteristics that are associated with the late Colonial period. These characteristics include fine craftsmanship and attention to detail. Weatherboarding was usually "beaded," that is, the lower edge of each board was curved and grooved, thus softening the sharp line created by overlapping boards. The lightest of verge boards substituted for eaves, and, as at Old Dominion (44), the verge board might be tapered, giving a lilt to the roof line. The eave closure, that is, the covering for each end of the horizontal eave, would likely be cut to match precisely the moldings of the boxed eave, as at Old Dominion. Such eave closures are good examples of the simple craftsman-like approach to a problem too often made overcomplicated in later architecture. Fairly small windows with small panes, usually 8″ by 10″, were typical. Important rooms might have larger windows than secondary rooms, and first floor rooms larger than those of the second floor. Window panes tended to be the same size throughout, variations in the size of windows resulting from varying numbers of panes used in the sashes. Frequently, six panes would be used in the lower sash, and nine in the upper fixed sash, the smaller one used at the bottom so it could be easily raised. This placement was sometimes reversed with the advent of window balances many years later.

Doors were most often of the batten or of the six-panel type. If batten, they would be carefully made of vertical boards held in place with wide chamfered battens. The boards themselves would have beaded edges. Usually heights of doors of this period were lower than the 6′ 8″ height which is standard today. The six-panel type, also called the Covenanter Door because the stiles of the upper portion resemble a cross and the panels of the lower part resemble an open Bible, were skillfully crafted, usually with high raised panels on one side, and flat panels on the reverse. Panels were rarely less than ⅞″ thick and the stiles rarely more than 1⅛″. Stiles of today's doors are a minimum of 1⅜″ since lighter stiles cannot accommodate modern mortise locks. At that time, locks were of the surface type and were of iron or wood with wood, iron or brass knobs. Ingenious devices with wood bars operated by latch strings were also used. Hinges were hand forged, and beautiful examples of H and L, and of strap hinges can still be found in the oldest houses in the area.

Interior walls might be of hand-planed boards with beaded joints, or, less often, of plaster with a wood wainscot consisting of extremely wide boards with simple moldings not unlike those of colonial times. The moldings seem to have been designed to unify the separate parts, and to have been applied so as to catch the least dust. The same restraint is noticeable in the design of the mantels, which were frequently integral with the wall panelling, and might have raised panels beneath, similar to the panels in the doors.

Ceiling beams were often exposed, in which case the hand-planed surfaces contrasted pleasantly with the beaded corners of the beams, the early builders rarely leaving sharp edges of timbers exposed.

Framing for the earliest buildings was of necessity hand-hewn, with the mark of the adze visible; if planed, the marks of the plane usually show. Construction was of the "braced frame" type, with corners well braced and the members heavier but more widely spaced than customary in the later "balloon frame" type. Framing members were mortised and tenoned, or dowelled, wooden pegs replacing scarce nails where possible.

This "colonial type" is noticeably similar to modest New England colonial houses and in many respects to those of colonial Williamsburg. Rooms were generally small and ceilings low. Though most of the older houses of the area eventually had porches these were in many cases later additions. When painted, it is likely that the colors were similar to those used in colonial New England and in Williamsburg. In contrast to the trim and precise architecture of such "colonial" types, is the indigenous architecture of the area well exemplified by the Harrison-Walker-Brown house. Such houses were of necessity built very simply of native materials, and designed primarily to protect from the exigencies of and to exploit the benefits of the local climate. Most of these were of log construction, a construction which inspired a more vigorous design than that of the so-called colonial type. Unpainted, with exposed rafters and wide eaves (even on the gable ends in many examples), with large chimneys and roofs with varying slopes like the hills around them, such houses seem to grow from the land and to blend into the landscape. This was the case with many of the early houses of the Oconee Area, and these are categorized as indigenous.

The Oconee Area, however, was settled by both frontiersmen and by men of established wealth and background. The stylish new capitol and the elegant Brown-Sanford house were built at the same time or even before many of the indigenous types. A curious aspect was the fact that wealthy aristocrats might live in the latter. Accustomed to plantation life and to yearly rigorous trips to the foothills or the seashore where they lived in the simplest of vacation houses to escape the heat and miasma of the older settlements, many wealthy landowners lived in surroundings almost as plain as those of Thoreau's Walden, happily oblivious that their houses appeared rude and unfinished to outsiders who had heard much of southern wealth and elegance.

Simple, unpretentious houses of the type classified herein as indigenous were built until the time of the Civil War, when the whole mode of life changed. In rural areas, particularly, the structure might well be of logs, and the possibilities and limitations of that type construction were an influence on the development of architecture in the area.

The size of individual rooms was frequently limited by the length of logs that could be practically handled, and the use of logs for interior partitions discouraged flexibility within. It was difficult to "throw rooms together"; instead each room tended to be a unit within itself, and of necessity, to be square or rectangular in shape. Frequently the separate rooms were built with a space between them, a space which could be roofed over and serve as a hall and kind of summer living room. These open-ended rooms, or "dogtrots" as they were called, gave the early houses a unity with the outdoors which was pleasing in the mild Oconee Area.

In the smaller houses, there might be a loft room hardly high enough for standing even in the center, but perfectly adequate for sleeping "a passell of hardy brats" who would have to climb a ladder to reach their quarters. Larger houses might have full-size rooms in the attic or a complete second story, the latter usually three rooms wide and one room deep, a scheme which gave admirable cross-ventilation to those rooms.

Most of the houses eventually boasted front and back porches, the full width of the house. Frequently these were additions, built a year or so after the main rooms and the dogtrot. The next change, and a logical one, would be to enclose one or both ends of either or both porches, forming extra small rooms which opened onto the porch. Construction of these rooms was frequently with sawed lumber, which clearly shows that they were later additions. According to tradition it was customary to leave one such room unlocked for the use of visitors who might wish to come in late without disturbing the owner. Nearly every country house boasted such a room, usually called "the prophets' chamber" because of the number of circuit-riding ministers who used the room overnight. Many porches on houses of the indigenous type had solid, square, wooden posts with chamfered corners and with mortised balusters which are an integral part of the overall design as in the Harrison-Walker-Brown house (42). Porch rafters, hand hewn with delicately beaded edges, were usually left exposed (43). Originally the log walls might be left exposed on the exterior, though they were sometimes protected with wood siding, frequently the board and batten type, placed vertically so as to be at right angles with the horizontal logs. For the same reason, interior panelling applied to the logs was most often vertical.

Glass windows, particularly in upper stories, were sometimes omitted, hinged wood shutters of the batten type being used instead. Otherwise doors, windows, mantels, and interior woodwork were similar to that in the "colonial type" houses, except that that of the indigenous type tended to be even simpler, and particularly in later examples, the workmanship bolder and less meticulous. Most houses of the indigenous type were left unpainted inside and out, though it is likely that some of those with board and batten siding were originally whitewashed, a method of painting which produces a sparkling white impossible to equal with oil-based paints.

The industrious early settler had a good stout fence around his house to keep the varmints out. Usually built of split saplings which were held upright by the interlaced trunks of vines, it was repeated in the graceful picket fences which surrounded the more finished antebellum homes. That there were settlers who omitted the fence is confirmed by contemporaries who wrote of the confusion of dogs, chickens, and children which were eternally scampering through the trot.

Though the development from dogtrot cabin to the plantation plain type (the latter with a one-room deep second story) had been completed in other sections before the Oconee Area was fully settled, examples still standing within the area illustrate the steps of that development, but not necessarily in chronological order. In its variations, the open dogtrot might be a hall, not infrequently with oversize double doors surrounded by glass so that the original relationship with the outdoors is emphasized. The solid chamfered posts of the prototype might be translated into carefully carpentered square columns, built of planks, and the woodwork painted, but the basic axial scheme that harks back to the dogtrot cabin is discernible in the plantation plain types, such as Jasmine Bower, as well as in those that are more obviously indigenous.

The Jordan-Pierson Cabin

Map. no. 13-5   Photo no. 34

Notable

DATE OF CONSTRUCTION   Circa 1790

LOCATION   Near Davisboro, Washington County

ORIGINAL OWNER   John Jordan

INTERIM OWNERS   Various members of the Jordan family

PRESENT OWNER   Leroy Pierson (1967)

34. *The Jordan-Pierson Log Cabin,* Washington County
KK

35. *The Jordan-Pierson House,* Washington County
KK

The Jordan-Pierson House
Plan of first floor

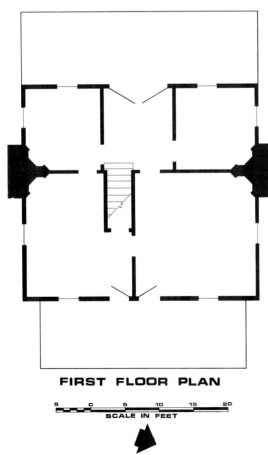

FIRST FLOOR PLAN

SCALE IN FEET

Typical of the dogtrot cabins of the first settlers, and probably as old as any now standing, the Jordan-Pierson cabin is thought to have been built as a temporary residence while the main house was under construction. The open space, or dogtrot, between the rooms served as a semi-outdoor living room during most of the year: meals were eaten here; churning, ironing, shelling peas—most of the minor chores became less onerous in the cool of the breezeway.

It is interesting to note that the dogtrot is almost on a north-south axis, as were so many of the older houses. The squared, skillfully notched logs indicate the care the builder took with his temporary home. Spaces between the logs were probably chinked with moss and mud during the winter, this being removed in summer for coolness.

The Jordan-Pierson House

Map no. 13-5   Photo no. 35

Valuable

DATE OF CONSTRUCTION   Circa 1795

LOCATION   Near Davisboro, Washington County

ORIGINAL OWNER   John Jordan

INTERIM OWNERS   Various members of the Jordan family

PRESENT OWNER   Leroy Pierson

ARCHITECTURAL DATA   See floor plan.

The Jordan-Pierson house is on the same site and about a hundred feet away from the cabin just described. At first glance the house gives the impression of a New England house perched on a Georgia hill. Compact, with conspicuous chimneys, a steep pitched roof, and crisp lines, its architecture implies a colder climate. A closer study reveals that it is admirably adapted to hot weather. In fact it seems designed expressly to direct the summer breezes throughout the house. Presumably because of the direction of the prevailing summer breezes, the newer house was oriented differently from the old log cabin, oriented to take full advantage of those breezes. The large back porch (now glassed in) runs almost the full width of the house. This replaced the dogtrot as the summer living room, and faced directly toward the prevailing summer breezes. A pair of impressively wide doors seems to scoop the breezes into a small central hall, whence they flow directly into every room of the original house.

As restored and modernized by the Piersons this example shows how well such old houses can be adapted to modern living. Having suffered years of occupancy by a series of careless tenants, and some years of total abandonment, it would not have seemed a happy choice for a future home.

Fortunately the Piersons were able to recognize an admirable plan, good lines, and sound construction under the apparent decay. With imagination, skill, and a genuine appreciation of its original qualities, they have rejuvenated the house, have installed bathrooms and a modern kitchen, and have meticulously restored the fine old woodwork. They have also saved a number of interesting artifacts found during the remodeling. These include an unused wooden peg with a head. It appears that all the pegs must originally have been thus shaped, and the heads cut off after being driven in place, an interesting and long forgotten facet of early construction methods.

A sample of the old heart pine flooring a full 1½″ thick taken from a place where it had not worn and another, worn until it is barely ¼″ thick but still strong and useable, illustrates the high quality of both the materials and the structure of the old house.

The most striking single feature of the house is the pair of wide double doors opening onto the back hall. Formed in the traditional colonial pattern, but with nine instead of six panels, these pine doors have been exposed to nearly two centuries of sun and blowing rain; this weathering has etched the grain of the wood into high relief and suffused it with a silvery sheen.

Minor changes have been made which should be recorded. As mentioned before, the back porch was closed in, making it useable the year around. The front porch, which previously had a low hipped roof, now has a shed type roof similar to the one on the back. Larger stationary windows have replaced original ones in the sides. These changes were made to adapt the house to modern conditions and taste.

Few houses built today can boast the charm and livability of this home which will soon begin its third century of use. The large back porch faces ESE.

The Buck-Archer House

> Map no. 13-6   Photo nos. 36, 37
> Valuable to Area

DATE OF CONSTRUCTION	Said to be 1847; appears to be older
LOCATION	Washington County, Route 24, Milledgeville to Sandersville
ORIGINAL OWNER	Probably Seaborn W. Buck
INTERIM OWNERS	Mrs. Wiley Shepard, daughter of Mr. Buck; then her sister, Mrs. Archer; now Mrs. Archer's son
PRESENT OWNER	(1967) W. A. Archer

> The house faces SSW.

36. *The Buck-Archer House,* Washington County

37. *Dogtrot,* Buck-Archer House
JL & KP

38. *The Dickerson-Miller House,* Monticello
RH

The development from the dogtrot cabin to this house is obvious. The breezeway of the prototype has been enlarged, as have the individual rooms, and the house is two rooms deep instead of one. Porches have been added, front and back, and there is a stairway instead of a ladder leading to the attic rooms. Basically, however, the house is an enlarged version of the Jordan-Pierson cabin.

There is a fine relation here between the house and the countryside. This is due in part to the sweep of the roof, at once logical in structure and harmonious with the hills around. It is due in part to the sheer delight of the wide porches. And it is due also to the subtle progression from the outdoors to the open porch, thence to the breezeway which is at once indoors and outdoors. It is this breezeway, relict of the old dogtrot, which is the heart of the house. It is a room, with the feel of a room, and with panelled walls and a staircase. But it is more than a room, because two of its walls are open, and the axis of the room passes through the open walls and the porches beyond, effectually making the room one with the countryside. The woodwork here displays the same restraint and fine craftsmanship noted in the Jordan-Pierson house.

It is as unusal as it is fortunate to find such a house preserved in its original form. No paint has marred the beauty of the panelling in the breezeway; instead it has mellowed with the years and boasts the patina of time. It could be assumed that the lack of paint was for economic reasons, but in all the years since this house was built, there were surely times when the occupants could have easily afforded to paint this woodwork. It is a tribute to them that they had the artistic sensitivity to refrain from so marring the natural wood.

Though many houses in the area were built with similar breezeways, most of the breezeways have long since been enclosed. These cool summer retreats can be frigid in winter, and occupants of the houses can hardly be blamed for closing in the summer rooms. If it is ever decided to so remodel this house, it is to be hoped that it will be done completely with glass and with the narrowest possible metal structural members. To make changes in a building with so much character, the designer would do well not to mimic that character, but instead to complement it, maintaining its integrity by contrasting the new with the old.

This house is particularly exciting to designers of contemporary architecture; basic principles used in its design are also basic to modern architecture. The adaptation to region and climate, the straightforward expression of structure, the subtle transition from exterior to interior space, and the high quality of craftsmanship combined with the appreciative use of natural wood, all display its kinship with the best of modern residential architecture. This is a delightful house as is; it could also be a delightful house if modernized. It is definitely worthy of preservation. Incidentally, there is in the front yard, the tremendous hollow trunk of what appears to be the most ancient of crape myrtle trees. There is a fringe of new shoots at the top.

Mark Twain inimitably and in detail described just such a house as the home of the aristocratic Grangerfords whose immaculate white shirts, white linen suits, and Panama hats impressed Huckleberry Finn almost as much as their high code of honor and their feud with the Sheperdsons.

The Dickerson-Miller House

Map no. 8-1   Photo no. 38

Notable

DATE OF CONSTRUCTION   Before 1850

LOCATION   13 East Washington Street, Monticello

ORIGINAL OWNER   Unknown

AMONG INTERIM OWNERS   Henry A. Dickerson

PRESENT OWNER   Mrs. Mary Anna Miller

ARCHITECTURAL DATA

PORCH POSTS   4½″ by 2⅝″ by 7′6″ high, chamfered above railing; railing missing

BEAM OVER POSTS   1⅝″ by 7½″, posts notched to receive beam

FRONT DOOR   3′ by 6′5″, 6-panel Covenanter type

WINDOWS   Formerly 8″ by 10″, 18-light

39. *Tompkins Inn,* Putnam County
KK

The 1850 census gives the following data for residents of this house.

	AGE	SEX	OCCUPATION	VALUE OF REAL ESTATE	PLACE OF BIRTH
Henry A. Dickerson	38	Male	Tailor	$1,000.00	Massachusetts
Sarah Dickerson	31	Female			Georgia
Alexander O. Daniel	25	Male	Tailor		North Carolina
James E. Wood	22	Male	Tailor		Georgia

The clean lines and straightforward structural expression, so reminiscent of Cape Cod, have been enhanced in this house by a skillful restoration using colors of the Colonial period.

Tompkins Inn

Map no. 11-1   Photo no. 39

Valuable

DATE OF CONSTRUCTION   Circa 1808

LOCATION   U.S. Highway 441 north of Eatonton, Putnam County

ORIGINAL OWNER   Nicholas Tompkins

PRESENT OWNER   U.S. Government

40. *The Wright-Phillips House,* Johnson County
    KK

41. *The Dickson-Hall House,* Wilkinson County
    JL & RH

As at the Dickerson-Miller house, the roof lines of this old inn perfectly reflect the room arrangement and the structure beneath; they also inadvertently and happily repeat the slopes of the surrounding hills. Porches and some of the lean-tos are obviously later additions or replacements.

Legend has it that at times as many as one hundred guests were bedded down here, most of them on pallets and cots. The original kitchen, a separate building, has been destroyed. The entrance, which appears to be in the original position, faces west, and the main porch extends across the west and the south sides of the house. There was another rear porch to the east, which has since been enclosed. These porches are much later additions, but may well be replacements of former porches.

The Wright-Phillips House

	Map no. 9-1 Photo no. 40
	Valuable
DATE OF CONSTRUCTION	Late eighteenth or early nineteenth century
LOCATION	The Buckeye Section, Johnson County
ORIGINAL OWNER	John B. Wright
AMONG INTERIM OWNERS	Daughter of John B. Wright, Mrs. Elizabeth Wright Martin
PRESENT OWNER	J. D. Phillips
	The house faces wsw, not quite parallel with the road.

This house has a picturesque and sturdy quality which immediately suggests the pioneer days during which it was built, built incidentally by the man for whom Wrightsville was to be named. Structurally the house is still sound. The porch posts and some of the rails that are mortised into them appear to be original. The porch posts are solid, 6″ by 6″ with chamfered edges. The rails are set into the posts. A 6″ by 12″ beam over the posts spans the length of the porch, and measures 47′ in length. The unpainted woodwork of the interior displays the fine craftsmanship of the period.

There is no ceiling over the kitchen, which is a one-story lean-to room on the back. The exposed rafters and underside of the roof are black with the smoke of more than a century's cooking. The second floor is one large room, and the shuttered windows appear never to have had glazed sash. It is a large pleasant room with hand-hewn exposed rafters and with the wood shingles of the old roof under the later metal roof, acting as ceiling. It would make a delightful recreation room if the house were to be restored.

The house was built by John B. Wright who became a

wealthy man in his day. He was the owner of many slaves, some of whose cabins are still standing. Evidently Mr. Wright never forsook his modest way of living: the house is still simple and sturdy, and far from pretentious. A Currier and Ives print entitled "Home to Thanksgiving" shows a house similar to this one.

John D. Phillips, the present owner, has lived here since 1912. He has twenty-seven children (the youngest about ten years old) and the present Mrs. Phillips is his third wife. Mrs. Phillips is a most industrious woman, and uses the second story as a storage room for strings of peppers, sacks of nuts, and the many jars of preserves and vegetables which she has canned, also baskets of buckeyes which she sells to customers as far away as Atlanta. They bring good luck, and she says that some say they cure arthritis, but this she will not guarantee.

The house is perfectly adapted to the owner's way of life. It could also be delightfully and unobtrusively modernized. The sound construction, the high quality of the woodwork, the panelled rooms, and the good simple lines of the exterior would assure its distinction and charm.

The Dickson-Hall House

Map no. 15-5   Photo no. 41

Valuable

DATE OF CONSTRUCTION	Probably early nineteenth century
LOCATION	Off Highway 112, Wilkinson County
ORIGINAL OWNER	William (Buck) Dickson
INTERIM OWNERS	Mrs. Frances Payne Dickson, Mrs. M. E. Hall, W. A. Hall, Mrs. Lillie Freeman Hall
PRESENT OWNERS	Heirs of Mrs. Lillie Freeman Hall

ARCHITECTURAL DATA

COLUMNS	7¾" square at bottom of shaft tapering to 6" at top, 8' 2" overall height; no cap or base.
CEILINGS	Porch varies from 8' to 8' 2" in height principal rooms of first story 8' 10" second story 7'
EXTERIOR DOORS	3' wide by 6' 6" high
WINDOWS	In two principal rooms 8" by 10", 15-light, 9 over 6; shutters only, no sash, in upstairs rooms nor in small rooms off porch; extra roof projection at porch 22½", may have been added.

House, which is remote from highway, faces wsw.

See floor plan.

The Dickson-Hall House

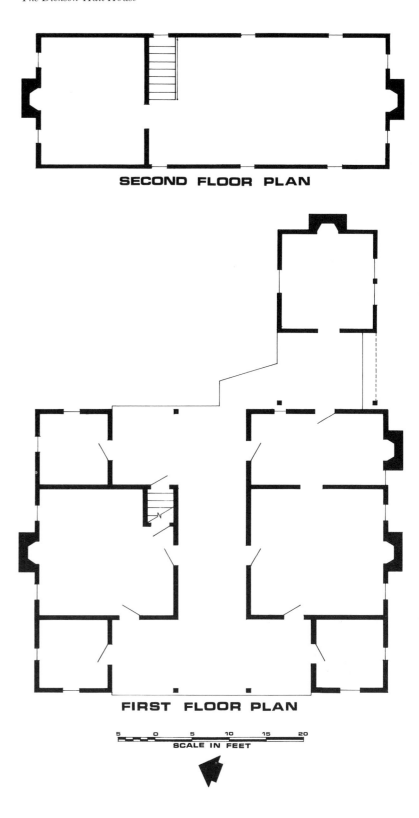

SECOND FLOOR PLAN

FIRST FLOOR PLAN

SCALE IN FEET

43. *Porch Post and Beam*, Harrison-Walker-Brown House
JL & RH

Built for coolness, the second story of this house is only one room deep, with windows on all sides. The rooms at either end of the wide spreading porch help funnel breezes through the open dogtrot, also into the interior rooms. Though rare today, such houses were once common throughout the area. It would be difficult to conceive a house plan better suited to the climate before the advent of air conditioning.

The present kitchen appears to be an old plantation office, moved next to the house and attached by an open porch. It is likely that the original kitchen was detached, both for the sake of coolness and as a precaution against fire. The beam over the porch is concealed within the roof structure, thus accentuating the plane of the ceiling in a manner that has been adapted by modern architects because of its apparent simplicity, and because exterior and interior appear to be more closely related without the divisive beam.

The Harrison-Walker-Brown House

Map no. 13-7　　　Photo nos. 42, 43

Nationally Important

DATE OF CONSTRUCTION	Probably very early nineteenth century
LOCATION	Washington County
ORIGINAL OWNER	———— Harrison
AMONG INTERIM OWNERS	Mrs. H. F. Walker, descendant of original owner
PRESENT OWNER	Mrs. Cecil Brown, descendant of original owner; always owned by descendants of original owner.

ARCHITECTURAL DATA

PORCH	41′ by 7′. The beam over the second story porch is one piece, 5¼″ wide, 7″ deep, and 45′ long. Hand-hewn rafters, beams, and ceiling boards are beaded.
PORCH POSTS	First story vary from 5¾″ square to 6¼″ square, and are 7′ 11″ high, the corners chamfered above the railing; second story vary from 4½″ to 5½″ square, and are 6′ 2″ high, the corners chamfered above the railing; posts are solid.
RAILINGS	Hand-split pickets in the railing vary from ¾″ to 1¼″ roughly square, set at 4″ on center; top of rail downstairs 2′ 11″ above the floor; upstairs 2′ 10″ above floor.
HALL	9′ wide (former dogtrot)
WINDOWS	Downstairs 8″ by 10″, 15-light, 9 over 6; upstairs 8″ by 10″, 12-light
	Gable eaves project beyond the chimney. The house faces slightly west of north.

The hall of the Harrison-Walker-Brown house was originally an open breezeway or dogtrot. The log walls of the house have recently been covered with asbestos siding, but the beautifully weathered woodwork of the porch still gives the house an air of mellowed antiquity.

Splendidly related to the climate and to the site, the house achieves distinction by the rhythmic repetition of vertical elements, primarily the strong rhythm of the porch posts and the lighter rhythm of the balusters. The balusters are square, and appear to be hand split. They are oblique to the railings so that a section through them would appear diamond shaped. The ends are rounded and set into the rails.

The clean-swept dooryard, with ancient cedars, is bounded by plants and wire fencing, but must once have boasted a picket fence which would strengthen the rhythmic effect of the porch work.

Because it so perfectly expresses the requirements of time, place, use, and climate; because its design is a harmonious synthesis of indigenous craftsmanship and sophisticated restraint; and because of its sheer graciousness, this house has been categorized as nationally important.

44. *Old Dominion,* Sparta
RH

Old Dominion

Map no. 6-1   Photo no. 44

Practically in ruins; otherwise would have been Valuable to Area

DATE OF CONSTRUCTION   Before 1806

LOCATION   Sparta, off Jones Street

ORIGINAL OWNER   John Lucas

House faces SSE or NNW depending on which was the original front.

Despite its age, and its decayed condition, the sensitivity and meticulous craftsmanship of early builders can be discerned in the ruins of Old Dominion. The verge board is tapered with the wide end toward the eave, thus giving a graceful lilt to the line of the roof: the closure at the end of the eaves is accurately scribed to the abutting moldings. The weather boarding is beaded, a refinement which was probably done one board at a time and by hand in the early 1800s. Such attention to detail was typical of the era.

The first North Georgia Conference of the Methodist Church was held at Old Dominion in 1806.

The Hall House

Map no. 15-6   Photo no. 45

With picket and rail fences: Valuable

DATE OF CONSTRUCTION   Before the Civil War

LOCATION   Highway 112 south, six miles from Toomsboro

45. *The Hall House*, Wilkinson County
KK

46. *The Henderson-Fore House*, Jasper County
KK

ORIGINAL OWNER	H. A. Hall
INTERIM OWNERS	Mrs. M. E. Hall, W. A. Hall, M. A. Hall, Sr.
PRESENT OWNER	M. H. Hall, Jr.

ARCHITECTURAL DATA

FENCE PICKETS	1½″ by 1½″, 5″ taper at top
GATE	4′ high to top of pickets, gate pickets 37″ high
GATE POSTS	53″ to top of diamond-shaped cap which is integral with post; diamond cap is 16½″ high, horizontal center line of diamond is 6″, above square part of post.

House is parallel to the road and faces SW.

The similarity of the Hall house and the older Dickson-Hall house which is nearby is apparent. The rooms under the porch have been omitted, and the dogtrot has become a hall, but the general layout is the same. The ornate porch work of the Hall house appears to be the result of postwar remodeling. The flush siding of the back porch walls has been painted to resemble cut stone work.

The picket fence is still standing—barely standing, but mostly upright, and there are still sections of the adjoining split rail fence. Unfortunately, there are no blinds at the windows. The picket fences and the horizontal lines formed by open blinds gave these houses a graceful quality which is lost without them. The house is in fair condition, and would be charming if restored.

The Henderson-Fore House

Map no. 7-2   Photo no. 46

Valuable

DATE OF CONSTRUCTION	Circa 1815
LOCATION	Jasper County
ORIGINAL OWNER	James Henderson (primitive Baptist preacher)
AMONG INTERIM OWNERS	William Henderson (son of James Henderson) and wife, Cynthia
PRESENT OWNER	Mrs. V. B. Fore

The house faces NE.

Houses similar to this group, with the upstairs only one room deep and a one-story porch across the front, were so popular in the South in antebellum days that they earned the designation of "plain plantation style." Still standing in South Carolina is a house named Middleburg, built in this style in the seventeenth century. Throughout the eighteenth and nineteenth centuries this style so suitable to southern living remained popular. The contemporary styles were frequently adapted to it, and there are numerous examples in the area with Greek Revival or Victorian porch work.

Jasmine Bower

Map no. 7-3   Photo no. 47

Valuable

DATE OF CONSTRUCTION   Circa 1830

LOCATION   Jasper County, Highway 142 north of Shady Dale

ORIGINAL OWNER   Harmon Geiger

INTERIM OWNERS   Randall Geiger (son of Harmon G.), Randall's sister, Celeste (Bowers), Oscar E. Lancaster

PRESENT OWNER   Alva Lancaster

The house faces ssw.

Originally there were seven varieties of jasmine in the door yard garden, whence the name "Jasmine Bower." The rock-bordered beds still remain, but the jasmine was dug up many years ago because a doctor of the time advised that it might endanger children's health. The picket fence has been replaced by an electric one, but the hospitable porch, the doorway as wide as many of the old dogtrots, and the large trees and quaint flower beds still augment the charm of the old house.

The three center bays of the porch are original, the end bays having been added at a later date.

47. *Jasmine Bower,* Jasper County
JL

48. *Rock Mill,* Hancock County
JL

Rock Mill

Map no. 5-12   Photo no. 48

Valuable to Area

DATE OF CONSTRUCTION   Circa 1815-1820

LOCATION   Road Jewell to Mayfield, east of Highway 248, Hancock County

ORIGINAL OWNER   William Shivers

AMONG INTERIM OWNERS   ——— Simpson, ——— Cason, Sonny Wheeler.

PRESENT OWNER   Dr. Olin Shivers

The house, which is remote from the road, faces south.

This great old mansion has a foundation of carefully fitted granite blocks, a raised brick basement floor, two full stories above that, and a large attic completely ceiled and plastered. At each end are two chimneys, the two curiously

joined together in the attic so that they emerge from the roof as one. The two chimneys contain flues for twelve fireplaces.

A two-story porch which was added about 1890, and which extended across the front has been removed, and is to be replaced by a restoration of the original small portico. The oval fan and sidelights at the main entrance are noteworthy, as are the classic egg and dart moldings and the acanthus leaf medallions in the principal rooms.

The mantels are Federal in style and the interior doors are Greek Revival, as was the original portico. Despite such stylistic elements, the character of the exterior with its majestic proportions and understated detail is more closely akin to that of the great houses of the eighteenth century than to contemporaneous architecture. Completion of the Greek Revival portico may alter this impression.

The house is listed in the National Registry. The present owner, a descendant of the original builder, is restoring the house and plans to open it to the public. Edward Vason Jones, an authority on American neoclassical architecture, is in charge of the restoration.

4. Oconee Federal and Transitional Architecture

Concurrent with the indigenous architecture, a unique architecture developed in the Oconee Area. Chaste and elegant, as was most Federal architecture, there were characteristics and features which were distinctly native.

In the Milledgeville vicinity, the houses tended to have narrow two-story pedimented porches expressive of the halls behind them, the porches having two columns only, and these columns heavier than usual for the Federal styles, though lighter than the Greek Revival. A delicately simple fan was frequently outlined against the flush wood siding of the tympanum. The floor plans and the fine wood and plaster work as well as the finish of the interiors of most of these houses are described and illustrated in Frederick Doveton Nichols's authoritative book, *The Early Architecture of Georgia*.[1]

The houses in this group have remained livable throughout the years. The rooms, though large, are not overwhelming as was too often true with Greek Revival houses. The delicate wood and plaster work is more in harmony with today's furnishings than is the more robust Greek Revival trim. Whether due to New England-born Daniel Pratt or to the taste of the owners (many of whom were from New England), we have here a type of architecture which is a unique and charming fusion of the South and New England, of traditional and indigenous architecture, combined with the Federal style, a style which had ended chronologically more than a decade before its use in some of the Oconee Area examples.

Because earlier architecture of the area was restricted to

49. *The Brown-Sanford House,* Milledgeville
KK

frontier building methods, the Federal style was more elaborate than that which preceded it. Rooms were larger and ceilings higher. Doorways with exquisite fan and side lights made their appearance, the higher ceilings sometimes permitting the fan light to be a full half-circle. A figure of the American eagle used at the pivotal center of some of the fan lights is a reminder of the intense national pride of the era.

The narrow two-columned portico seems to have been unique to the Milledgeville vicinity during this period, though two-columned porches of the colossal style were not unusual during succeeding periods. The traditional porch with a shed roof extending the full width of the house was more often used even within the Oconee Area. This type might be two stories high but in such cases there would be separate columns for each floor, unlike the two-story columns used with the narrow gabled porches.

Classic elements were freely handled, and occasionally there were startling misinterpretations as indicated by the delightfully naive Ionic capitals of the Coleman house. More often, the changes were deliberate, and were made to attain a lighter expression which would be more in keeping with the wood construction and the domestic scale of a residence. Typical and indicative of this, is the portico of Boykin Hall. Not only has the portico been reduced in size so that the pediment can be supported by two comparatively slender columns, but the entablature has been lightened by the omission of the traditional frieze. A simple band of truncated cones under the cornice gives the sparkle and interest usually furnished by the minor elements of the classic entablature. Similar variations are found in buildings of the Federal period throughout the area, changes from precedent that made the architecture more appropriate for its use, and more expressive of its construction.

The treatment of gable ends usually followed colonial precedent, with simple, narrow, possibly tapered verge boards substituting for eaves. Beaded weather boarding was used more often than not, though flush siding might be used on walls occurring under porch roofs. Windows, too, tended to follow the earlier patterns, with the narrowest possible casing and usually with small 8″ by 10″ panes. Larger panes were becoming available, and were used extensively in fashionable eastern cities, but these were still rare in the Oconee Area.

A distinct departure from indigenous precedent can be noted in the hallways of most of the houses attributed to Daniel Pratt. In these, the rear of the hall is terminated by the stairway, thus reducing the through circulation and the axial effect basic to the older scheme. In some of the houses, the hall is divided into two parts, the front serving as an entrance hall, the rear enclosing a graceful circular stair.

Stairway balusters of the period were nearly always simple rectangular pickets (most often ⅝″ by 1⅛″) and spaced one or two to a tread, depending on the width of the tread. Average spacing was 5″ to 6″ on center. The sheer simplicity of the pickets and of the simple round hand railings accentuated the grace of the stairways, particularly of the curving stairway so popular at the time.

Mantels, frequently with slender pilasters or colonettes, might have rococo motifs reminiscent of the late eighteenth century. More often, their decoration consisted of sunburst motifs and reeding typical of the Federal period. The acanthus leaf remained a favorite decorative motif, as its heavier version would continue to do throughout the succeeding Greek Revival period.

Moldings of the period, crisp and delicate, exhibit at smaller scale the same spirit of sophisticated simplicity noted in the stairways. Extremely fine ornamental plaster work is found in some of the houses and buildings, always handled with the grace and restraint so typical of the period.

Interior colors were frequently muted and very dark colors were not uncommon. Research has revealed the use of such colors at the Brown-Sanford house, colors sometimes touched with gold leaf. Careful scraping of layers of exterior paint on the Brown-Sanford house indicates that it was first painted a buff or putty color, and that later, but still at an early date, it was painted in shades of gray. Doors were often painted to resemble woods more exotic than the native pine, and woodwork was sometimes marbelized. When fully restored, this house promises to be an authoritative source as to colors used during that era.

The Masonic building in Milledgeville which was built during the transitional period is pictured and described in Chapter 1 of this book.

The Brown-Sanford House

Map no. 4-10   Photo nos. 49, 50

Of National Importance

DATE OF CONSTRUCTION	Circa 1812
LOCATION	West Hancock Street at South Jackson, Milledgeville
ORIGINAL OWNER	George T. Brown
INTERIM OWNERS	John T. Brown, Sam Beecher, Erasmus Brown, D. B. Stetson, Stetson Sanford, and Daniel and Marah Sanford
PRESENT OWNER	Old Capitol Historical Society
ARCHITECT-BUILDER	John Marler (also spelled Marlor)

ARCHITECTURAL DATA

PORCH   25' 5" by 8' 4"; height, first story, 10' 8"; first story pilaster shafts, 14" at bottom, 12½" at top; second story pilaster shafts, 12" at bottom, 10½" at top; pilasters 9' overall height; architrave second story 7½" deep; pilasters first story Doric, second story Ionic; columns first story not original, second story Doric, which may have been moved from first story; flush siding under porch up to 18" wide.

DOORS   Entrance, first story 3' 7" wide by 7' 6" high; front, second story 3' 7" wide by 7' 1" high; fanlights both doors 6' wide by 1' 11" wide.

STAIRWAY   Continuous curving stringers under stairway with hand-split laths and plaster over; pickets ¾" by 1"; top of rail 37" above upstairs floor.

MANTEL   Shelves are subtly curved; sunbursts and motifs are wood, hand carved.

WINDOWS   First story 10" by 12", 18-light; second story 10" by 12", 15-light.

See floor plan.

50. *Fanlight,* Brown-Sanford House
KK

The Brown-Sanford House
Plan of principal floor

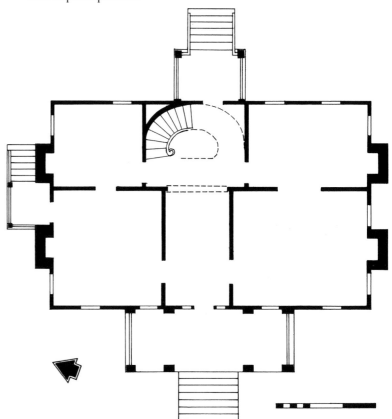

The Brown-Sanford house is one of the few Early American houses to incorporate successfully the Palladian arch into a large portico. Although the columns of the lower floor have obviously been replaced with later substitutes, the urbane quality of the design still dominates. The plan with a large entrance hall opening onto an even wider stair hall with a circular stair might have been the inspiration for some of the plans of houses attributed to Daniel Pratt.

The interior, like the exterior, is delicate and sophisticated. The stair railing has unembellished, rectangular-shaped pickets, their simplicity accentuating the curve of the stairway itself.

The portico, wider than the entrance hall, extends over a window in each adjoining room. This was a problem that was to become common in Greek Revival architecture, the desirable size for the piazza usually being wider than the hall, thus leaving the designer with the alternative of truthfully expressing the interior with a small porch, or, on the exterior, visually separating windows that are related within. Here the architect has mitigated the effect by relating them to the architectural treatment of the uniquely beautiful portico. It is interesting to note that the entrance door does not center the portico, but is 17" nearer one side than the other. Quite a difference, but one that is not noticed unless it is pointed out.

The house was originally located on Wilkinson Street, where it was slated for destruction. Under the leadership of the Old Capitol Historical Society, and with help from many

51. *The Terrell-Stone House,* Sparta
KK

52. *Doorway,* Terrell-Stone House
Library of Congress Photo

53. *Kitchen,* Terrell-Stone House
RH

sources, the house was moved to its present location, and is in the process of being restored. Photographs of this house are included in the Historic American Buildings Survey. These and photographs made by the survey of other houses are available from the Superintendent of Documents, U.S. Government Printing Office in Washington, D.C.

The Terrell-Stone House

Map no. 6-2   Photo nos. 51, 52, 53

Valuable to Area

DATE OF CONSTRUCTION	Circa 1820
LOCATION	839 Jones Street, Sparta
ORIGINAL OWNER	Dr. William Terrell
INTERIM OWNERS	Edgar G. Dawson, Dr. Thomas Jefferson Jones, Mr. and Mrs. Carleton Stone
PRESENT OWNER	Mrs. Carleton Stone (granddaughter-in-law of Dr. Jones)

ARCHITECTURAL DATA

FRONT DOOR OPENING	5′ 6″ wide by 8′ high
WINDOWS	Opening onto porch, 10″ by 12″, 32-light, 16 over 16.
	House fronts on ENE and faces the highway.

Another house displaying strong Palladian influence is the Terrell-Stone house, with its Palladian entrance and window, and its low roof with the delicately beautiful parapet completely around it. The porch was added, the original one having been smaller. The old kitchen, built of large granite blocks, still stands in the back yard as do the remains of a small classic building that was originally an office, but was unfortunately converted to a garage. There was also a large conservatory, long since gone, and magnificent formal gardens to the rear. Photographs of this house are included in the Historic American Buildings Survey.

The Cheely-Coleman-Moore House

Map no. 5-3   Photo nos. 54, 55, 56

Of National Importance

DATE OF CONSTRUCTION	Circa 1825
LOCATION	In Hancock County, near Shoals
ORIGINAL OWNER	Thomas Cheely
AMONG INTERIM OWNERS	Henry Coleman (son-in-law of Thomas Cheely), James Hunter Coleman, Warren Coleman, Mrs. Warren Coleman
PRESENT OWNER	Mrs. Warren Moore (formerly Mrs. Warren Coleman)
ARCHITECT-BUILDER	Said to be John Marler (also spelled

Marlor). The naive handling of classic details indicates a less highly trained designer.

ARCHITECTURAL DATA

PORCH   Architrave second story 6″ deep; no architrave first story.

COLUMNS   Tapered round, first story 10½″ diameter at base, 8′ 10″ overall height; second story 8¼″ diameter at base, 8′ 10″ overall height.

STAIRS   Pickets ⅝″ by 1⅛″

WINDOWS   8″ by 10″, 24-light, 12 over 12, 4 lights wide

House faces east.

54. *The Cheely-Coleman-Moore House,* Hancock County
KK

55. *Porch Stairway,* Cheely-Coleman-Moore House
KK

56. *Porch Columns and Cornice,* Cheely-Coleman-Moore House
RH

In plan, detail, and sheer ingenuity, few houses offer more of interest and delight to the student of Early American architecture than does the Cheely-Coleman-Moore house. A fairly large house, it retains the open dogtrot and has a curved stairway open to the porch. The dogtrot, which is a misnomer in this case, is closed at the rear with louvers which completely fill the arched opening there. These louvers, though apparently quite old, were probably added after the house was built as they do not match the louvered blinds, blinds which are unique in that each slat protrudes about half an inch beyond the frame of the blind. They appear to be the work of a skilled craftsman who had seen louvered window blinds, but could not remember precisely how they worked. The louvers in the elliptical archway are the adjustable type.

The house has two stairways, the curved one on the porch leading to the boys' quarters; the other one, which is accessible only from the master bedroom, leading to the bedrooms used by the daughters of the house. The arrangement suggests that there has been a change in the mores of the area as well as in the architecture.

An intriguing feature of the house is the elliptical arch under the porch stairway, the arch curving in two planes to accommodate the steps. The porch balustrade of the second floor has been altered, the pickets there being more widely spaced than are the notches to receive them. The first floor columns are a craftsman's version of the Tuscan column, those on the second floor a delightfully naive interpretation of the Ionic order. The cornice is embellished with a board decorated with repetitive holes and scallops, a treatment which lightly conveys the idea of a classic fret with dentils, but which is more appropriate to the wood structure.

The rear view is chaste and simple, and one wonders if this was once the front. In any case, the present front with its two-story porch with curving stairs and its marvelous indoor-outdoor relationship sets this house apart from all the others.

Major General Judson Kilpatrick, Federal Cavalry leader, and members of his staff apparently used the house as headquarters when they passed through the area on their march to the sea. On a bedroom wall is written, "May all the names engraved here, in the golden book appear," signed by General Kilpatrick and members of his staff.

57. *Mount Nebo,* Baldwin County
Destroyed by fire about 1940
Library of Congress Photo

58. *The Grantland-Stevenson House,* Milledgeville
KK

Mt. Nebo, also called *McComb's Mount*

Map no. 3-3   Photo no. 57
Destroyed by fire about 1940

DATE OF CONSTRUCTION	1823
LOCATION	Baldwin County
ORIGINAL OWNER	Governor David B. Mitchell
AMONG INTERIM OWNERS	Robert McComb, Annie McComb Chandler, Frank Chandler

The house faced south.

In his excellent book, *The Early Architecture of Georgia,* Frederick Doveton Nichols[2] notes that Mt. Nebo seemed to be the only house in Georgia which was inspired by the same source as Brandon in Virginia, Morris's *Select Architecture.* The floor plan of Mt. Nebo is included in Nichols's book; additional photographs and drawings are included in the Historic American Buildings Survey.

Fans similar to the one in the porch pediment at Mt. Nebo were used in the pediments of several Oconee Area houses of the period, usually in a simplified form.

Several outbuildings and ruins of the old gate still remain. A few crape myrtle trees and giant cedars are all that remain of the once-famous gardens, all, that is, except the magnificent view from the site of the old house. One understands why the name was changed from McComb's Mount to Mt. Nebo, when it is remembered that it was from Mt. Nebo that Moses viewed the promised land.

The Grantland-Stevenson House

Map no. 4-11   Photo no. 58
Valuable

DATE OF CONSTRUCTION	Circa 1820
LOCATION	510 Allen Memorial Drive, Milledgeville
ORIGINAL OWNER	——— Grantland
INTERIM OWNERS	——— Bailey, ——— Smith, ——— Johnson, ——— Green, ——— Ennis, ——— Harper, O. T. Pounds
PRESENT OWNER	Eugene Stevenson

59. *The Homestead*, Milledgeville
KK

ARCHITECTURAL DATA

DIMENSIONS	Width of house, 60′ 3″; width of porch 56′ 9″
PORCH	Lattice 11/16″ by 2″ at 6″ on center
COLUMNS	11″ face by 6½″ sides at bottom of shaft tapering to 10″ face by 6″ sides at top of shaft; height 9′ 9″ overall; 8½″ from porch cornice to bottom of architrave; cornice slopes with roof.
FRONT DOOR	3′ 6″ by 7′ 2″; fanlight 6′ wide
WINDOWS	10″ by 12″, 18-light, 9 over 9

The Grantland-Stevenson house was moved to its present location from Smith's Mount. Originally there was a ballroom in the basement; this was not moved with the rest of the house. The widespreading one-story porch is reminiscent of the indigenous type, but the exquisite doorway with its elliptical fanlight is pure Federal. The proportions of the columns are closer to those of Greek Revival architecture than to Federal, and these might have been changed since the house was built. The fact that some sections of the porch railings have square balusters and others turned balusters indicates that changes have been made to the porch. The pleasant lattice screen may be of a later period, although such screens were frequently used during the antebellum time, and this one adds much to the usefulness of the porch and to the beauty of the house.

The Homestead

Map no. 4-12   Photo no. 59

Valuable to Area

DATE OF CONSTRUCTION	1818
LOCATION	Washington Street at Liberty, Milledgeville
ORIGINAL OWNER	Peter J. Williams
AMONG INTERIM OWNERS	"Miss Sue" Jones, Mrs. David Ferguson, Miss Betty Ferguson, great-great-granddaughters of original owner.
PRESENT OWNER	Miss Frances Lewis

ARCHITECTURAL DATA

PORCH	Floor 19′ by 9′ 5″
COLUMNS	18¾″ diameter at bottom of shaft; bases project (10″ one side, 5″ other side) beyond porch floor, the piers being corbelled out to accommodate them; 21′ 4″ overall height; irregularities and cracks suggest that columns are tree trunks.
DOORS	Front, 4′ by 7′ 6″
WINDOWS	10″ by 12″, 18-light, 9 over 9

60. *The Cedars,* Milledgeville
JL & KP

61. *Stairway,* The Cedars
RH

The Homestead is the oldest of a number of great houses in Milledgeville that have the comparatively narrow two-story portico which so well expresses the arrangement of the rooms within the house. A first impression is that the houses are Greek Revival, and they have many features in common with that style. Closer study reveals more delicate proportions than was common with Greek Revival architecture, while the interiors reveal a wealth of late Georgian or Federal-type wood and plaster work. Frederick D. Nichols, in *The Early Architecture of Georgia,*[3] characterizes such houses as Early Republican.

Besides housing a fabulous collection of antique furniture and art, the Homestead boasts the original boxwood gardens and wisteria planted by its first mistress. It also has a ghost, who appears as a little old lady dressed in brown and is usually seen in the garden about dusk. Though hardly comparable with the glamorous Sylvia of Panola Hall, she has her good points. She is loyal and faithful, and has followed the family all the way from Wales to New England, and thence to Georgia. She also attends to her ghostly duties, though in a rather lackadaisical way. She has been known to appear to members of the family just before they died, or before there were deaths in the family. Mostly, however, she just putters about the garden.

The Homestead may well be the first house in America to utilize a narrow colossal-type portico with only two columns. Though never widely used, the style became so popular in the Milledgeville area that it is frequently referred to as the Milledgeville-Federal type of architecture. Though not indicated thus individually, as a group these houses would certainly be considered of national importance. Photographs of these houses are included in the Historic American Buildings Survey.

The Cedars

Map no. 4-13   Photo nos. 60, 61
Valuable to Area

DATE OF CONSTRUCTION	Various dates ascribed from before 1820 to as late as 1830
LOCATION	131 North Columbia Street, Milledgeville
ORIGINAL OWNER	Charles W. Howard
INTERIM OWNERS	Dr. William A. Jarrett, William H. Scott, —— Prosser, Charles Moran, Dr. E. A. Tigner, Miss Hallie Smith
PRESENT OWNER	Mrs. James I. Garrard
ARCHITECT	Probably Daniel Pratt

ARCHITECTURAL DATA

PORCH   18′ 5″ by 5′ 10″; architrave 1′ 7″ deep (there is no frieze)

COLUMNS   Reeded instead of fluted; 17½″ diameter at bottom of shaft, with 18 "reeds" or "convex flutes"; reeded pilasters are 17¾″ at bottom of shaft, 6 reeds wide; 18′ 6″ high overall; Ionic capitals are hand carved, of wood.

FRONT DOOR   4′ by 7′ 6″; the doorway is recessed in a unique and charming way, which might be the result of a misinterpretation of the architect's drawing.

Various dates have been ascribed to this house. There is a tentative quality about the architecture, which indicates that it was designed before the other houses in the area that were attributed to Daniel Pratt. This could indicate that it was built in the very early 1820s.

The Cedars formerly faced Clark Street, and had a circular drive bordered with cedars; there were also gardens which were laid off by an Irish landscape gardener named Patrick Cane. The house has been beautifully and skillfully restored by the present owner.

As on the very old houses of the area, the siding except under the portico is beaded, and a delicately tapered verge board was used instead of eaves on the gable ends. The graceful fan in the porch pediment is similar to several others in the area, but its simple form may be unique to this section of Georgia. Photographs of this house are included in the Historic American Buildings Survey.

The Williams-Sallee House

Map no. 4-14   Photo nos. 62, 63, 64

Of National Importance

DATE OF CONSTRUCTION   Circa 1822

LOCATION   251 South Liberty Street, Milledgeville

ORIGINAL OWNER   John Williams

INTERIM OWNERS   Grantland, Orme, Crawford

PRESENT OWNER   Mrs. J. O. Sallee

ARCHITECT   Probably Daniel Pratt

ARCHITECTURAL DATA

PORCH   18′ 9½″ by 9′ 10½″

COLUMNS   Solid unfluted tree trunks, worked to the Roman Tuscan order, have a diameter of 20″ at bottom of shaft.

62. *The Williams-Sallee House,* Milledgeville
RH

63. *Detail of Door and Fanlight,* Williams-Sallee House
Library of Congress Photo

64. *Doorway and Fanlight, Interior View,* Williams-Sallee House
Library of Congress Photo

65. *Boykin Hall*, Baldwin County
JL & KP

66. *Porch Detail*, Boykin Hall
RH

PILASTERS   19″ at bottom of shaft, 20′ 7″ overall height; there is the Milledgeville-type fan in the pediment.

Another of the houses generally attributed to Daniel Pratt, the Williams-Sallee house has a delicate balcony instead of a second story porch, permitting the magnificent fanlighted doorways to show to full advantage. Like all houses in the group, it has the comparatively narrow porch, expressive of the hall behind.

There are amusing anecdotes about the encounter between the Massachusetts-born mistress of the house (Mrs. Abigail Adams Edgarton Orme) and members of Sherman's invading army, but space does not permit their inclusion here. They are charmingly recounted in *White Columns in Georgia* by Medora Field Perkerson.[4]

Most of the antebellum furnishings are still in the house, though handsome prints of Confederate Army officers have been placed over the hall sofa where occupying Federal officers once rested their arms. The heirlooms, in addition to John Adams's walking cane which conceals a dagger within, include several from Massachusetts which Mrs. Orme inherited. Many photographs of this house are included in the Historic American Buildings Survey.

Boykin Hall

Map no. 3-4   Photo nos. 65, 66, 67, 68

Valuable to Area

DATE OF CONSTRUCTION   Circa 1830

LOCATION   Highway 24, twelve miles east of Milledgeville, Baldwin County

ORIGINAL OWNER   Dr. Samuel Boykin

INTERIM OWNERS   William Whitaker, Samuel F. Whitaker, Sam Walker, Mrs. John V. Shinholser (daughter of Sam Walker), Mrs. Helen McHenry Shinholser

PRESENT OWNER   Bennett Giles

ARCHITECT   Probably Daniel Pratt

ARCHITECTURAL DATA

PORCH   17′ at junction with house; 17′ 6″ outside face of pier to outside face of pier; 10′ 10″ deep.

COLUMNS   Of Tuscan order, 19½″ diameter at bottom of shaft; 20′ 9½″ overall height; shafts 18′ 7″; capital 12″ high including abacus; 24 flutes; 7 flutes on pilasters.

EXTERIOR DOORS   First story, 3′ 6″ by 7′; fanlight 6′ wide by 3′ high; second story, 3′ 3″ by 6′ 10″.

WINDOWS   8″ by 10″, 18-light, 9 over 9

ROOF   Tapered verge board instead of eaves on gable end

STAIRWAY   Pickets of the interior stairway (the only stairway in the group of houses attributed to Daniel Pratt which is not curved) ⅞" by 1". It is possible that this is not the original stairway.

House which is remote from the highway faces ssw.

Situated at the end of a straight drive which is cut through thick woods and which is nearly half a mile long, Boykin Hall is still a thrilling sight, though the house is run down and the vista somewhat obscured by the untrimmed trees. The exterior is almost identical with the exterior of the Blount house, though Boykin Hall lacks the flanking pilaster on the facade, and is only one-room deep upstairs.

The wood and plaster work, particularly in the room to the right of the entrance hall, is light and delicate. There is an Adam-type mantel in this room, with a decorative plaster arch over it and flanking concave niches on either side. The window trim is finely detailed, the panels under the windows being exceptionally beautiful.

Some of the plaster work is broken and missing. Many of the windows are broken, and, though basically sound at this time, the house is fast deteriorating. It is urgent that the windows and doors be boarded up and protected until the house can be restored.

Being of reasonable size, in good structural condition, and with most of its exquisite wood and plaster work intact, it is unthinkable that this house should go indefinitely without an appreciative owner who can afford to restore and live in it. Until such time, it is to be hoped that it will not be permitted to deteriorate further.

Boykin Hall was originally called the "White House," it being the only house painted white in the immediate vicinity. It may also have been the only painted house, however it predates the era when white was considered the only color for such a house. Photographs of this house are included in the Historic American Buildings Survey.

The Gordon-Blount-Banks House

Photo no. 69

Valuable to Area

DATE OF CONSTRUCTION   Circa 1828–1833

ORIGINAL LOCATION   Jones County near Milledgeville

ORIGINAL OWNER   Governor John Gordon

AMONG INTERIM OWNERS   —— Blount, Mrs. W. C. Lamar, Dr. L. C. Lindsley

67. *Fireplace Wall with Niches*, Boykin Hall
RH

68. *Mantel Originally in Boykin Hall*
Photo courtesy of Mrs. E. W. Allen, Sr.

69. *The Gordon-Blount-Banks House*
Originally in Jones County, removed to Newnan, Georgia
JL & RH

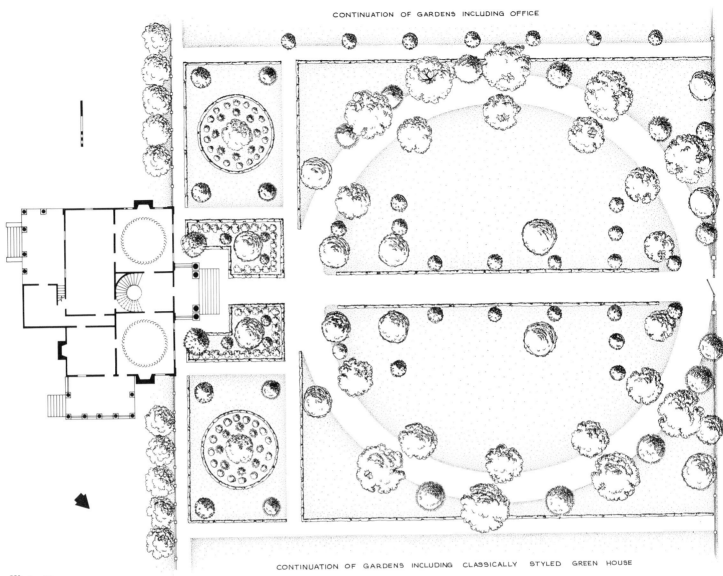

CONTINUATION OF GARDENS INCLUDING OFFICE

CONTINUATION OF GARDENS INCLUDING CLASSICALLY STYLED GREEN HOUSE

Westover
Plan of principal floor and adjoining gardens

PRESENT OWNER William N. Banks

ARCHITECT Probably Daniel Pratt

ARCHITECTURAL DATA

PORCH Floor 16′ 9″; outside of pier to outside of pier 18′; projects 11′.

COLUMNS Tuscan order, 22¼″ diameter at bottom of shaft, 22 flutes with sharp arrises.

PILASTERS On porch, 22″ wide (7 flutes); project 1 flute; pilasters at front corners of house do not return on side.

House faces east.

Though originally in Jones County, just outside the Oconee Area, this house of the Milledgeville Federal type is too closely related to those in and around Milledgeville to omit. Its similarity to Boykin Hall is marked. The house has recently been moved to Newnan, Georgia.

Westover

	Map no. 3-5 Photo no. 70
	Destroyed by Fire
DATE OF CONSTRUCTION	Circa 1822
LOCATION	Meriweather Road, six miles from Milledgeville, Baldwin County
ORIGINAL OWNER	Probably Colonel Lee Jordan
PRESENT OWNER	Mrs. L. C. Lindsley
ARCHITECT	Probably Daniel Pratt

70. *Westover*, Baldwin County
Destroyed by fire about 1942
Library of Congress Photo

Destroyed by fire since the photographs were taken, Westover has been replaced by a simplified version of the old house. The once-famous garden with its circular drive and box parterres is being gradually restored. Remnants of the original fences and garden buildings still remain.

Frederick Doveton Nichols, in *The Early Architecture of Georgia*,[5] considered the exterior of Westover the most academic of those in this group, and his book contains many illustrations of the fine interiors as well as of the exterior. Photographs and measured drawings were also made by the Historic American Buildings Survey. This is the only one of the group attributed to Daniel Pratt that had two sets of paired columns instead of two single columns supporting its portico.

Because of the masterful interrelationship of the interior of the house and of the design of the gardens, a plan of the main floor of the house and of part of the gardens is included.

The shape of the porch floor and of the rectangular space around the porch complement the apsidal shape of the entrance hall, seeming to serve as a proscenium for the curving stairs therein.

That interrelationship was emphasized and reemphasized by the repetion of similar elements within and without. The circular stairway repeated the movement and the shape of the circular drive, the arched doorway repeated in a vertical plane the horizontal plan of the hall, and the design of the ornamental plaster ceilings with floral motifs repeated the shapes of the round box-bordered flower beds. It is likely that the patterns of the rugs and carpets were likewise interrelated with the design of the gardens. The geometry of the flower beds and of the topiary echoed the architecture of the house.

The large room at the rear was a ballroom and was added in 1852. It probably replaced a porch which would have faced southeast.

71. *The Paine-Jones House*, Milledgeville
JL & RH

72. *Hand-Carved Pilaster Capital*, Paine-Jones House
JL & RH

The Paine-Jones House

Map no. 4-15   Photo nos. 71, 72

Valuable to Area

DATE OF CONSTRUCTION   Circa 1820

LOCATION   201 South Liberty Street, Milledgeville

ORIGINAL OWNER   Dr. Charles I. Paine

AMONG INTERIM OWNERS   Sara Ann Rockwell

PRESENT OWNER   Miss Elizabeth Jones

ARCHITECTURAL DATA

PORCH   22′ 4″ by 8′; architrave 1′ 2″ deep

COLUMNS   Spacing 7′ 2″ on center, 6′ 9½″ (center to center of center columns), 7′ on center; overall column height 20′ 7″; bottom of tapered column shaft 10⅝″.

PILASTERS   20′5″ overall height including pedestal, pedestal 2′10½″; bottom of tapered pilaster 10⅝″

FRONT DOOR   3′ 6″ by 7′ 4″

WINDOWS   8″ by 10″, 18-light, 9 over 9

Built about the same time as the group of houses attributed to Daniel Pratt, the Paine-Jones house has the same delicacy and restraint, but its two-story porch (too light for the technical term "colossal") has four widely spaced columns and is wide enough to include a window of each of the rooms flanking the hall. Ionic pilasters resting on pedestals suggest that the present columns of Doric persuasion are not the original ones, charming though they are. The pedestals also suggest that there might formerly have been a balustrade.

In the rear, there is an addition with a pleasant porch, delightfully trimmed with scroll saw work of a later period.

There were doubtless many other houses of the Federal style in the Oconee Area. Some have probably been overlooked. Others were destroyed or remodeled. The Clark-Bentley house, built by Governor John Clark about 1815 near Milledgeville, and once occupied by the Seaton Grantlands and by the DuBignon Richardsons, is said to have boasted a Milledgeville-type portico, lost in a later remodeling. One of the many additions to the Scott-Smith house at Scottsboro was likewise said to have been in this style, but it too was remodeled at a later date. The area as a whole, however, and Milledgeville in particular, is fortunate to have such a wealth of this type architecture.

5. Greek Revival Architecture of the Antebellum Era

After the frontier was established, and in the palmy days before the war, architecture in the Oconee Area attained a rare synthesis of indigenous and classic design. The era coincided with a fashionable admiration for things Greek, especially for ancient Greek architecture. Whether this architecture was particularly suitable to the South, or whether the builders and architects of the area were unusually skillful in adapting the style to good basic plans already developed, the synthesis of the Greek Revival style and of southern architecture was usually a happy one.

Numerous architectural books gave every literate builder ample opportunity to follow the rules worked out by archeologically oriented architects of the day. Luckily most of the builders of the Oconee Area accepted the rules without undue reverence, rarely letting them interfere with the "comfort, commodity or delight" of the building.

84. *Glen Mary,* Hancock County. See page 58.
RH

73. *The Hitchcock-Walker House*, Monticello
JL

Reflecting the architecture of ancient Greece, Greek Revival architecture had a simple grandeur, frequently described as "noble" by writers of the time. The most obvious characteristic was the use of columns, usually of Greek Doric or of Tuscan influence, though the Ionic and Corinthian orders were sometimes used. Like their prototypes, columns of the Greek Revival period were heavy, particularly compared with those of the Federal or Early American periods. Trim and moldings were larger, simpler, and more vigorous. Ornament, when used, was likewise bolder (some critics say coarser), and was usually based on Greek motifs, favorite ones being the acanthus leaf and the anthemium (honeysuckle) motif. A favorite architectural book, and a very good one, was Asher Benjamin's *The Builder's Guide*. This was published in many editions over a long period of time, and appears to be the source of most of the designs for moldings, ornaments, mantels, and millwork.

The grand scale is evident throughout. Rooms are larger, ceilings higher, and doors and windows of greater scale. Windows were frequently floor length, particularly when they opened on porches, and could be used as doors. Window panes in the finer houses were larger, those at Lockerly being 13″ by 19″.

Entrance doors were often 8′ high, some exceeded 9′ and were correspondingly wide. Four-panel doors, similar to the Covenanter or six-panel doors but without the small panels at the top, were most used. Doors with only two vertical panels were also used, a handsome type rarely used in other periods. The fanlight so popular during the Federal Period was superseded by a straight top transom, partly because arches were rarely used in ancient Greece. Patterned frosted glass was frequently used in the transoms and sidelights, and occasionally stained glass or a type of patterned glass which was part frosted and part stained. A particularly beautiful example of the latter was used at the Slade-Harris house in Eatonton.

Trim for doors and windows tended to be heavy, simple, and grand. Instead of being mitered at the corners, the wide casing was frequently butted against corner blocks. The heaviness and boldness of the moldings and casings sometimes concealed defects, craftsmanship not always being on a par with that of the preceding eras. Mantels reflected the trend toward heaviness and simplicity. Though not always beautiful in themselves, they were in harmony with the heavy walnut and rosewood furniture of the period, and provided the right foil for the light rococo Victorian furniture which was also much used. Marble mantels, heavy, simple, and severely classic, or delicate, ornate, and romantic were both used, frequently in conjunction with cast iron grates of elaborate design.

Because of the quality of the work of this period, and because so much of it is still in existence, more space has been given to Greek Revival architecture than to that of other periods. The photographs in this section illustrate the development of the style. The buildings are not shown in chronological order insofar as precise dates are concerned. Instead, they are shown in an architectural sequence which shows how the style progressed from vernacular architecture to what could be called "High Greek Revival." The fact that some of the early types were built after types in the latter category (and vice versa) indicates the erratic progression of architectural style, but does not refute the overall sense of evolution. Painting, decorating, and landscaping of the Greek Revival period are discussed in conjunction with other antebellum styles in Chapter 7.

The first series of photographs illustrates development of the Greek Revival cottage, the second the two-story Greek Revival house or mansion.

74. *The Weedon-Bell House,* Sandersville
RH

The Hitchcock-Walker House

Map no. 8-2   Photo no. 73
Notable

DATE OF CONSTRUCTION	Before 1821
LOCATION	North Warren Street, Monticello
ORIGINAL OWNER	William Hitchcock
PRESENT OWNER	Estate of James N. Walker

This attractive cottage is said to be the first brick house built in Monticello. Except for being of brick, it is typical of numerous houses built in the area throughout the nineteenth century. It is not Greek Revival, but is included here to show the close affinity of Greek Revival cottages with their predecessors.

The Weedon-Bell House

Map no. 14-1   Photo no. 74
Valuable

DATE OF CONSTRUCTION	Circa 1850
LOCATION	428 West Church Street, Sandersville
ORIGINAL OWNER	William H. Weedon
AMONG INTERIM OWNERS AND OCCUPANTS	Miss Ernestine Davis, Miss Beebe Davis; occupied continuously by members of Weedon family until 1900.

75. *Anonymous Cottage*, Wilkinson County
JL

PRESENT OWNER	Mrs. Frank L. Bell
ARCHITECT	Attributed to John Washington Renfroe, brother-in-law to W. H. Weedon

The house faces south, oblique to the road and oblique to the surrounding houses.

The Weedon-Bell house is another which might not be considered Greek Revival. The center hall and the original square columns have been changed. The sweeping roof lines, common to indigenous and much of the Greek Revival architecture, and the general form are the same, however, and illustrate the close relation of the two types of architecture.

Originally the porch had banisters, and there was a picket fence around the dooryard. The delicate repetitive quality of these two elements counterpointed by the heavier rhythm of the columns must have enhanced the easy charm of the old house.

Anonymous Cottage

Map no. 15-7   Photo no. 75

Worthy of Mention

DATE OF CONSTRUCTION	Unknown
LOCATION	Highway 57, Wilkinson County near Washington County line

House faces SSE and is parallel with the highway.

This cottage is interesting because of features which point both backward and forward in the evolution of architecture and architectural styles. The carefully detailed chimney cap is reminiscent of brickwork of the seventeenth and very early eighteenth century in this country, the decorative course of angled brick being unusual and a carry-over from very early times. This type brick work would be discarded in the Greek Revival architecture which was to follow, but would reappear later as Victorian Gothic.

The front porch is most intriguing because of latent elements of Greek Revival architecture. The roof structure projects completely beyond the edge of the porch floor and is supported by independent posts in front of the floor along the edges where it is normally vulnerable to decay. Esthetically, the change emphasizes the verticality and importance of the supporting posts, posts which are obviously plain tree trunks. It is interesting to note that the first Greek temple columns were developed from tapered tree trunks.

Other elements which are frequently found in southern

Greek Revival architecture are the flush siding under the porch, and the casual placement of the windows and door. Protected as it was by the roof, there was no need to overlap the weatherboarding as was done elsewhere, and the smooth wall of flush siding gives a pleasant "interior" character to the porch. The cavalier placing of the off-center door and the windows is a characteristic which bothers bookish critics, but one which frequently lent a delightful sense of informality to a style which could become boring by too close conformity to classic precedent.

It could hardly be claimed that this cottage is a thing of beauty. It is more like an awkward adolescent, clumsy and probably a little ridiculous, but displaying possibilities of beauty when developed.

The Rivers-Harris House

Map no. 15-8   Photo no. 76

Notable

DATE OF CONSTRUCTION   Thought to have been 1821

LOCATION   Highway 18, south from Gordon, Wilkinson County

ORIGINAL OWNER   Joel Rivers

INTERIM OWNERS   ———— Lott, Dan Lee, Walter Dennard, E. J. Jones

PRESENT OWNER   I. V. Harris

ARCHITECTURAL DATA

DIMENSIONS   House 44′ 4″ wide

PORCH   41′ 6″ wide; height of porch 6′ 8″; no visible beam or architrave.

COLUMNS   11″ square at bottom; like Greek Doric columns, they have no base and rest directly on a pier; beam over columns concealed in roof.

House faces SE.

76. *The Rivers-Harris House,* Wilkinson County
KK

If the Rivers-Harris house was built in 1821, as the records indicate, the handsome porch columns must have been substituted for an earlier type during the Greek Revival period. This was a common practice, and indicates the ease with which the indigenous architecture could be transformed into the southern version of Greek Revival. Like the Weedon-Bell house, this one likely had banisters at one time, and a picket fence about the dooryard. And like those of the Anonymous Cottage, the columns gain importance by being placed in front of the porch floor.

77. *The Smith-Baugh House,* Baldwin County
JL

The Smith-Baugh House

Map no. 3-6   Photo no. 77

Valuable to Area

DATE OF CONSTRUCTION	1840 or earlier
LOCATION	Gordon Road (Highway 243) five miles from Milledgeville, Baldwin County
ORIGINAL OWNER	L. D. Smith
INTERIM OWNERS	John G. Polhill, Harriett A. Polhill (1858–1866), W. Stevens estate (1866–1892), Annie E. Brewer (1892–1918), M. S. Barnes (1918–1922), L. D. Smith (1922), W. E. Baugh estate (1922–1958)
PRESENT OWNERS	Major and Mrs. Joseph R. Baugh (since 1958)

ARCHITECTURAL DATA

PORCH	48′ by 8′
COLUMNS	Rectangular in section and vary slightly in size; the faces vary from 9¾″ to 10″ and the sides from 8¼″ to 9¼″; 9′ in height.
CEILINGS	12′
BATTENS	⅝″ by 2¼″ plus or minus and from 12 to 13″ on center
FRONT DOOR OPENING	6′ 9″ wide by 9′ 4″ high
WINDOWS	12″ by 18″, 12-light
	House is approximately parallel to highway and faces ESE.

As delightfully as any in the area, this house exhibits the merging of indigenous and Greek Revival architecture. The sloping roof, the central hall, the wide porch, and the board and batten siding are all indigenous to the region. The larger windows and window panes might be the result of climate and improved technology, but the columns, deliberately heavier than those of earlier times, the plain heavy trim, and the simple vigorous moldings are pure Greek Revival. The fact that the change in style occurred at a time when skilled labor was being replaced by slave labor unaccustomed to the precise work required for the earlier styles does not lessen the charm of such houses.

Many of the trees in the yard date back to antebellum times. Then, as now, there were walnut and pecan trees, cedars, elms, and fig trees. Flowering shrubs included crape myrtles and cape jasmine, now called gardenia. Some of the old grape vines still remain, and the owner, who lived there as a child, remembers the original herb garden where mint, garlic, sage, and bay were among the plants included.

Union troops set fire to the house, but left in time for the residents to come out of hiding and extinguish the fire. Little damage was done though the burn marks are still visible.

The Lingo-Bridges House

Map no. 15-9   Photo no. 78

Valuable

DATE OF CONSTRUCTION	Between 1850 and 1855
LOCATION	Highway 57, three miles from Irwinton, Wilkinson County
ORIGINAL OWNER	John T. Lingo
INTERIM OWNERS	James Lingo, Lovie Lingo
PRESENT OWNER	R. T. Bridges

ARCHITECTURAL DATA

COLUMNS — 12½″ square at bottom of shaft tapering to 6½″ at top; edges chamfered; columns are placed on masonry piers which are 7″ in front of porch floor.

House faces ESE.

Another step in the constant evolution of architecture can be seen in the Lingo-Bridges house, where fanciful woodwork has been used with Greek Revival columns whose powerful expression belies their comparatively small size.

It would be interesting to know whether the lattice and scroll saw work on the porch of this cottage were part of the original design or were added to relieve the classic severity of a Greek Revival cottage. In either case, gratitude is due the subsequent owners for maintaining this charming example of Victoriana. Actually the lattice probably serves the very practical purpose of helping to shade the porch, and the scroll saw brackets add a pleasantly frivolous contrast to the classic facade. It is gratifying to see houses such as these, which have been kept in good condition for more than a hundred years, still being enjoyed and appreciated.

78. *The Lingo-Bridges House*, Wilkinson County
RH

79. *The Newman House*, Sandersville
RH

The Newman House

Map no. 14-2   Photo no. 79

Valuable

DATE OF CONSTRUCTION	Circa 1855
LOCATION	245 North Harris Street, Sandersville
ORIGINAL OWNER	Major Mark Newman
INTERIM OWNERS	J. D. and J. W. Newman, sons of Major Newman
PRESENT OWNER	Mrs. H. H. Newman

ARCHITECTURAL DATA

COLUMNS	Shaft 10½″ diameter at bottom tapering to 9″ at top; 12 flutes with sharp arrises; 7′ 2½″ overall height.
WINDOWS	12″ by 18″, 12-light, 6 over 6

The Newman house was extensively remodeled shortly before the Civil War. The whole front portion was added to the original and there is a change of floor level at the juncture. The combination of unorthodox Greek Doric columns with exposed rafters is as charming as it is unorthodox, and in spirit closer to the early forms of Greek architecture than is the usual academic type.

80. *The Old Parsonage (now the Bell House),* Milledgeville
Library of Congress Photo

The Old Parsonage

Map no. 4-16   Photo no. 80

Valuable

DATE OF CONSTRUCTION	Before the Civil War
LOCATION	140 North Columbia Street, Milledgeville
ORIGINAL OWNER	Methodist Church
AMONG INTERIM OWNERS	Thrweatt-Trippe
PRESENT OWNER	Frank Bell

There is a curious relation between this house and Magnolia Manor, both in Milledgeville. The body of the Old Parsonage has a deep entablature, but only a cornice and the suggestion of an architrave (or beam) over the porch. Magnolia Manor has a deep entablature over the porch, and only a cornice over the body of the house. The Old Parsonage house has five openings on the front of the house and only three spaces between the columns. Magnolia Manor has only three spaces between the columns, with five openings behind. Photographs of this house are included in the Historic American Buildings Survey.

Magnolia Manor

Map no. 4-17   Photo no. 81

Valuable

DATE OF CONSTRUCTION Circa 1859

LOCATION 731 Habersham, Milledgeville

ORIGINAL OWNER Lewis Kenan

INTERIM OWNERS ——— Jarrett, Dr. Gustav Lawrence

PRESENT OWNERS Misses Lucetta and Roberta Lawrence

ARCHITECTURAL DATA

PORCH 41′ 2″ by 7′ 6″; ceiling 9′ 1″; architrave and frieze 3′ deep.

COLUMNS 11¼″ square at bottom of shaft tapering to 10″ at top, 8′ 8″ overall height.

DOORS Entrance 3′ by 7′

WINDOWS 12″ by 20″, 12-light

Interesting comparisons may be made between this house and the Old Parsonage, photo no. 80.

The Wescoloski-Bryan House

Map no. 13-8   Photo no. 82

Notable

DATE OF CONSTRUCTION Circa 1850

LOCATION Main Street, Riddleville, Washington County

ORIGINAL OWNER Wescoloski

INTERIM OWNERS Stephen T. Jordan, Lurian Jordan Fulgham, William Henry Fulgham

PRESENT OWNERS Mr. and Mrs. John Y. Bryan

ARCHITECTURAL DATA

PORCH Railing 2′ 3″ above floor; pickets ¾″ square, 4¼″ on center

COLUMNS 10¼″ square, 10′ 3″ overall height

DOORS Entrance 3′ by 7′

WINDOWS 10″ by 12″, 18-light, 9 over 9

Another of the many variations of the one-story Greek Revival cottage, this well-cared-for house must appear very much as it did in antebellum days. It overlooks a spacious lawn with a fine grove of trees.

The original owner of this house was one of the early Jewish residents. He sold the house to Stephen T. Jordan in 1867; it has since been continuously owned by Jordan's descendants.

81. *Magnolia Manor*, Milledgeville
RH

82. *The Wescoloski-Bryan House*, Riddleville, Washington County
KK

83. *The Howard-Dean House,* Milledgeville
KK

The Howard-Dean House

Map no. 4-18   Photo no. 83

Valuable

DATE OF CONSTRUCTION	Circa 1833
LOCATION	121 East McIntosh Street, Milledgeville
ORIGINAL OWNER	Homer A. Howard
INTERIM OWNERS	DeLauney, White, Gaas, Lamar, Winsor, McQueen, Bass
PRESENT OWNER	Mrs. Ione Bass Dean

ARCHITECTURAL DATA

PORCH	Beaded siding
WINDOWS	8″ by 15″, 12-light

The house was originally on the corner of McIntosh and Jefferson Streets. Restored by its present owner, it maintains a quality peculiar to Greek Revival architecture, a quality combining Greek dignity with pleasant informality.

Glen Mary

Map no. 5-4   Photo no. 84, p. 49

DATE OF CONSTRUCTION	Circa 1853
LOCATION	Sparta to Linton Road, Hancock County
ORIGINAL OWNER	Theophilus Jackson Smith
INTERIM OWNERS	General and Mrs. Ethan Allen Hitchcock, then various members of the Nicholls family
PRESENT OWNERS	Miss Elizabeth Nicholls and Mrs. James Frederick Nicholls

ARCHITECTURAL DATA

PIERS	Lower floor 2′ 2½″ wide, 1′ 6″ thick; corner piers 2′ 2″ by 2′ 2″.
	Almost parallel to highway, house faces ESE.

The inclusion of Glen Mary under "cottages" might well be questioned, its size and dignity suggesting a different category. It is, however, of a type frequently referred to as a "raised cottage," and because it so well illustrates the culmination of the development from vernacular cottage to classic architecture, it is included here. Its relation to the preceding cottages is obvious, while the flat roof, precise proportions, full entablature, and Greek detail clearly indicate that it was designed according to classic rules. Its style might well be called High Greek Revival.

Unlike the vernacular prototypes, Glen Mary does not

seem to be a part of the countryside. Instead, it rises grandly above the hills in consummate contrast.

Surprisingly for a house which appears so academically correct, it is comfortable and eminently suitable to the area. Rooms and porches on the raised main floor not only have an unexcelled view of the countryside, they also catch every cooling summer breeze, breezes which are channeled through the house by way of the shaded porch and oversize windows and doors. The two-foot thick walls of the lower floor and the high ceiling of the upper floor accentuate the effect of coolness.

The transom and sidelights of the principal entrance door of the upper floor are of "cranberry" glass; white marble mantels and ornamental plaster ceilings further enrich the interior. The plaster work is signed by the plasterer: Francis McDermott.

Glen Mary has been in the possession of members of the same family since 1869, and it is good to know that two of them, Mrs. James Frederick Nicholls and Miss Elizabeth Nicholls, are restoring the grand old house, adding modern conveniences, and planning to live there when the work is complete.

85. *The Lane-Duggan House,* Hancock County
Destroyed by fire, 1968
JL & RH

The Lane-Duggan House

Map no. 5-5   Photo no. 85
Valuable to Area

DATE OF CONSTRUCTION	Antebellum
LOCATION	Granite Hill, Hancock County
ORIGINAL OWNER	Jeffrey Lane
AMONG INTERIM OWNERS	Colonel Andrew Lane, Mrs. Fleetwood Maddox, Mrs. Charles Rogers, ———— Duggan
PRESENT OWNER	Unknown, house destroyed 1968

ARCHITECTURAL DATA

PORCH	30' 8" by 10'; bottom of architrave to porch ceiling 5½".
COLUMNS	Spacing 9' 5" on center, 9' 11" on center, 9' 5" on center; 1' 9" diameter at base of shaft; 12' 7½" overall height.
PILASTERS	1' 6" at base of shaft; 12' 5½" high
DOORS	Entrance 3' 6" by 7' 1"
WINDOWS	12" by 20", 12-light
	The house, which was remote from the highway, faced NW.

As with Glen Mary, the inclusion of the Lane Duggan house under "cottages" is questionable. The reasons for its inclusion are the same. And here, too, the flat roof, classic

86. *The Brown-Northington House,* Davisboro, Washington County
    RH

87. *Column Detail,* Brown-Northington House
    RH

proportions, meticulous detail, and elegantly correct columns and entablature place the house in the High Greek Revival category.

There was a tendency for Greek Revival architecture to become cold and sterile, particularly in northern regions where the large porches were frequently unsuitable. The style often reflected the seemingly arbitrary rules of academicians instead of the needs of the client and the appropriateness to the region. In this case, adherence to the rules produced a house of classic serenity, while the large windows with their louvered blinds, the comfortable porch, and the inviting stairs transform its formality into sheer graciousness. It is interesting to note that the walls of the lower floor are of granite, quarried within a short distance of the house. So also are some of the out buildings.

This house is reputed to be one of the stopping places where Robert Toombs spent the night during his flight from the Yankees after the fall of the Confederate government.

The Brown-Northington House

Map no. 13-9   Photo nos. 86, 87

Valuable to Area

DATE OF CONSTRUCTION	Circa 1840
LOCATION	Davisboro, Washington County
ORIGINAL OWNERS	Turner L. and Cynthia Brown
AMONG INTERIM OWNERS	W. R. Kitchens
PRESENT OWNER	Mrs. Sarah Kitchens Northington

ARCHITECTURAL DATA

PORCH	46′ 4″ by 8′ 1″ (extends across entire front of house); ceiling 8′ 8½″; soffit of cornice 10″, bottom of cornice to bottom of architrave 4″, architrave 5¾″ wide; horizontal railings 3½″ by 3½″, set oblique.
COLUMNS	10¼″ square, no taper; 8′ 3½″ overall height.
DOORS	Entrance, originally double door opening 6′ wide by 7′ high.
WINDOWS	10″ by 12″, 18-light, 9 over 9

House faces SE.

As it developed in the Oconee Area, Greek Revival architecture took two distinct and divergent courses. One was the process already described and illustrated wherein the architecture started with indigenous types, became more and more academic, increasingly adapting its character to Greek prototypes and classic rules, and finally culminated in that type referred to as High Greek Revival.

The other course of development, which we will term Vernacular Greek Revival, embodied the spirit rather than the precise forms of Greek architecture. Logic, clarity, and simplicity are its Greek characteristics. The indigenous forms developed by the early settlers were still logically suitable, and the Greek Revival architecture of this category maintained its indigenous character. Wood construction was logically expressed as wood structure, not as marble forms copied in wood. (The Greeks themselves were not always so logical, having expressed the forms of wood prototypes in their marble temples—marble temples which were frequently recopied in wood in this country.) In this second category, the principal changes made from the indigenous architecture of the Oconee Area were the added emphasis on the columns and an overall simplification of form and detail, which gave clarity and stateliness to the basic forms already in use. Columns were enlarged, and sometimes set independently in front of the porch floor in keeping with the new emphasis on them. They were likely to be square, expressive of the fact that they were built of boards and hollow within. Windows and doors were likely to be larger, the windows with larger and fewer panes than in the earlier examples, and the doors with fewer and larger panels, all in keeping with the simplicity and new scale of the Greek-inspired architecture. Moldings especially were simplified, losing their former delicacy, but reflecting the strength and vigor of the Greek prototypes. The sloping roof, the wide intercolumniation, and the mere suggestion of a beam or architrave over the columns were maintained as in the older examples, affirming the wooden structure.

The Brown-Northington house is a beautiful example of this type architecture. Like the earlier indigenous types, it seems a part of its surroundings, almost as though it grew out of the ground. It is distinctly southern in character and classic in spirit. Its frank architectural expression of time and place, of structure and material, of deliberate simplicity, link this with the best of modern architecture.

It is interesting to compare this house with the preceding one at Granite Hill. Though the basic plans are similar, the architectural philosophies behind the two designs seem to be antithetical, that of the Lane-Duggan house based on the rigid rules of classic architecture, rules that deal primarily with esthetic aspects of archeology, proportion, and detail, while the architectural philosophy behind the design of the Brown-Northington house reflects a frank expression of function, climate, structure, and locale, all unified by a free and easy adaptation of Greek forms.

It is interesting to note that the examples of High Greek

88. *The Francis Plantation House*, Washington County
JL & RH

89. *Entrance Doors,* Francis Plantation House
JL

90. *Well House and Dairy,* Francis Plantation
JL

Revival shown are eminently livable and suited to the area; also that the examples of Vernacular Greek Revival frequently have a serene stateliness that is the essence of classic Greek architecture.

The Francis Plantation

	Map no. 13-10 Photo nos. 88, 89, 90
	With plantation buildings: Valuable to Area
DATE OF CONSTRUCTION	Circa 1856
LOCATION	Near Davisboro on Josey Church Road, Washington County
ORIGINAL OWNER	Cordall Francis, who obtained the land in 1783. The house has been in the Francis family continuously since.
PRESENT OWNER	Mrs. Sarah Eugenia Francis Josey
BUILDER	Captain W. B. Francis

ARCHITECTURAL DATA

COLUMNS	12″ square; 10′ 8″ from architrave to pier; pier 1′ 3″ above porch floor level.
DOOR OPENING	Entrance 5′ by 8′; frosted patterned glass in sidelights and transom
	Remnants of old garden in front. House faces west.

The Francis Plantation boasts an unusual number of antebellum outbuildings still standing and some in use. The house itself is a variation of the Greek Revival cottage, raised high off the ground, with some of the delicate wood lattice still in place between stuccoed masonry piers. Heavy stone abutments on each side of the entrance steps are obviously modern additions. The double front doors with raised octagonal panels framed with unusually heavy moldings are an outstanding feature of the house. The small size of the front porch is compensated by a tremendous back porch which connects with the kitchen. This back porch was evidently the center of plantation life, a kind of combination outdoor living room, dining room, work room and office. Though dilapidated, the well house with a dairy on one side and larder on the other, is still a charming outbuilding, located only a few feet from the back porch. The commissary, built of large squared logs beautifully fitted together, is still in prime condition and looks as though it should last another hundred years. Other outbuildings still standing include a dovecote, a barn, a work shed, and several old cabins, all in varying degrees of decay.

The house itself is almost grand because of its scale and simplicity: four huge rooms, two on each side of the hall, plus a large dining room on the back, and a tremendous porch with connecting kitchen. It is in fair condition, and one would like to see it and at least the well house and dovecote restored. It would take real imagination and perhaps a change in living habits, however, to adapt from a contemporary house with its many small rooms to one with so few and such large ones.

The Hurt-Rives Plantation House

Map no. 5-6   Photo nos. 91, 92

With plantation fence and buildings: Valuable

DATE OF CONSTRUCTION	West part very early 1800s. East part with gallery begun before the Civil War, but not finished until the 1870s.
LOCATION	About six miles from Devereux, Hancock County.
ORIGINAL OWNER	William Hurt, who built west portion in early 1800s
INTERIM OWNERS	G. S. Rives who bought the plantation in 1836 or 1840, and descendants of G. S. Rives
PRESENT OWNER	Sidney B. Rives, Jr.

Though it was in a dismal state of repair when the photograph was made the house is being restored. It probably has more of the original plantation buildings still standing than any other antebellum plantation in the Oconee Area. Remnants of the old picket fence still surround the house, which is now (1971) in the process of being restored. The house itself is an indigenous type, classified here as Greek Revival by virtue of its simplicity and some of the details. The lower floor is of rough masonry, plastered over, probably with kaolin, a kind of white clay found in the area. The main floor, raised a full story above the ground, is of wood with a delightfully wide front porch which follows the L-shape of the house.

A row of slave cabins, each with its own fenced area, still stands with a strange high building called "the jail" at one end. According to Mrs. Robert Woodall (née Susan Rives) who has carefully researched the plantation records, this building was originally a smoke house, but was later used as quarters for county prisoners who worked on the plantation in the 1880s and 1890s. Its peculiar form is similar to that of the cotton gins shown on the drawing of the Harris-Rives Plantation. The interiors of the cabins are suprisingly pleasant, particularly considering the dilapidated appearance from the outside. The ceilings with exposed round pole beams have been whitewashed with the kaolin clay previously

91. *The Hurt-Rives Plantation House*, Hancock County
RH

92. *Fireplace in Slaves Quarters*, Hurt-Rives Plantation
RH

93. *The Evans-Boyer House*, Linton, Hancock County
JL & KP

The Evans-Boyer House
Plan of principal floor

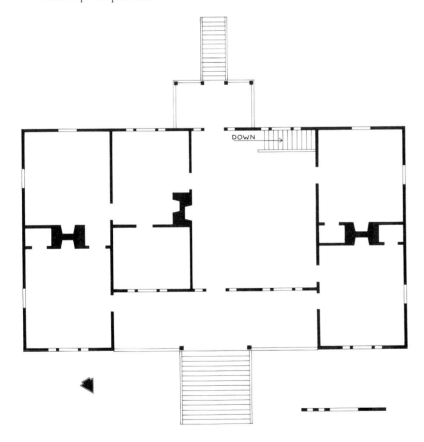

mentioned; and so have the tremendous open fireplaces which have received so many coats over the years that the original rough masonry is smooth and rounded, and pleasant to the touch.

The Evans-Boyer House

	Map no. 5-7 Photo no. 93
	Valuable
DATE OF CONSTRUCTION	Antebellum
LOCATION	Linton, Hancock County
ARCHITECTURAL DATA	See floor plan.

The predecessor for this unusual house is the log cabin with the "prophets' chambers" at each end of a wide front porch. Though the semi-enclosed porch fails to catch shifting breezes as does a more open type, the plan has many advantages. Breezes are pulled through the large central room, which has the added advantage of being sheltered from the sun. The porch itself is so protected that it can be used from early spring until late fall, and even on mild days during the winter. The enclosed quality of the porch is accentuated by its smooth walls which are plastered like an interior room, giving it the piquant quality of being a space that is at one time both indoors and outdoors. The proportions, detail, and overall composition are pure Greek Revival: the unusual plan indicates the freedom of design possible within the seemingly rigid rules of that style.

The house is said to have been built to be used as a residence by a professor at Linton Academy, and also as a dormitory for students who boarded with him. This probably accounts for the unusual size of the large central room which could have been used as a student dining room and meeting hall as well as a living room.

A partition, evidently added shortly after the house was built, now divides that space into two rooms. The added partition is not shown on the floor plan.

The house appears to be unused, but in good condition. It could probably be restored with modern conveniences added for the same price (or possibly a little less) as a modern house with the same number of rooms. Very few houses built today could equal its charm and livability if properly restored.

The Kirby House

	Map no. 15-10 Photo no. 94
	Worthy of Mention
DATE OF CONSTRUCTION	Probably antebellum

LOCATION   205 Baggett Street, Gordon, Wilkinson County

PRESENT OWNER   ——— Kirby

Though it has many features that might be classified as Greek Revival, this small cottage has others that indicate a reaction against the style. The flat wood arches are but a step removed from Victorian scroll saw work. The house has an overall quality that is intimate in scale, a quality which is closer to Victorian romanticism than to Greek discipline. With blinds replaced, and banisters restored, this could again be a quaint and charming cottage. Add to those a well-proportioned picket fence, and it would be, in the words of the women's magazines, irresistible.

Two Cottages Facing the Town Square

Map no. 12-1   Photo nos. 95, 96

(1) The Gerdings-Young House

Notable

DATE OF CONSTRUCTION   Probably about 1850; addition to rear before 1885

LOCATION   103 Sumpter Street, Eatonton

ORIGINAL OWNER   Julius Gerdings

INTERIM OWNERS   ——— Boss, R. B. Nisbett, ——— Adams, ——— Shaw, Robert Young

PRESENT OWNER   H. A. Young

94. *The Kirby House,* Gordon, Wilkinson County
JL & KP

95. *The Gerdings-Young House,* Eatonton
KK

96. *The Floyd-Greene House,* Eatonton
KK

ARCHITECTURAL DATA

PORCH   Banister pickets 1½″ by 1½″ at 3½″ on center; bottom of cornice to bottom of architrave 2′.

COLUMNS   8″ face by 6″ deep by 13′ high; corner columns L-shaped, 8″ on face sides, 6″ deep.

DOORS   Double opening 4′ by 8′; doors have heavy Greek Revival moldings.

FENCE   Known to be pre-twentieth century, probably antebellum; pickets 1½″ by 1½″ at 3″ on center; typical pickets 32″ high plus pointed end; baseboard (replacement) 7½″; total height 41″ plus or minus; rails 2½″ by 2¾″ wide.

(2) The Floyd-Greene House

Worthy of Mention

DATE OF CONSTRUCTION   Original part probably very early nineteenth century; porch probably about 1850.

97. *The Mosely-Adams House,* Eatonton
RH

LOCATION	105 Sumpter Street, Eatonton
ORIGINAL OWNER	—— Floyd
AMONG INTERIM OWNERS	Cate Greene, Thad Greene
PRESENT OWNER	Greene estate

ARCHITECTURAL DATA

PORCH	Ceiling 10′ 3″, slopes and varies; bottom of cornice to bottom of architrave 11½″.
COLUMNS	6½″ face by 4½″ deep by 9′ 1″ high
DOORS	Double opening 4′ by 6′ 6″
WINDOWS	8″ by 10″, 18-light, 9 over 9
	Fine mantels with delicate reed work and exquisite moldings.

These houses were built close to the street as were so many village houses in the days when towns were for living and streets were for visiting. These houses further illustrate the versatility of the Greek Revival idiom.

The Gerdings-Young house must have been designed by an architect. Commodious, with large-scale Greek Revival-type columns, windows, doors, and trim; and with all parts unified, it presents an interesting comparison with the similar, but smaller house next door, a house with some disparate elements.

The smaller Floyd-Greene house appears to be very old. The beaded weatherboarding, the low doors, the small paned windows and the delicate woodwork, particularly that of the unusually fine mantels, indicate that this must have been built very early in the nineteenth century. The would-be Greek porch was certainly a later addition, and the bits of scroll saw work on the porch, still later. The porch might have been changed about the time that the Gerdings-Young house was built, with the idea of keeping up with a stylish neighbor. The change was probably a mistake in view of its proximity to the newer house. If the porch was originally of the shed type, as is likely, the contrast would have been especially pleasing, while the present porch invites an unfair comparison.

The Mosely-Adams House

Map no. 12-2   Photo no. 97

Valuable to Area

DATE OF CONSTRUCTION	Circa 1837
LOCATION	200 Church Street, Eatonton
ORIGINAL OWNER	—— Mosely
PRESENT OWNER	Hammond Adams

98. *The Adams-Hume House,* Eatonton
KK

ARCHITECTURAL DATA

COLUMNS   Shaft 19⅝″ diameter at base; 14′ overall height.

House faces SSE approximately parallel with street.

The stately beauty of the Mosely-Adams house affirms the validity, when handled with skill and restraint as in this case, of the ancient principles inherent in Greek Revival design.

The Adams-Hume House

Map no. 12-3   Photo no. 98

Valuable

DATE OF CONSTRUCTION   Antebellum

LOCATION   416 North Jefferson Avenue, Eatonton

ORIGINAL OWNER   ——— Adams, father of John L. Adams

AMONG INTERIM OWNERS   John L. Adams, Howell Hearn

PRESENT OWNER   Ben L. Hume

ARCHITECTURAL DATA

DIMENSIONS   Front of house 38′ 4″ wide

PORCH   29′ 9″ (outside of pier to outside of pier) by 10′; floor 30′ by 10′ 4″; bottom of cornice to bottom of architrave 17½″; bottom of architrave to porch ceiling 17½″.

COLUMNS   Shaft 17½″ diameter at base, 16 flutes; overall height varies from 12′ 2″ to 12′ 5″; spacing 10′, 8′ 11″ (center), 9′ 8½″ on center.

FRONT DOOR   3′ 6″ by 8′

WINDOWS   12″ by 22″, 12-light

House faces WSW approximately parallel to street.

The classic gable, with its precise slope, raking cornice, and entablature below, proclaim the Greek Revival influence in this house, just as do the Doric columns and the serene proportions.

129. *The Mansion*, Milledgeville. See page 86.
   KK

6. From Indigenous Two-Story House to Greek Revival Mansion

As with cottage architecture, many features of the Greek Revival mansion are not products of the classic era but are rooted in the indigenous architecture of the early settlers. It was the magnificent fusion of the two that gave Greek Revival architecture its particular glory. A case in point was the practice of using smooth walls, either by placing the boards flat or by plastering, a practice which antedated the Greek Revival, but which was followed so extensively during that period that it became a characteristic of the style.

One feature of the native two-story house which lost favor during the period was the southern practice of having the second story only one-room deep, presumably to take advantage of summer breezes. Though the type was too appropriate to be completely abandoned, the Greek columns were likely to appear ponderous with so shallow a house. Because of this, and because increasing prosperity brought a demand for more rooms, the practice of having the second story only one-room deep became less common.

99. *The Jackson House,* Wilkinson County
KK

The Jackson House

Map no. 15-11   Photo no. 99

Valuable to Area

DATE OF CONSTRUCTION	Probably early nineteenth century
LOCATION	Highway 112, Wilkinson County (three miles from Highway 57)
ORIGINAL OWNER	The Jackson family moved to the district in the early 1700s. This house has been in their possession continuously since it was built.
PRESENT OWNER	Mrs. Pittman M. Jackson, Sr.

The house faces sw.

The Jackson house is more indigenous than Greek Revival, and it could be that the central hall was once an open dogtrot. The house was included in this section to show the close relationship between Greek Revival and indigenous architecture in the Oconee Area. The classic proportions and simplicity of detail would, in any case, justify its inclusion with houses of the Greek Revival period.

100. *The Torrance-Cline House,* Milledgeville
Destroyed 1969
RH

101. *The Harley-Rives House,* Sparta
KK

The Torrance-Cline House

Map no. 4-19   Photo no. 100

DATE OF CONSTRUCTION — Circa 1820; demolished in 1969 for a parking lot

LOCATION — 131 North Jefferson Street, Milledgeville (prior to demolition)

ORIGINAL OWNER — Probably H. Torrance

AMONG INTERIM OWNERS — ——— Lamar, ——— Hubbar, ——— Tranor, Miss Mary Cline, John J. Cline III

ARCHITECTURAL DATA

PORCH — Flush siding underneath; some of the other siding beaded, with much apparently replaced with square edge siding; cornice to bottom of architrave, and ceiling to bottom of architrave, both 7½"; soffit of architrave 6⅜", in line with outer face of columns.

COLUMNS — 10" square at bottom tapering to 8" at cap, 8' 9" overall height; originally no base; plain square-tapered columns of Greek Doric inspiration.

PILASTERS — 9¾" at bottom, 8" at cap, 8' 10" overall height, no base

DOORS — Entrance 3' 6" by 7' 2"; slats in door blinds ¼" by 3", adjustable slats in (original) window blinds ¼" by 2½".

Greek Revival exterior trim at front

Front yard paved with old brick, laid herringbone fashion, and without mortar. Possibly paved in later times, but pleasant in any case.

The Torrance-Cline house further illustrates the kinship of the Oconee Area Greek Revival and its indigenous prototype. This house predates the Greek Revival period and still has the old beaded siding on the north side of the house. The window and door trim, the door itself with its two vertical panels, and the columns were evidently changed at a later date to conform to the current style. Such changes are minor, almost superficial, and the indigenous plan and comfortable arrangement remained. The same old plan and arrangement were likewise used in many of the contemporaneous Greek Revival houses being built at the time this house was being remodeled.

The Harley-Rives House

Map no. 6-3   Photo no. 101
Valuable

DATE OF CONSTRUCTION — Circa 1850

LOCATION — 720 Elm Street, Sparta

ORIGINAL OWNER	William Isaiah Harley and his wife Mary Battle Harley
AMONG INTERIM OWNERS	DeLamar Turner, Bishop George F. Pierce, Moses Harris
PRESENT OWNER	George S. Rives

So close to Oconee indigenous architecture are the classic details of the Harley-Rives house that they might go unnoticed, but the low-pitched roof and the full entablature which crowns the main part of the house proclaim its studied classicism. As is true of some beautiful people, the house is not photogenic, and should be seen to be appreciated.

The house was built with slave labor, and most of the materials, including the wood for the solid walnut doors, was obtained from the plantation of the owner.

The Bass-Foster House

Map no. 5-9   Photo no. 102
Notable

DATE OF CONSTRUCTION	Circa 1817
LOCATION	Highway 16 near Granite Hill, Hancock County
ORIGINAL OWNER	Unknown
AMONG INTERIM OWNERS	——— Bass, John Sanders
PRESENT OWNER	Mrs. John Foster

ARCHITECTURAL DATA

COLUMNS	15″ square, 9′ 10″ overall height
DOORS	Entrance 3′ 4″ by 6′ 10″, 6-panel Covenanter type
WINDOWS	8″ by 10″
	House faces south, oblique to the highway.

This house is indigenous to the area, but the heavy wood columns must have been inspired by the Greek Revival style. It is quite possible that the body of the house, the porches, and the rooms under the porch roof were all built at different times. During the course of repairs, the roof of the one-story wing was temporarily removed, and the date 1817 found inscribed on the adjoining chimney.

It is interesting to compare this house with the similar but more sophisticated Evans-Boyer house at Linton.

The Fort-O'Connor House

Map no. 4-20   Photo no. 103
Valuable

DATE OF CONSTRUCTION	Circa 1820
LOCATION	Corner Liberty and Green Streets, Milledgeville

102. *The Bass-Foster House,* Hancock County
RH

103. *The Fort-O'Connor House,* Milledgeville
KK

ORIGINAL OWNER   Dr. Tomlinson Fort

AMONG INTERIM OWNERS   The Methodist Church used house as parsonage, Miss Mary Cline

PRESENT OWNER   Mrs. Edward O'Connor

ARCHITECTURAL DATA

PORCH   46' 6" by 8' plus 3" floor overhang; ceiling 10'. Weatherboarding lapped even under porches, possibly further indication that porches were added.

COLUMNS   Spacing beginning from left: 9' 7", 9' 5", 7' 4½" (center), 9' 1", 9' 11" on center; unorthodox version of Greek Doric; 14" diameter at base of shaft, 10 flutes; square bases probably not original; shaft 9' 5" overall height, capitol 3⅝", base 1½", overall 9' 10¼".

DOORS   Entrance 3' 2" by 6' 11"

WINDOWS   First story, 10" by 12", 18-light, 9 over 9; second story 8" by 10", 18-light, 9 over 9.

Tapered verge boards on gables.

The easy comfortable beauty of the Fort-O'Connor house is due in large part to additions made over a period of years. The second story porch with its ornate banisters which contrast pleasantly with the classic first story porch is an obvious addition, but even the Greek-inspired columns of the first story porch must be later than the 1820 date of construction. Additions to the rear of the house are further evidences of the growth of this house.

The Dozier-Faulkner House

Map no. 7-4   Photo no. 104

Valuable

DATE OF CONSTRUCTION   Circa 1812; the porch possibly a pre-Civil War addition

LOCATION   Jasper County

ORIGINAL OWNER   Dozier

AMONG INTERIM OWNERS   ——— McDowell, Arthur Faulkner

PRESENT OWNER   Daughter of Arthur Faulkner

ARCHITECTURAL DATA

COLUMNS   15½" face by 15" deep at base, slightly tapered

DOORS   Entrance 2' 9" by 6' 5"

WINDOWS   First floor 8" by 10", 18-light, 9 over 9; second floor 8" by 10", 15-light, 6 over 9; possibly 9 over 6 originally.

House faces NW, and is parallel with highway.

104. *The Dozier-Faulkner House,* Jasper County
RH

The plan of this house and the natural slope of the roof are rooted in the indigenous architecture of the area. The heavy, square wood columns indicate the Greek Revival influence. The formal planting design of the front yard can still be traced, despite some gaps, by fine boxwood that has survived through the years.

105. *Turnwold,* Putnam County
KK

106. *The Reese-Sorensen House,* Monticello
RH

Turnwold

Map no. 11-5   Photo no. 105

Valuable

DATE OF CONSTRUCTION   Antebellum

LOCATION   Putnam County, six miles from Eatonton

ORIGINAL OWNER   Joseph Addison Turner

PRESENT OWNERS   Mr. and Mrs. Mike Dunn

The house pictured faces sw.

"Here from 1862 to 1866, Joel Chandler Harris, author of *Uncle Remus,* lived and worked as a printers' apprentice on what was probably the only newspaper ever printed on a southern plantation. *The Countryman,* a weekly newspaper edited and published by Joseph Addison Turner, owner of Turnwold. Mr. Turner, planter, lawyer, scholar, and writer, encouraged his youthful apprentice in writing and the use of the large plantation library. In the slave quarters the boy Harris heard African animal legends and the true Negro folklore of the Old South, which he immortalized in his *Uncle Remus* stories" (from the Georgia Historical Commission marker erected at Turnwold). This very pleasant house, set far back from the road and surrounded by ancient trees, appears as welcoming today as it proved to be to Joel Chandler Harris when he worked on the plantation as a boy. It has been completely modernized and the stucco columns appear to be replacements for older wooden ones. The original porch was probably one-story.

Within a few hundred yards is another antebellum house, now in ruins, but apparently once finer than the one pictured.

The Reese-Sorensen House

Map no. 8-3   Photo no. 106

Valuable to Area

DATE OF CONSTRUCTION   Circa 1820

LOCATION   25 Green Street, Monticello

ORIGINAL OWNER   Dr. David A. Reese

INTERIM OWNERS   Dr. Thomas C. Davis (1851–1858), Eli S.
Glover (1859–1866), Emily B. Fish

107. *The Stone-Boyer House,* Linton, Hancock County
KK

108. *The Morton-Alford House,* Putnam County
JL & RH

(1867–1876), Benjamin W. Peurifoy (1877–1920), Charles Harvey.

PRESENT OWNER   Alfred Sorensen

ARCHITECTURAL DATA

PORCH   38′ 6″ (outside of column to outside of column) by 9′ 6″; bottom of porch cornice to bottom of architrave 22″. The Greek Revival porch is almost certainly of later date than the rest of the house.

COLUMNS   22″ square, 17′ 6″ overall height, 4 flutes per side

DOORS   Entrance 2′ 10″ by 6′ 10″, 1 panel (rare)

WINDOWS   10″ by 12″, 18-light, 9 over 9

The house faces WNW.

The fine qualities of this house seem to be enhanced by the fact that it is not parallel to the street, and by the fact that the usual view is from the side. A plaque on the ground reads in part, "Here lived Dr. David Addison Reese, born in Mecklenburg County, son of a Revolutionary soldier and grandson of a signer of the Mecklenburg Declaration of Independence . . . in politics, a Whig, he succeeded Alexander Stephens as Congressman in 1835."

The Stone-Boyer House

Map no. 5-10   Photo no. 107

Valuable

DATE OF CONSTRUCTION   Circa 1837

LOCATION   Linton, Hancock County

ORIGINAL OWNER   Dr. John Stone

INTERIM OWNERS   Gus Buck, Johnny Boyer

PRESENT OWNER   Bernard Boyer

Evidently weathered for a hundred years, this old house appears sound and livable. Rarely were such elegant houses left unpainted, but when the wood remains sound, and weathers as graciously as here, one would be reluctant to cover it with paint. Though the architecture is almost severely classic, a description of this house with its grand old trees would have to include the word "romantic."

The Morton-Alford House

Map no. 11-6   Photo no. 108

In Ruinous Condition

DATE OF CONSTRUCTION   1857

LOCATION   Route 300, near Rock Eagle, Putnam County

ORIGINAL OWNER   Henry Morton

INTERIM OWNERS   Samuel Arnold Morton, Henry Jones
PRESENT OWNER   Harold Alford

Still standing in 1967 were the melancholy ruins of this deserted mansion. The ingenious and ingenuous adaptation of Greek motifs to local construction methods is worthy of study.

The Denham-Andrews-Birchall House

Map no. 11-7   Photo nos. 109, 110
Valuable to Area

DATE OF CONSTRUCTION   Circa 1840
LOCATION   Greensboro Highway, four miles east of Eatonton, Putnam County
ORIGINAL OWNER   Denham
AMONG INTERIM OWNERS   Dr. H. H. Cogburn, ——— Jones, A. D. Freeman
PRESENT OWNERS   Mrs. Alice F. Andrews and Mrs. Eloise F. Birchall

ARCHITECTURAL DATA

PORCH   Ceiling 18′ 8″
COLUMNS   17′ 6″ overall height; bottom of shaft 20″ in diameter.
House faces NW, and is parallel to the highway.

There are old photographs which show this house with a handsome picket fence around it. The picket fence was replaced by the present fence in 1927, but otherwise the house is little changed. Its architecture is basically indigenous with Greek Revival features including the magnificent porch, where Greek columns and details have been logically transmuted to conform to local construction methods.

The Stovall-Conn House

Map no. 4-21   Photo no. 111
Valuable

DATE OF CONSTRUCTION   Circa 1825
LOCATION   Corner Wilkinson and Greene Streets, Milledgeville
ORIGINAL OWNER   Joseph Stovall
INTERIM OWNERS   O'Brien, Beecher, DeGraffenreid, Calloway
PRESENT OWNER   W. T. Conn
BUILDER   Possibly John Marler (also spelled Marlor).

The Stovall-Conn house is another which "jes' growed." The original part was built during the Federal-Transitional

109. *The Denham-Andrews-Birchall House,* Putnam County
KK

110. *Porch Detail,* Denham-Andrews-Birchall House
RH

111. *The Stovall-Conn House,* Milledgeville
RH

112. *The Springer-Holten House,* Sparta
Photo courtesy Mrs. Holten

The Springer-Holten House
Plan of principal floor

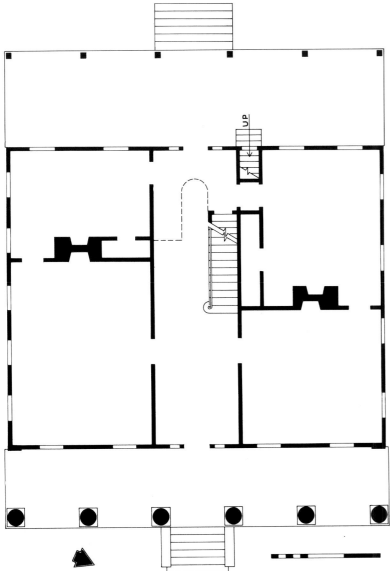

period, but it is the Greek Revival additions which dominate. Many times the southern builder took a cavalier attitude toward academic rules, and such was the case here where a magnificent portico was flung around the two street fronts of the house with little regard for symmetry, and even less regard for the proper joining of the porch entablature to the body of the house. Roof lines more or less took care of themselves. The capitals of the columns are a personal interpretation of the Ionic order. And in spite of, or because of, this disregard for pedantry, the result is a casually beautiful house with exactly thirteen columns which are said to represent the thirteen original colonies. Photographs of this house are included in the Historic American Buildings Survey.

The Springer-Holten House

Map no. 6-4   Photo no. 112

Valuable to Area

DATE OF CONSTRUCTION	Antebellum
LOCATION	Jones Street, Sparta
ORIGINAL OWNER	William G. Springer
INTERIM OWNERS	Burrell Wynn, Edgar G. Dawson, Colonel Henry Atkinson Clinch, Will Burgamy
PRESENT OWNER	J. W. Holten
	House faces east, parallel to the highway.
ARCHITECTURAL DATA	See floor plan.

Set far back from the street, and rising grandly from a hill, the classic Springer-Holten house typifies the popular concept of a southern plantation house. The scale throughout is large and grand. Like the exterior, the woodwork of the interior is Greek Revival, simple and somewhat massive. Such large and simple interiors are disappointing when the rooms are empty, but provide the perfect foil for mid-nineteenth century Victorian furniture.

The axial floor plan is typical of most of the Greek Revival houses of the area, and representative of the final phase that evolved from the dogtrot cabin to the planter's mansion with its great hall. Large enough to be used as a ballroom, and with oversize doors surrounded by glass at either end, the hall like the dogtrot, remained the center of plantation life, closely related to the out-of-doors, because it was, in effect, an extension of the main exterior walk right through the house.

The house is said to have been built before 1823, but the Greek Revival porch and woodwork would indicate a later date. It is reassuring to know that the present owners are in the process of restoring this fine old mansion.

Panola Hall

Map no. 12-4   Photo no. 113
Valuable

DATE OF CONSTRUCTION	Antebellum
LOCATION	400 North Madison Avenue, Eatonton
ORIGINAL OWNER	John Trippe
AMONG INTERIM OWNERS	Dr. Benjamin W. Hunt
PRESENT OWNER	M. L. Lyles
BUILDER	Probably Greene Alford

ARCHITECTURAL DATA

COLUMNS	31″ diameter at bottom of shaft, 22′ overall height; the "flutes" have flat faces; fine wooden version of Greek Doric order; bottom of cornice to bottom of architrave 4′ 8″.
DOORS	Transom and sidelights at front door have panes, with a pattern of frosted and amber glass.

The whole area around North Madison Avenue in Eatonton is pleasant with trees, and fine old homes such as this, as well as attractive and comfortable ones of later vintage. Most are conveniently near the center of town, but for this very reason, the section is in danger of being usurped by the usual and too common succession of small office buildings, then stores and filling stations. It is hoped that definite steps will be taken to save this section before it is too late.

Panola Hall is one of many fine Greek Revival houses in the area. The heavy parapet above the entablature helps conceal an almost flat roof. Treating such roofs in a classic manner was a problem that often plagued designers of the era.

In addition to its mortal occupants, the house is the habitat of a wistful ghost named Sylvia. She has been seen only by aristocrats, to whom she appears as a beautiful young woman, always wearing the same white hoopskirted dress and with a damask rose in her dark hair. For more than a hundred years now the various occupants of the house have graciously accepted her presence, and Sylvia, in turn, has ever been the perfect ghost, her one apparent fault being that she is something of a snob.

The Reid-Stubbs House

Map no. 12-5   Photo no. 114
Valuable

113. *Panola Hall*, Eatonton
RH

114. *The Reid-Stubbs House*, Eatonton
RH

DATE OF CONSTRUCTION	Antebellum
LOCATION	114 North Madison Avenue, Eatonton
ORIGINAL OWNER	Andrew Reid
INTERIM OWNERS	Frank Leverette, James M. Rainey (1894), E. F. Bronson, Mrs. E. F. Bronson
PRESENT OWNER	Mrs. F. M. Stubbs, daughter of E. F. Bronson

ARCHITECTURAL DATA

PORCH	Bottom of porch cornice to bottom of architrave 3′
COLUMNS	33½″ at bottom of shaft, 19′ 6″ overall height; Greek Doric.

Possibly the most successful method, both esthetically, and functionally, of handling the tremendous porches of Greek Revival mansions is to carry them all the way around as was done at the Reid-Stubbs house. Not only is the simple repetition of heroic scaled columns invariably magnificent, but the problem of relating and joining the colonnade to the house is eliminated. In addition, windows can be left open without danger from sudden showers, and if the weather is at all decent, a pleasant area can always be found on the hospitable porch. Such porches are and were expensive to build. The Reid-Stubbs house is a good example of the type, and appears to be in a good state of repair; even the attractive brick lattice under the porch is still in place.

Such large houses are not only expensive to build; they are likewise expensive to keep up. If remodeled into apartments, the apartments must be of a particularly high quality, and arranged with deference to the exterior, or the elegance becomes shoddy. In some cases where upkeep has become prohibitive for use as a residence, such houses have been successfully converted into prestige-type office buildings. It is to be hoped that this house will continue to be used as a private residence. If the time comes when this is unfeasible, it is near the center of town, is possessed of true elegance, and could well be converted into such an office building, or into quality apartments.

The Slade-Harris House

Map no. 12-6   Photo no. 115

Of National Importance

DATE OF CONSTRUCTION	1836
LOCATION	206 Madison Avenue, Eatonton
ORIGINAL OWNER	Daniel Slade
AMONG INTERIM OWNERS	Terrell Wingfield

115. *The Slade-Harris House,* Eatonton
RH

PRESENT OWNER   Mrs. V. V. Harris, daughter of Terrell Wingfield

ARCHITECTURAL DATA

COLUMNS   34″ diameter at base of shaft, 24′ 6″ overall height including octagonal granite bases; Greek Ionic order.

DOORS   Transom and sidelights at front door have panes with a pattern of frosted and amber glass.

Greek Revival architecture seems to have reached a certain classic perfection in the Harris house. The Ionic columns of the portico are repeated in the smaller columns of the entrance. Floor-to-ceiling windows with louvered blinds suggest the cool spacious interiors. Lattice brick walls and the most delicate of cast iron fences frame the yard, while trees and vines cast shadows on mellow brick walls.

Lockerly

Map no. 4-22   Photo nos. 116, 117

Valuable to Area

DATE OF CONSTRUCTION   Circa 1839

LOCATION   Irwinton Road, Milledgeville

ORIGINAL OWNER   Judge Daniel R. Tucker

INTERIM OWNERS   Emma Irwin Sibley, Dr. T. O. Powell, George Hollingshead, R. W. Hatcher

PRESENT OWNER   Edward J. Grassmann

ARCHITECTURAL DATA

PORCH   58′ 10″ (outside of pier to outside of pier) by 11′ (from wall to outside of base); floor projects 4″.

COLUMNS   Spacing 11′, 10′ 8″, 11′ 4″ (center space), 10′ 10″, 11′ on center; shafts 40″ diameter at base, 20 flutes; bases 4′ square, 7½″ high; 25′ 6″ overall height; Greek Doric order; back porch 13″ diameter at base of shaft, 12 flutes, 10′ 8¾″ high overall.

WALLS   Stucco over brick; blocked 14″ by 40″.

DOORS   Entrance 3′ 4″ by 8′, walnut, 4 flat panels.

WINDOWS   First story windows under porch 13″ by 19″, 18-light, 6 over 6 over 6.

House faces NW.

A truly outstanding example of Greek Revival architecture in its most classic form, Lockerly is owned by Edward J. Grassmann, who not only is restoring the house, but is plant-

116. *Lockerly,* Milledgeville
JL & KP

117. *Parlor,* Lockerly
RH

ing extensive gardens to be known as the Lockerly Foundation Arboretum. The house is of the finest quality throughout. The masonry walls are stuccoed over and a heroic Doric portico extends across the entire front. Inside, carefully executed trim frames solid walnut doors. The stairway has a mahogany railing and balusters, while the risers are ivory color, marbelized.

The illustration of the parlor shows what a wonderful foil the almost severe Greek Revival interiors were for the crystal chandeliers, ornate pier mirrors, and Victorian furniture of the period. Fine lace curtains were usually hung to soften the contrast between exterior and interior. Photographs of this house are included in the Historic American Buildings Survey.

118. *Pomegranate Hall,* Sparta
KK

119. *Side View,*Pomegranate Hall
RH

Pomegranate Hall

Map no. 6-5   Photo nos. 118, 119
Valuable to Area

DATE OF CONSTRUCTION	Circa 1830
LOCATION	322 Adams Street, Sparta
ORIGINAL OWNER	Nathan Sayre
AMONG INTERIM OWNERS	Judge Seaborn Reese, ——— Oliver
PRESENT OWNER	Cleveland M. Kale

ARCHITECTURAL DATA

DIMENSIONS	House 40′ 3″ wide
PORCH	42′ by 7′ 8″
COLUMNS	23½″ diameter at base of shaft, 23′ 6″ overall height; base is in two parts, the lower part square 8½″ high, the upper part octagonal 7½″ high; columns are not round, but have 14 flat sides; unorthodox version of Doric order.
PILASTERS	23½″ side at bottom of shaft
FRONT DOOR	3′ 6″ by 7′ 10″
WINDOWS	12″ by 18″, 18-light, 6 over 6 over 6; slats in blinds on porch 3¾″ wide, stationary.

Pomegranate Hall, sometimes called "The Half-House" because legend has it that this is half of a house that was inherited by Mr. Sayre and another legatee. According to the story, Mr. Sayre dismantled his half, had it transported from New York or New Jersey, and recreated in Sparta about 1830. Houses similar to this, and frequently called "half-houses" were built throughout the country during the second quarter of the nineteenth century. Many were built with the idea that balancing rooms were to be added later, so that the hall, and therefore the entrance, would eventually be in the center of the house. Others were deliberately designed to have the hall and entrance to one side. The beauty of this and similar houses proves that symmetry was not essential to good Greek Revival architecture. A close study of this house would reveal some of the weak as well as the strong points of this style architecture. The junction of the porch cornice with that of the house is awkward, and though the sloping parapet rising above the entablature suggests a gabled roof, it is not truly expressive of the roof behind. This criticism is not meant to be disparaging; the inconsistencies of the architecture of Pomegranate Hall are a part of its character and add interest to the house.

The original entablature of the porch appears to have been repaired at a later date by being covered with clapboards. Though unconventional, the treatment is in harmony with the architecture of the house. The columns themselves are not round, but are fourteen-sided, made up of flat tapered boards gracefully expressing their wood structure and Doric spirit. Incidentally some of the proto-Doric columns were themselves chamfered instead of round.

The beauty of the columns, the graceful fanlighted door, and the long windows of the front are at once apparent. Equally lovely is the play of color, texture, and shadow on the sides of the house. Handmade brick painted white over a base of unpainted stone; vigorously designed louvered blinds, dark green in color and suggesting coolness within; windows with rippled glass and delicate wood muntins, together with the weathered out-buildings are vibrant in their setting of grass and sky.

The Reid-Griffith House

Map no. 12-7   Photo no. 120

Valuable

DATE OF CONSTRUCTION	Circa 1848
LOCATION	200 South Washington Street, Eatonton
ORIGINAL OWNER	——— Reid
AMONG INTERIM OWNERS	Walter Griffith
PRESENT OWNER	Mrs. Walter Griffith

ARCHITECTURAL DATA

PORCH	18′ 2″ by 10′ 4″, steps recessed into porch 1′ 3½″.
COLUMNS	29¼″ square at base of shaft, 18′ 7″ overall height; stucco over brick; tapered.
DOORS	Entrance recessed 11″; double opening 4′ 10″ by 7′ 2″; interior door casing has unique corner blocks of vigorous and incisive design.

Dining room has unusual cabinets.

120. *The Reid-Griffith House*, Eatonton
KK

121. *The Gibson-Sapp House,* Wilkinson County
JL

122. *The Marler-Humphrey House,* Milledgeville
JL & RH

This is one of four mansions built in Eatonton by the Reid brothers. Simpler than the Reid-Stubbs or the Reid-Lawrence house, this one derives its beauty from a straightforward expression of plan and structure more than from classic precedent.

The Gibson-Sapp House

Map no. 15-12   Photo no. 121

Notable

DATE OF CONSTRUCTION	Before 1854
LOCATION	Highway 18, three miles south of Gordon, Wilkinson County
ORIGINAL OWNER	Evidently James S. Gibson
AMONG INTERIM OWNERS	David Solomon, W. H. Fitzpatrick, Carrie S. Lee
PRESENT OWNER	Mrs. Albert Sapp

ARCHITECTURAL DATA

COLUMNS	19½" square at base of shaft, 19' overall height; 4' between center columns, 3' between end columns.

House faces sw parallel to highway.

Most of the antebellum houses of the Oconee Area were built by the owners without the aid of architects. Many of these were delightful, their inconsistencies having a certain piquant charm. Others have features which bother us today, features which we may not appreciate because of changes that have occurred to the house or to the setting over the years, or because of changes that have occurred in our sense of values. This house is a case in point. Certainly the columns appear terribly heavy. Could the builder have based the dimensions on a frontal view, unaware that the diagonal dimension of a square column is the one that counts visually? And did the fact that the returning architrave of the porch rests partly on a window opening bother him, or is this quibbling? When it was new and freshly painted, and complete with blinds and trees and grass, the sheer power of the portico might well have obviated such criticism.

The Marler-Humphrey House

Map no. 4-23   Photo no. 122

Valuable to Area

DATE OF CONSTRUCTION	Circa 1830
LOCATION	Corner North Wayne and McIntosh Streets, Milledgeville
ORIGINAL OWNER	John Marler (also spelled Marlor)
AMONG INTERIM OWNERS	John Marler, Mrs. Mary Marler Bethune, Oscar M. Cone

PRESENT OWNER   Mrs. W. C. Humphrey

ARCHITECT   John Marler

ARCHITECTURAL DATA

PORCH   18′ 9″ by 7′ 10″; steps recessed into porch; ceiling 22′; ceiling and bottom of porch cornice to bottom of architrave 2′ 6″.

COLUMNS   Spacing 3′ 8¾″, 9′ 3¾″ (center), 2″ 7¾″ on center; 24½″ diameter at bottom of shaft; 20 flutes.

PILASTERS   24½″ at bottom of shaft; 19′ 6½″ overall height.

The Marler-Humphrey house was built by the architect-builder, John Marler, who likewise built the Masonic building in Milledgeville. The comparatively narrow two-story porch of the Greek Doric order adheres closely to classic precedent, but the influence of the earlier Milledgeville-Federal type is apparent, not only in its plan and overall proportions, but in the delicate balcony over the entrance, in the fan in the gable, and in the graceful circular stairway within.

The Newell House

Map no. 4-24   Photo no. 123

Valuable

DATE OF CONSTRUCTION   Circa 1825

LOCATION   201 South Clark Street, Milledgeville

ORIGINAL OWNER   Isaac Newell

INTERIM OWNERS   Thomas Newell, Mary Newell, Colquit Newell

PRESENT OWNER   Miss Colquit Newell

One of few houses which has been continuously occupied by members of the same family for well over a hundred years, the Newell house is similar in some respects to the Marler-Humphrey house. It is likely that the Greek Doric columns with the heavy entablature over them and the massive doorway are due to changes, as they are distinctly Greek Revival in character, of a type later than the 1825 date of the house. In front of this house is a crape myrtle of an unusually beautiful shade of pink. During the summer it blooms continuously and in winter its gnarled limbs and white bark add interest to the landscape.

Rockwell

Map no. 4-25   Photo nos. 124–127

Valuable to Area

DATE OF CONSTRUCTION   1834

LOCATION   19 Allen Memorial Drive, Milledgeville

123. *The Newell House,* Milledgeville
JL

124. *Rockwell,* Milledgeville
JL & RH

125. *Fence and Gate*, Rockwell
JL & RH

126. *Interior Doorway*, Rockwell
Library of Congress Photo

ORIGINAL OWNER	Samuel Rockwell
INTERIM OWNERS	Prince, Johnson, Myrick, Morris, Bland
PRESENT OWNERS	Mr. and Mrs. Oscar Ennis
ARCHITECT	Joseph Lane

ARCHITECTURAL DATA

PORCH	19′ 7″ by 8′ 4″; ceiling 24′ 10″; flush siding under porch; bottom of cornice to bottom of architrave 3′.
COLUMNS	25″ diameter at base of shaft, 24 flutes, 21′ 10″ overall height; Greek Ionic order; pilaster caps are Doric; spacing 3′ 6″, 9′ 7¼″, 3′ 6″, on center.
DOORS	Double opening 4′ 8″ by 8′ 5″
WINDOWS	10″ by 24″, 24-light, 12 over 12, 4 lights wide
BALCONY	Curved
STAIRS	Pattern cut in wooden stair risers
FENCE	Retaining wall about 17″ high; 37″ from bottom of lower rail to top of upper rail; 41″ to top of cresting; about 58″ from sidewalk to top of cresting.

House faces SSE approximately parallel to street.

The plan of the Rockwell mansion, or Beauvoir as it was once called, the size of its porch, the arched doorway, and the circular stairway indicate its close relationship to the older Milledgeville Federal houses. The columns, entablature, and pediment are, however, pure Greek Revival, heavier than the Federal type and, in scale, closer to those of Hellenic Greece. Of Greek inspiration also is the wood fret around the balcony floor. Interior doorways are especially fine, with crisp moldings and carved frets and anthemion motifs of Greek inspiration. The iron fence at the front was cast in Milledgeville, and further enhances the rare beauty of the house and grounds. Photographs of the interior and exterior of the house are included in the Historic American Buildings Survey.

The Reid-Lawrence House

Map no. 12-8   Photo no. 128

Valuable to Area

DATE OF CONSTRUCTION	Before 1840
LOCATION	Wayne Street, Eatonton
ORIGINAL OWNER	Alexander Sidney Reid (1840–1895)
INTERIM OWNER	T. G. Green (1895–1957)
PRESENT OWNER	George Lawrence

ARCHITECTURAL DATA

PORCH   36′ 3″ by 12′; 37′ 9½″ outside of pier to outside of pier, 12′ 5″ wall to outside of pier; roof so constructed that no weight rests on columns.

COLUMNS   29″ diameter at base of shaft, 25′ 3″ overall height, 24 flutes; Corinthian order with hand-carved wooden capitals: columns evenly spaced; small columns at doorway 13½″ diameter at base of shaft, 24 flutes: Corinthian order.

DOORS   Entrance 3′ 7″ by 8′

House faces ENE, parallel to street.

Magnificently situated at the end of Wayne Street, and framed by the trees that border that street, the Reid-Lawrence house is so related to its surroundings that it is as though the house plan had been continued out-of-doors—or the street plan continued into the house. The vista from the avenue is repeated by the long front walk, a brick walk which is bordered by boxwood of such size that the rows on either side nearly meet at the center. The vista almost terminates at the Corinthian portico which is, in a sense, repeated in miniature by the entrance with its smaller Corinthian columns. Inside the axis of the street and walk is restated by the long hall and symmetrical floor plan.

The following information was contributed by the present owners, Dr. and Mrs. Lawrence. The house was built by one of the Reid brothers. These brothers built five houses in Putnam County, and four of them are still standing (1967). Alexander Sidney Reid spent ten years gathering materials for the house, and three years were spent in actual construction. The foundation was allowed to settle for a year before the house was completed. The crossbeams in the attic are about sixty feet long, and are hand hewn with no break in them. The porch roof is self-supporting, so that the weight of the roof does not rest on the columns. Wood pegs were used to fix the framing members. The original plaster work including three ceiling medallions in downstairs rooms is still in good condition. The medallions and marbled painting were done by Italian craftsmen when the house was built. The total cost of the house when built was fourteen thousand dollars. The stained glass window in the upstairs hall was an 1890 or early twentieth-century embellishment. Some of the woodwork was painted in the combed and grained style at about the same time. A kitchen was added to the rear in 1895, the original kitchen having been a separate building.

127. *Stairway*, Rockwell
Library of Congress Photo

128. *The Reid-Lawrence House*, Eatonton
JL & RH

129. *The Mansion*, Milledgeville
KK

130. *Interior View of Dome*, The Mansion
RH

131. *Mantel*, The Mansion
Library of Congress Photo

The Mansion

Map no. 4-26   Photo nos. 129–132

Of National Importance

DATE OF CONSTRUCTION   1838

LOCATION   120 South Clark Street, Milledgeville

Home of State Governors from 1839 to 1869.

Home of President of Georgia College at Milledgeville since 1889.

ARCHITECT   Credited both to John Pell and Timothy Porter; also to Charles B. Cluskey

ARCHITECTURAL DATA

See floor plan.

PORCH   32′ 4″ by 10′ 8″

COLUMNS   35½″ diameter at base of shaft, 23′ to 24′ overall height, base 1′ 8″ high; Greek Ionic order; columns equally spaced.

DOORS   Entrance 3′ 8″ by 8′

WINDOWS   12″ by 18″, 12-light

Granite trim said to be imported from Vermont.

The Mansion
Plan of principal floor

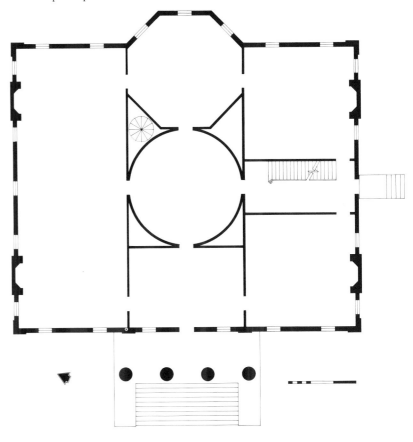

Probably the most academic of all the Greek Revival mansions of the area, the old Governor's Mansion is an acknowledged masterpiece. Though the dome is visible from the exterior, it is not an outstanding feature. Instead it is the facade with its granite-trimmed walls and shallow but monumental portico, the two so closely and classically related that they count as one and dominate the exterior. Thus it is usually with surprise that the visitor, after passing through the foyer, enters the rotunda, with its high domed ceiling and subtle overhead lighting.

The sophisticated floor plan differs markedly from that of contemporary mansions in the area. Precedents for the circular domed hall are numerous, however, and include the Villa Rotonda by Palladio and Thomas Jefferson's Monticello, both of which are frequently cited as the source of the architect's design. Regardless of its origin, the design of the Mansion exhibits a masterful handling of space and of the classic principles of architectural design.

The structure of the Mansion was built to last, but much of the finish and plasterwork deteriorated over the years. This has recently been restored, the restoration completed in 1967.

The Mansion is described in detail in *The Early Architecture of Georgia* by Frederick Doveton Nichols.[1] Photographs are also included in the Historic American Buildings Survey.

132. *Old Kitchen,* The Mansion
RH

133. *The Sayre-Shivers House,* Sparta
RH

The Sayre-Shivers House

Map no. 6-6   Photo nos. 133, 134, 135
Valuable to Area

DATE OF CONSTRUCTION	Begun in 1829, finished 1839
LOCATION	118 West Broad Street, Sparta
ORIGINAL OWNER	Robert Sayre
INTERIM OWNERS	Colonel Thomas M. Turner and descendants, since the mid-1840s
PRESENT OWNER	W. O. Shivers, descendant of Thomas M. Turner

Frequently referred to in Sparta as the twin houses, this house and the Bird-Campbell house built on adjoining corner lots are strikingly similar, and were built about the same time.

Both are extremely fine mansions. Ten years were required to complete the Sayre-Shivers house. The foundation is of 2′ by 4′ granite blocks. Windows are panelled, and have both interior shutters and exterior blinds. Mantels on the main floor are of Italian marble, and the ceilings have rich plaster moldings and medallions. The overdoors are carved with acanthus leaf designs. The doors themselves are mahogany, as is the stair rail. Within the newel post of the stair rail

134. *Interior View of Entrance Doorway,* Sayre-Shivers House
Library of Congress Photo

135. *Mantel,* Sayre-Shivers House
Library of Congress Photo

is set one of Mr. Sayre's mother of pearl cuff links, a feature which used to be known as an "amity button."

In Nantucket, similar buttons of ivory were imbedded in the newel post when all the debts incurred in building a house were paid. They were called "mortgage buttons" and signified that the house was mortgage free.[2]

Originally the grounds were more extensive, and formally landscaped. They were surrounded by a fence which repeated also in wood, the sheaf of wheat design of the entrance porch balusters. This was later replaced by a picket fence, but there were two panels of the original remaining within the memory of Mr. Shivers, the present owner. In time the picket fence, too, deteriorated and was taken down. Mr. Shivers remembers the design of the grounds, the front yard having consisted mostly of boxwood-bordered flower beds. Other plants remembered are violets and white hyacinths. Unusual for the time and place was *festuca glauca* and a cactus hedge. In the back a 60' euonymus hedge-bordered walk led to the orchard, where naturally, there was a scuppernong arbor. It is a shame that there is no extant plan of the grounds as they were originally. Perhaps some day one will turn up, as they must surely have been designed and drawn by a landscape architect, or a landscape gardener as they were called in those days.

Photographs of the house and the interiors are included in the Historic American Buildings Survey.

The Bird-Campbell House

Map no. 6-7   Photo no. 136

Valuable to Area

DATE OF CONSTRUCTION	Circa 1834
LOCATION	204 West Broad Street, Sparta
ORIGINAL OWNER	Wilson Bird
AMONG INTERIM OWNERS	Lovick Pierce, ——— Moore
PRESENT OWNER	Estate of Mrs. Effie B. Campbell

ARCHITECTURAL DATA

COLUMNS	11' 2" overall height; round columns 18⅝" diameter at bottom of shaft, capitals 2' 1½" high; square columns 15" square from railing down, 14½" square above railing, corners chamfered; capitals 2' 6" high, top of railing 29½" above floor.
DOORS	Entrance, double opening, 4' 4" by 8' 10"
WINDOWS	18" by 25", 8-light, 4 over 4 (on porch)

As previously mentioned, the Bird-Campbell and the Sayre-Shivers houses, placed on adjoining corner lots, are frequently called the "twin houses" in Sparta. Being similar in plan, size, and proportion, and being further united by powerful Greek Revival architectural forms, the title is apt, despite the difference in the porches. A study of the Bird-Campbell porch reveals that originally, it too must have been only an entrance porch and about the size of that of the Sayre-Shivers house. At that time, the similarity would have been even more striking, and the sobriquet probably dates from then, when the only marked difference would have been in the orders used for the entrance porches: Doric for the Sayre-Shivers house, Corinthian for the Bird-Campbell.

Not as high as their girth would normally indicate, the center columns have exquisitely carved capitals in an intriguing variation of the Corinthian order. The design for the capitals was likely taken from one of the builders' guide books of the time, but it is one with which the writer is not familiar.

Equally delightful are the capitals on the columns of that part of the porch which is assumed to be an addition. Obviously scroll saw versions of the central columns, they are expressive of the wood structure and of the machine tools of the time. As is the case with several houses in the area, the pilasters are of a different order from the columns; in this case the pilasters seem to be a local interpretation of the Doric order.

The Cuthbert-Benton House

Map no 7-5   Photo no. 137

Valuable

DATE OF CONSTRUCTION	Antebellum
LOCATION	Two and a half miles north of Highway 16, Eatonton to Monticello, Jasper County
ORIGINAL OWNER	Senator Alfred Cuthbert
PRESENT OWNER	L. O. Benton

ARCHITECTURAL DATA

PORCH	Extends around the NW, the NE, and the SE sides of the house.
COLUMNS	11″ square
DOORS	Entrance faces NE.

The Cuthbert-Benton house was reputedly prefabricated, a practice more widespread during the mid-nineteenth

136. *The Bird-Campbell House*, Sparta
RH

137. *The Cuthbert-Benton House*, Jasper County
KK

century than is generally realized. California houses of that time were commonly fabricated in the east, shipped in sections to the west coast, and assembled on arrival.

Ready cut would be a more likely term for the Cuthbert-Benton house, however. The plaster walls and brick piers and chimney would of necessity have been applied and built according to conventional methods. The millwork, weatherboarding, and hand-hewn framing might all have been factory assembled, and there are peculiarities which suggest that this was the case. The attic timbers are much more widely spaced than was customary, with unplaned boards nailed flat to them, these boards substituting for ceiling joists. The laths are nailed to the face of the boards. On the exterior, pilasters could conceal vertical seams. And, despite the surrounding porch and the Greek Revival columns and moldings, the house does not have the feel of an Oconee Area house. Wherein lies or does not lie this intangible quality, or whether the lack is good or bad is a difficult question. It may result from the preconceived idea that the house was prefabricated. At any rate, this house sits high on a hill, is spacious and airy, surrounded by a columned porch, and is altogether delightful.

7. Antebellum Grounds, Interiors, and Diverse Architectural Styles

So appropriate was Greek Revival architecture to the antebellum southern way of life, and so strong was its appeal to the southerner, that the style has become the very symbol of those far-off days.

Yet houses in other styles were built during that period. By the 1840s Andrew Jackson Downing's popular books were inveighing against the Greek Revival style with its forced symmetry and imitation marble forms. By the end of

the 1840s the Greek Revival was losing favor except in the South. There the new styles were occasionally accepted, sometimes twenty to forty years after their designs had appeared in the plan books. Frequently the designs selected included the wide porches and cool halls, so much a part of the older houses. Sometimes the old forms were maintained, the new style being acknowledged only by scroll saw work on the porch. Such decoration was also added to update existing

138. *The Old State Capitol*, Milledgeville
    Photo about 1936 by Eberhart Studios

houses. The conservatism of the area at that time makes it difficult to date the houses architecturally, particularly the neo-Gothic and "Italian Villa" styles which were used both before and after the war.

Whether because the plans were frequently similar, or because Classic proportions were common to most, or because all the building materials of the era were harmonious; because the same basic type doors and windows were common to all, or because the powerful Greek Revival architecture provided the perfect foil for the almost frivolous Victorian decoration; for whatever reasons, existing southern antebellum houses seem always to be in harmony with each other.

Several houses built prior to the Civil War had additions of a later pre-Civil War period. Where no single style dominated, such houses are included in this section, though parts could be otherwise classified. Two factors which vitally affected the finished architectural structure were the use of exterior color and the color and furnishings of the interior. A real study of these factors is beyond the scope of this book, but a brief review of color and furnishings is in order, if only to encourage further research.

Many of the antebellum houses were unpainted inside and out. The high quality of lumber obviated the need of paint as a preservative, and such houses, like the Buck-Archer house (36), have grown more beautiful through the years as the wood has acquired the patina of age.

Until the advent of the Greek Revival, houses were painted a variety of colors. This was particularly true in very early days, as research at Williamsburg has proven. Laborious removal of layers of paint from the Brown-Sanford house has revealed early coats of buff and gray. One coat of a color is not absolutely conclusive. Then as now, a cheap primer coat of a different shade might be used. Doubtless, too, the owner occasionally changed his mind between coats of paint. It was the fashion of the times, however, to paint wood in the colors shown on prints of contemporary English and European examples. Since such examples were generally of stone, colors used tended to soft yellows, buff, beige, and gray.

During the Greek Revival period, the idea of white marble temples swayed the fashion to white. Most of the older houses were repainted to conform to the current style, although there were exceptions. Writers of the time commented on the gaily painted houses of the Charleston waterfront, but Charleston was ever different and would accept or spurn a style as she pleased.

Wealthy planters along the Mississippi likewise experi-

mented with more exotic colors, pale yellow with white columns, soft apricot with ivory trim, dull pink with faded blue woodwork were among them.[1]

As in most of the country during the Greek Revival era, white houses with dark green blinds predominated in the Oconee Area. The combination is particularly appropriate to the South, where a white house gleaming within a green grove is a cooling and refreshing sight.

With the Italianate and Gothic Revival styles, came a return to the use of color.[2] Andrew Jackson Downing, style arbiter of the day, decried the use of white and made a great case for muted colors, particularly a color called "drab," also "fawn," and several shades of gray. He likewise recommended that stuccoed or cemented houses be painted to resemble some mellow stone, such as Bath or Portland stone, and that cottages and villas be painted a "cheerful, mellow hue to harmonize with the verdure of the country." It is likely that many of the Italianate and Gothic Revival cottages and houses were originally so painted.

In some sections of the South it was customary to paint all interior walls, ceilings, and trim white, partly because of the cooling effect of white interiors, also because of the cheapness of lime or kaolin base paints, as in the slave cabins of the Hurt-Rives Plantation (92). Another custom, rigorously followed in many sections, was that of removing draperies, rugs, and heavy fabrics during the summer. Bare floors, white curtains, and chintz covers for furniture imparted psychological if not actual coolness. During post-Civil War years, the use of straw rugs and matting became popular, but the writer does not know whether this dates back to the antebellum custom of separate decorating schemes for winter and summer.

Another factor which should be mentioned was the completely different approach to landscaping home grounds in antebellum days. So-called foundation planting was unheard of. In many cases, the foundations of the houses were an especially attractive feature in themselves, frequently including delicate wood lattice work. Several houses in the area still boast the original lattice "underpinning," the Alston-Wiley house being a particularly fine example. Even when the foundation was of plain masonry or stucco, there was no attempt to hide it. There might be one or two favorite flowering shrubs planted against the house, but the practice of concealing the foundation as if it were something shameful is twentieth-century false modesty, not Victorian.

The front yard might be a grass lawn, or swept earth, or a formal garden with boxwood parterres. From a distance, the boxwood gave the impression of a carpet of deepest green, while at closer range the pattern of the beds repeated, not literally but in essence, the formal treatment of the interior, and the axis of the interior would be aligned with the axis of the garden. In nearly all cases the dooryard or grounds were protected with a fence, which gave visual unity to the house and grounds.

The delicate summer houses, usually built of wood and exposed to the weather, as were the fences, have virtually disappeared. Vines were much used during antebellum days on fences, summer houses, porches, the house itself, and on trees. Some of the hardier ones such as English ivy, wisteria, scuppernong, and the Lady Banksia, and Cherokee Roses still survive from those times. Native vines including yellow jessamine, woodbine, and autumn clematis—called Virgin's Bower in those days—were likewise used.

Important to most of the southern antebellum gardens was *Euonymus japonica,* a large dense shrub with very dark and lustrous leaves, not dissimilar to burfordi holly. It could be sheared, and was most often used as a very high hedge, frequently high enough so that arched gateways could be cut through it as in English yew. The Euonymus hedge at the Sayre-Shivers house is said to have been more than fifteen feet tall. *Euonymus japonica* fell victim to a scale during the early part of the twentieth century, and though it is possible to control this by constant spraying, such spraying is expensive and troublesome. If a botanist could develop a scale-free type, he would restore to the South one of its finest shrubs, one which once served as a lustrous and living wall to many an antebellum garden.

Ornamental plants used in antebellum gardens were too numerous to list in this study, but some were used so frequently and have survived for so long that their presence may indicate the site of a long-forgotten garden. Such plants include flowering shrubs, among them *lonicera fragrantissima,* appropriately called breath of spring, forsythia or golden bells, chaenomeles or flowering quince, crape myrtle, and several types of roses. Flowering bulbs which persist include varieties of daffodils, jonquils, and narcissi, small blue hyacinths, leucojum or snowflakes, and star of Bethlehem. Among other flowers that might be found in the vicinity of an antebellum garden are iris, formerly called flag lilies, daylilies, violets, and trailing vinca. Native cedar trees (*juniperus virginiana*), ancient and gnarled, are much in evidence around the old houses as well as in the vicinity of the gardens.

In the southern and eastern parts of the area, gardenias formerly known as cape jasmine, azaleas, and camellias still remain from antebellum gardens. Lilacs, which were much used, rarely survived the intervening years. According to one authority, bridal wreath spirea, nearly always associated with the old gardens, was a later addition, not having been cultivated until 1864.[3] Another authority gives 1843 as the date of its introduction to this country.[4]

Except at the McKinley house which is described in this chapter, there is little indication that any of the houses were deliberately landscaped in the "informal manner" which had been practiced in England for more than a century, and which was advocated by Downing. It is possible that some grounds were so successfully landscaped in the informal or naturalistic manner that the artistry of the design has not been recognized.

The Old State Capitol

Map no. 4-1   Photo no. 138

Of National Importance

DATE OF CONSTRUCTION	Begun 1805, north wing added 1828, south wing 1836, porticos 1850, gates mid-1860s.
LOCATION	Milledgeville
ORIGINAL USE	Used as State Capitol until after Civil War.
PRESENT USE	Forms campus and buildings for Georgia Military College.
ARCHITECTS	Smart and Lane

The logical and grand evolution from the dogtrot cabins and the farm houses of the early settlers to the magnificent but still indigenous architecture of the Greek Revival is the dominant theme of the architectural history of the area. Throughout the development, there were innumerable variations, some closely related and some in direct contrast to those previously shown. A case in point is the old Capitol in Milledgeville, the first part of which was finished in 1807. Though Baldwin County had been open to settlement for only four years at that time, the style selected for the Capitol building was a contemporary version of Gothic. An occasional house had been built in this style before, but this seems to be the first public building in the United States to be built in the neo-Gothic style. This was the avant-garde style of its day, and in many ways a superficial one. As with most of the early examples, the plan was symmetrical and classic, as was the building itself. The Gothic style was expressed only in details such as the pointed arches of the openings, the parapet around the roof, and the profile of stone moldings copied in wood and stucco. The overall effect, though not Gothic, was both magnificent and practical. The parapets may have been unnecessary for protection, but silhouetted against the sky, they are a thrilling sight and convey the idea that the government does offer protection. The stucco surfaces hardly resembled their stone prototypes, but until damaged by fire in 1941 the aged walls, partly lichen-covered, were equally beautiful.

There were doubtless other isolated examples, but the Gothic style was rarely used again until the 1840s, when it would reappear as one of the popular styles of the day, and would provide delightful contrast to the even more popular Greek Revival architecture. It is interesting to note that the gates were not built until the mid 1860s when Gothic architecture was at the height of its popularity in this country; also that they were designed and built under the supervision of Federal Army Colonel B. W. Froebel—a different sort of memorial from the occupation forces, and one that has added to the beauty of Milledgeville for more than a century.

The McKinley House

	Map no. 3-7 Photo no. 139
	Valuable to Area
DATE OF CONSTRUCTION	1856
LOCATION	Highway 22 and 24, near Milledgeville, Baldwin County
ORIGINAL OWNER	Colonel William McKinley
INTERIM OWNERS	Mrs. Anne Andres McKinley, Guy Cumming McKinley, Archibald Carlisle McKinley, and Pauline del McKinley, Archibald Carlisle McKinley.
PRESENT OWNER	Mrs. Archibald Carlisle McKinley
ARCHITECTURAL DATA	See floor plan.

Built in the Gothic style in 1858, the McKinley house has been owned by the same family ever since, and descendants of the original owner still occupy the fine old brick house. With a perfectly symmetrical facade, the Gothic influence is apparent in such features as the steep pitch of the roof, the double chimneys, the flat arches, and by the carved barge boards of the gables. The setting with a tree-bordered drive, open lawn, and old trees, is idyllic.

A drawing of a house and house plan similar to this is illustrated and described in *The Architecture of Country Houses* by A. J. Downing,[5] and this may have served as the basis for the design of the McKinley house.

In explaining the design of the house, Downing wrote: "It will be seen at a glance that this design is in the English Gothic or pointed manner, yet it is no copy of any foreign cottage in this style." He went on to explain that it was de-

signed for living in the middle United States, and that architectural features such as broad and large windows, tracery, and picturesque gables which were expressive of the English climate had been altered to a "simple, earnest, and local expression for the Northern States...in a simple country house in the pointed style, we prefer to adapt the window openings to the climate by making them plain, and covering them with shutter blinds."

It will be noted that with the McKinley house, this adaptation to climate has been carried further, the rooms have been made larger and airier, the chimneys simplified, and the oriel window over the entrance changed to a southern type bal-

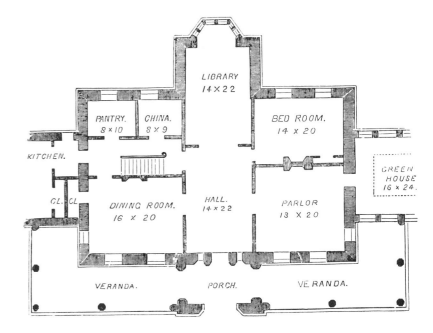

A Country House in the Pointed Style
Reproduced from figure 134 (opposite p. 304) of *The Architecture of Country Houses* by A. J. Downing (New York: D. Appleton, 1850)

139. *The McKinley House,* Baldwin County
RH

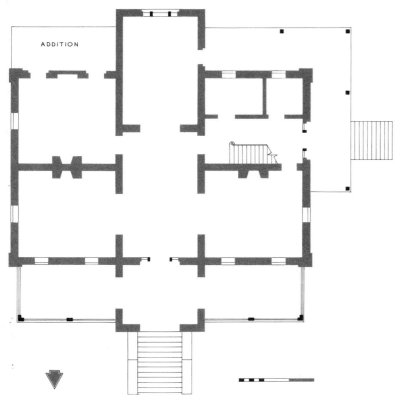

The McKinley House
Plan of principal floor

cony, all in keeping with Downing's philosophy of adapting borrowed styles to local climate and expression.

A copy of the illustration for the house by Downing and also a plan of that house are included.

The Ethridge-DuBose-Peck House

Map no. 6-8   Photo no. 140
Valuable to Area

DATE OF CONSTRUCTION	Circa 1853
LOCATION	513 Boland Street, Sparta
ORIGINAL OWNER	Probably Olney Ethridge
INTERIM OWNER	Charles W. DuBose family from 1856 to 1944
PRESENT OWNER	Colonel Marvin W. Peck since 1944
ARCHITECTURAL DATA	See floor plan.

The owners of this house through the years have had the good sense to recognize its unique charm, and have resisted the temptation to remodel it into a current style. It is only in recent years, and then by a younger generation, that such delightful Victorian houses have again been generally appreciated.

It is interesting to read the plan books of that era and to study the logic behind such designs, which were extolled

140. *The Ethridge-DuBose-Peck House,* Sparta
RH

The Ethridge-Dubose-Peck House
Plan of principal floor

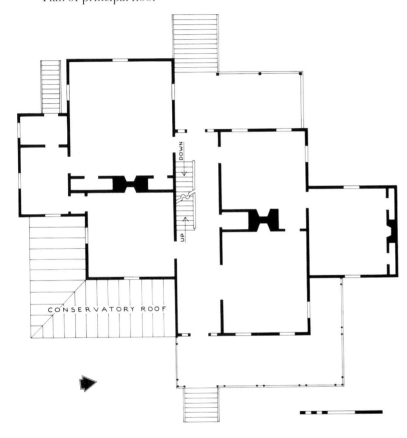

CONSERVATORY ROOF

141. *The Deese-Bruner Cottage,* Toomsboro
JL

because, unlike much Greek Revival design, the materials of those houses was honestly expressed, wood particularly being expressed as wood. Certainly it would be hard to find a better expression of the beginning of the machine age than in the fanciful scroll saw work of the Ethridge-DuBose-Peck house.

In several ways the seeds of modern architecture can be found in such houses. First of course is the insistence upon honest expression of the materials used, and recognition of the machine as a vital force in design. Even more important was the freeing of the plan from the rigid symmetry of classic precedent. Though some of the best of the Greek Revival buildings were asymmetrical, symmetry was basic to most. The deliberate nonsymmetry of this "Swiss Chalet"-type house and of many of the neo-Gothic and Italianate houses of the era, introduced a new freedom to planning which continues to the present day.

The Deese-Bruner Cottage

Map no. 15-13   Photo no. 141

Worthy of Mention

DATE OF CONSTRUCTION   Antebellum

LOCATION   Toomsboro, Wilkinson County

ORIGINAL OWNER   Joel Deese

INTERIM OWNERS   H. A. Hall, Mrs. M. E. Hall, Mrs. Mary Ware, W. W. Thompson

This house was originally of logs and had a separate kitchen connected by a walkway. It was moved to Toomsboro from the country, and the kitchen moved to another location. It is similar to the many Georgia cottages that have a shed roof porch across the front and lean-to rooms across the back, a type exemplified by the Buck-Archer and the Hitchcock-Walker houses. The house does, however, have a unique picturesque quality because the outer eave board across the front porch is scalloped, thereby giving the indigenous cottage a Victorian cast.

The Lane-Walker House

Map no. 6-9   Photo no. 142

Valuable

DATE OF CONSTRUCTION   Before 1856

LOCATION   Corner Elm and Hamilton Streets, Sparta

ORIGINAL OWNER   Probably the Lanes of Granite Hill

INTERIM OWNERS   Dr. George W. Walker, Julia Dixon, Mr. and Mrs. John Holmes, Sr., J. D. Copeland

PRESENT OWNER   Mrs. John D. Walker, Jr.

Another of those houses whose appeal defies analysis, this house, as Mrs. Terrell Moore noted in an article for the *Georgia Magazine,* simply "has charm."[6] It has had a varied history as well. It is believed to be the old house from Granite Hill Plantation, moved to Sparta when the new one, the Lane-Duggan house, was completed. At one time, it was used as a bordello. Today, without a suggestion of its boisterous middle years, it is the serene and tranquil cottage on the corner of Elm and Hamilton Streets.

The Eli Glover House

Map no. 8-4   Not illustrated.

Worthy of Mention

DATE OF CONSTRUCTION   Before 1829

LOCATION   Washington and Hillsboro Streets, Monticello

ORIGINAL OWNER   Eli Glover

INTERIM OWNERS   Continuously in Glover family.

The scroll saw work and the gables in the front indicate that this cottage was remodeled after its early date of construction. At one time the present kitchen was used as a post office.

The Hurd-Edwards House

Map no. 8-5   Photo no. 143

Worthy of Mention

DATE OF CONSTRUCTION   Circa 1855

LOCATION   25 Washington Street, Monticello

ORIGINAL OWNER   William S. Hurd

INTERIM OWNERS   Thomas J. Comer (1857–1860), Maxmilian H. Hutchinson (1860–1874), John H. Kelly (1874 to circa 1900), several owners since.

PRESENT OWNER   H. T. Edwards

This is one of the few houses in the area with a mansard roof. Known to have been once remodeled, the central dormer and ornate porch might have been additions.

The Dubignon-Brown House

Map no. 4-27   Photo no. 144

Notable

DATE OF CONSTRUCTION   Circa 1850

LOCATION   Corner Columbia and Hancock Streets, Milledgeville

ORIGINAL OWNER   Fleming Dubignon

INTERIM OWNERS   Perrin W. Brown, Julian S. Brown

PRESENT OWNER   Mrs. Julian S. Brown

142. *The Lane-Walker House,* Sparta
RH

143. *The Hurd-Edwards House,* Monticello
RH

144. *The Dubignon-Brown House,* Milledgeville
JL

145. *The Rossiter-Little House,* Sparta
Library of Congress Photo

146. *The Rossiter-Little House,* Sparta
Library of Congress Photo

Treillage such as that on the Dubignon-Brown house is too generally unappreciated and a rapidly disappearing feature of many antebellum homes. It is likely that the banisters were originally of a similar type with the motif within the posts, known as the "sheaf of wheat" design, repeated there.

The yard with its tile-bordered flower beds and swept walks will bring nostalgic memories to many older Georgians. Mrs. Brown, the present owner, remembers her late husband saying that he helped lay out these beds when he was a boy, probably in the 1890s.

The Rossiter-Little House

Map no. 6-10   Photo nos. 145, 146

Valuable to Area

DATE OF CONSTRUCTION	Before 1812
LOCATION	223 Broad Street, Sparta
ORIGINAL OWNER	Dr. Timothy Rossiter
AMONG INTERIM OWNERS	Elias Boyer (purchased house in 1812)
PRESENT OWNER	Mrs. Sarah Frank Little (house has been in her family for more than 130 years)

Built before 1812, and remodeled several times, this house too has the "sheaf of wheat" treillage, a light and delicate but unexpectedly sturdy type lattice which seems particularly suitable to the South. The projecting wings are pleasant features, indicative of a plan that not only assures maximum ventilation throughout, but that manages to scoop the breezes into the house. Both the treillage and the projecting wings are of later vintage than the original house. The sturdy roof lines of the older part dominate the side view.

The house was photographed for the Historic American Buildings Survey.

The Hardwick-Overstreet House

Map no. 13-11   Photo nos. 147–149

Valuable to Area

DATE OF CONSTRUCTION	Before 1850
LOCATION	Davisboro, Washington County
ORIGINAL OWNER	William P. Hardwick
PRESENT OWNER	Hoke Overstreet

ARCHITECTURAL DATA

PORCH	Posts 2¾″ by 8½″, 7′ 1½″ high; beam over porch posts 1⅞″ by 8¾″; railing 29″ high; rafters 2″ by 2⅞″, beaded.

House faces ssw.

Probably built in the days when the passing of the gaily painted new trains through the village of Davisboro was the exciting event of the day, the Hardwick house blandly turns its side to the main street, overlooks a tremendous garden, and faces the railroad tracks. It is still a good view, because from that distance the objectionable features are negligible, and despite newer ways of travel and changes in the trains themselves, a train passing through the countryside is still a thrilling sight, at once nostalgic and romantic.

The house set high on a full basement story, with its porch overlooking all, gives the impression that it was imported straight from the West Indies, or at least coastal Georgia. The whitewashed masonry of the first floor, the gracious steps leading to the main floor, the play of light and shadow on the balustrade, the casual and perhaps deliberate way the columns of the second floor were not placed over those of the first floor, give the front of this house an easy timeless beauty.

The porch itself is sheer delight—exposed rafters overhead, flat columns with corbel caps, lattice at the end for privacy and shade, potted plants, rocking chairs and a railing at foot-propping height.

The garden is planted with old-fashioned shrubs, mostly glossy evergreens. Underneath the shrubs, the ground appears clean swept, its sandy surface cool and white. This is not a house that can be described in technical terms, and the writer realizes that the description is flowery. The house and grounds inspire extravagant description.

The house was severely damaged in a hurricane many years ago, and part of its charm may date from changes made at that time.

147. *The Hardwick-Overstreet House,* Davisboro, Washington County
RH

148. *Front Porch,* Hardwick-Overstreet House
RH

149. *Column Detail,* Hardwick-Overstreet House
RH

The Newton-Wade House

Map no. 7-6   Not illustrated
Notable

DATE OF CONSTRUCTION	Circa 1856
LOCATION	Highway 83, Machen, Jasper County
ORIGINAL OWNER	Willis Newton
INTERIM OWNERS	Paul Roby, Edwin F. Perry, Sr.
PRESENT OWNER	J. D. Wade

Some details of the very pleasant porch of this house appear postbellum. It is likely that minor changes were made in the course of repairing or otherwise during the hundred-year period since this house was built.

The Jordan-Bellew House

Map no. 8-6   Photo no. 150
Valuable

DATE OF CONSTRUCTION	Circa 1838

150. *The Jordan-Bellew House,* Monticello
     KK

151. *The Jordan-Benton House,* Monticello
     RH

LOCATION	Madison Road, Monticello
ORIGINAL OWNER	Fleming Jordan (Georgia State Legislature 1841–1844)
INTERIM OWNERS	Gray, Towns
PRESENT OWNER	Robert Bellew

What was known as the Italianate influence is apparent in the details of this foursquare southern house with its surrounding porch. The hipped roof with wide eaves supported by brackets, the turned balusters, the suggestion of an arch at the end of the porch beams, and the arched insets in the porch columns are typical mid-nineteenth-century American versions of Italian Renaissance details. To us today, and doubtless to Europeans of that day, the house is as American as Yankee Doodle and as southern as magnolia blossoms. The wide eaves over the second story windows, and the comfortable porch which relates to the adjoining rooms with oversize windows down almost to the floor, are appropriate to the area. The interior woodwork is handsome, and includes a freestanding curved stairway. The house is being restored by the present owners; the photograph was taken during restoration.

The Jordan-Benton House

Map no. 7-8   Photo no. 151

Valuable

DATE OF CONSTRUCTION	Circa 1858
LOCATION	Highway 83, one mile sw of Monticello city limits, Jasper County
ORIGINAL OWNERS	William F. Jordan and wife Jane Goolsby
INTERIM OWNERS	J. D. Benton, William Brazey, Mrs. Rosalyn Fitzpatrick
PRESENT OWNER	L. O. Benton III
	House faces NW.

The architectural similarity of the Jordan-Benton house to the Jordan-Bellew house is as noticeable as the similarity of their designations. Plan books of the time usually referred to the style as "the bracketed style" and mentioned Italian influence. The use of brackets instead of the mutules and dentils of the more familiar classic cornices dates back at least as far as the Farnese Palace by Vignola. In America such cornices were sparingly used until the 1840s and it is likely that in the Oconee Area they were first so used in the cornice of the Masonic building in Milledgeville (28).

Their continued popularity was due in part to the fad for the Italian Villa style, with which they were considered requisite. Regardless of style, their use was appropriate and logical. The traditional elements of the classic entablature, that is the mutules, dentils, etc., were not easily adapted to the very wide eaves which were desirable as protection from both sun and rain. Brackets, however, could be used with the widest eaves and not become ponderous. Those used on the Masonic building at Milledgeville are Renaissance in character, suggestive of their marble prototypes. As the style progressed, the brackets became lighter, and evolved into a new and original form which was expressive of the good frame structures so popular at the time. They were also expressive of the burgeoning machine age, which at this early date was almost symbolized by semi-mass produced scroll saw work. As developed and used in the Jordan-Bellew and the Jordan-Benton houses, they are delightfully expressive of the construction methods of the time.

The Trawick House

Map no 5-11	Photo no. 152
Valuable	
DATE OF CONSTRUCTION	Circa 1860
LOCATION	Linton, Hancock County
PRESENT OWNER	Continuously owned by members of the Trawick family

Not quite completed at the outbreak of the Civil War, some of the upstairs rooms remained unfinished until recent years. Formerly there were two summerhouses placed symmetrically on either side of the front yard. There were also windows with louvered blinds in the cupola. Such cupolas, though rare in the Oconee Area, were frequently used in other sections of the South both as ventilating devices and as lookouts for supervising farming operations.

Like the Evans-Boyer house, this house was built to accommodate Linton Academy boarding students. The two downstairs rooms on the right of the hall were originally one large dining or commons room.

Monticello Female Institute

Map no. 8-7	Photo no. 153
Notable	
DATE OF CONSTRUCTION	1850
DESTROYED	1970
LOCATION	North Warren Street, Monticello
ORIGINAL OWNER	Monticello Female Institute
AMONG INTERIM OWNERS	——— Campbell, ——— Hill, O. H. Banks

Though it appeared that the exterior had been somewhat altered, this house with its elaborate brackets and arched

152. *The Trawick House,* Linton, Hancock County
KK

153. *Monticello Female Institute*
Destroyed 1970
RH

154. *The "Convenience," Dickerson Plantation,* Wilkinson County
     JL & RH

155. *The Hicks-Herrington House,* Johnson County
     KK

156. *Dovecote,* Hicks-Herrington Plantation
     KK

windows maintained something of the Italianate character it must have displayed when it was first opened as a fashionable boarding school for females.

The "Convenience," Dickerson Plantation

	Map no. 15-14 Photo no. 154
	Worthy of Mention
DATE OF CONSTRUCTION	Antebellum
LOCATION	Near Toomsboro, Wilkinson County
ORIGINAL OWNER	Dickerson family
INTERIM OWNERS	Members of Dickerson family
PRESENT OWNER	Mrs. Benita Dickerson Brannen (descendant of original owner)

One of several outbuildings remaining after a disastrous fire which destroyed the plantation house and heirloom furnishings, this once stylish "convenience" had accommodations for three. All buildings on the plantation including the "big house" and the slave cabins had similarly scalloped boards at the eaves.

The Hicks-Herrington House

	Map no. 9-2 Photo nos. 155, 156
	Valuable
DATE OF CONSTRUCTION	Circa 1850
LOCATION	One mile from Wrightsville on U.S. 319, Johnson County
ORIGINAL OWNER	Dr. Henry Hicks
INTERIM OWNERS	R. P. Hicks, Wilson Marshall, Otis Hall
PRESENT OWNER	Bronson Herrington

ARCHITECTURAL DATA

PORCH	Beam over porch columns concealed; columns tapered.
EXTERIOR	Stucco blocked off.
	House faces ESE, not parallel with the present road.

The influence of the old dogtrot cabin is at once apparent in this stuccoed brick house. Built in two parts like its log predecessor, the space between was obviously closed in at a later date. There may once have been a second story porch over the central portion. It is possible that the scroll saw work was added after the house was completed. Time and weather have eaten away the stucco and brick walls at ground level, and there is some danger that they will fall if not soon repaired. It would be a shame should this happen, as the house is basically sound otherwise, and with its good proportions and fine materials, it is most adaptable to restoration.

The house is approached by a long elm-bordered drive, which must have seemed to continue right through the house if the hall was once an open breezeway, as appears to be the case. It would be difficult to imagine a more effective way of relating house and grounds.

To one side of the driveway is the old family cemetery. Also to one side and in front of this house is a charming shingled dovecote, which may be of later date.

The Benton House

Map no. 7-9   Photo nos. 157, 158
Valuable

DATE OF CONSTRUCTION	Original part circa 1812; second story and additions circa 1860.
LOCATION	Jasper County, one-half mile off Highway 11, north of Monticello.
ORIGINAL OWNER	Abba Benton
INTERIM OWNERS	James Benton, L. O. Benton
PRESENT OWNER	L. O. Benton, Jr.

ARCHITECTURAL DATA

PORCH   Posts 8″ face by 6″ deep, corners chamfered; rafters (curved) 2″ wide by 3″, beaded; sheathing, underside of which is porch ceiling, beaded on the underside.

House faces ESE and does not face the present road.

Owned by the same family since 1812, the Benton house still boasts ancient boxwood and a handsome log smoke house. The porch with its lightly curving roof provides a happy contrast to the sturdy lines of the old house. The unusually delicate porch rafters are exposed, as is the underside of the roof sheathing. Both rafters and sheathing are hand planed and have beaded edges. The sheen of the paint reflects the plane marks, giving a rich texture which can best be compared with that of beaten silver.

The Fisher-Carswell House

Map no. 16-1   Photo no. 159
Valuable

DATE OF CONSTRUCTION	Circa 1835
LOCATION	Irwinton
ORIGINAL OWNER	Dr. William Fisher
INTERIM OWNERS	Mrs. Mary Fisher Smith, Dr. Joshua Wood, George H. Carswell, George H. Carswell II
PRESENT OWNER	Mrs. Julia Carswell

157. *The Benton House,* Jasper County
KK

158. *Log Joints of Smoke House,* Benton Plantation
RH

159. *The Fisher-Carswell House,* Irwinton
JL & RH

This pleasant white house with green blinds was used as headquarters by General W. F. Smith, brigade commander under Sherman. Though probably antebellum, the inviting porch may have been added, or at least remodeled, after the house was built, while the masonry piers which form the lower part of the columns are undoubtedly twentieth century.

The Alston-Wiley House

Map no. 6-11   Photo no. 160

Valuable

DATE OF CONSTRUCTION	Before 1817, remodeled before Civil War
LOCATION	509 Rabun Street, Sparta
ORIGINAL OWNER	Robert West Alston
INTERIM OWNERS	J. H. Burnet (about 1830), Charles Whitehead (son-in-law of J. H. Burnet), Richard Bolling Baxter
PRESENT OWNER	Robert C. Wiley, Jr.

The inviting porch of this simple and grand house, proves that the charm of the basic type which dates back to the early farmhouses, does not necessarily lie in classic detail. It would be hard to imagine a more delightful house than this, with the green lattice underpinning, the Victorian porch, and the happy combination of dark green blinds and white wood siding. The house is said to have been remodeled several times. It is hard to believe it could ever have been more beautiful.

The original house was L-shaped with the entrance to the north, facing Short Street. When last remodeled, shortly before the Civil War, the entrance was changed to the west, facing Rabun Street. The former entrance was changed to a bay window at that time. The original L-shaped plan, the roof lines, and the mutule blocks of the main cornice are strikingly similar to those of the historic Brumby house in Athens, Georgia. Both houses are thought to have been built between 1815 and 1820, and both were later remodeled with graceful porches added before the Civil War.

The Harris-Vinson House

Map no. 4-28   Photo no. 161

Valuable

DATE OF CONSTRUCTION	Circa 1832
LOCATION	421 Montgomery Street, Milledgeville
ORIGINAL OWNER	Judge Iverson Harris
INTERIM OWNER	W. H. Hall
PRESENT OWNER	Honorable Carl Vinson

160. *The Alston-Wiley House,* Sparta
KK

161. *The Harris-Vinson House,* Milledgeville
RH

162. *The Ballard House*, Monticello
KK

This house was purchased and restored by the Honorable Carl Vinson in 1922. The grounds were originally about two blocks square, with gardens and an avenue of trees leading to the first owner's downtown law office. The Victorian Italianate woodwork again gleams white and lovely in pleasant contrast to the black fence and window sash, and to the dark green blinds.

The Ballard House

Map no. 8-8   Photo nos. 162–164
Valuable to Area

DATE OF CONSTRUCTION   Antebellum
LOCATION   49 Forsyth Street, Monticello
ORIGINAL OWNER   Unknown
INTERIM OWNERS   A. S. Thurman, Greene F. Johnson
PRESENT OWNER   Speights Ballard, Sr.

ARCHITECTURAL DATA

PORCH   42' 9" by 9' 11"

COLUMNS   18" face by 12½" deep at bottom of shaft, 17' 7" high (shaft only); 5 flutes on face, 4 flutes on side.

FRONT DOOR   3' by 7' (possibly later than rest of house)

WINDOWS   12" by 18", 12-light, 6 over 6

From the beginning of the Greek Revival period, there were architects who questioned the propriety of duplicating the marble forms of classic architecture in wood. Practical consideration likewise encouraged a change from classic precedent. Whatever the reason, the interpretation of an architecture of marble into one of wood inspired new forms which added to the rich variety of antebellum architecture. Where the Doric order was used as the basic type architecture, the

163. *Brackets*, Ballard House
KK

164. *Column Detail*, Ballard House
RH

165. *Brightside*, Sparta
RH

change to wood was usually expressed by a simplification and lightening of the original order, as in the Brown-Northington cottage at Davisboro (86). When the Corinthian order was used, as at the Ballard house, a richer treatment was called for. Here the builder substituted sawed wood brackets for the heavier and more intricate detail that is customarily a part of the Corinthian entablature. As has been mentioned before, brackets were earlier used in the entablature of the Masonic building at Milledgeville, and a few years thereafter on most of the Italianate houses of the period. At the Ballard house, they are of an unusually light and delicate type, expressive of wood construction.

The columns, as in so many examples, are square, obviously and easily made of wooden boards. The acanthus leaves of the capitals have been even further stylized, so that they could be sawed out of straight boards. As a result, the light wood columns and the entablature so obviously constructed of wood, are in harmony with the wood frame house. The new forms have a richness and delicacy that is Corinthian in spirit and truthfully expressive of the constructive methods of its day. The changes are the work of a creative designer, and the house a lovely and exciting example of southern Italianate architecture.

Brightside

	Map no. 6-12 Photo no. 165
	Valuable
DATE OF CONSTRUCTION	Antebellum
LOCATION	562 Hamilton Street, Sparta
ORIGINAL OWNER	George W. Davis
AMONG INTERIM OWNERS	Bishop George Foster Pierce, John T. Mullalay
PRESENT OWNER	Descendants of John T. Mullalay
ARCHITECT	Thought to have been designed and built by John T. Mullalay.

Brightside, thought to have been built shortly before the Civil War, is reminiscent of eighteenth-century New England houses. Its beauty derives from the fine proportions, admirable window spacing, and good, clean lines. An interesting refinement is the use of thin, very narrow clapboards on the front facade. At one time there was a porch across the front and sides of the house.

The Abercrombie-Skinner-Morris House

	Map no. 6-13 Photo no. 166
	Notable
DATE OF CONSTRUCTION	Circa 1805 or 1810

LOCATION   525 Rabun Street, Sparta

ORIGINAL OWNER   Either Willie Abercrombie or James Oliver Skinner

INTERIM OWNERS   J. I. Berry (1835), members of the Berry-Morris family since 1835

PRESENT OWNER   Mrs. M. E. Morris

Many times changed and remodeled, the Abercrombie-Skinner-Morris house is far too charming not to be included. Chimneys of handmade brick, windows with small panes of rippled glass, and fine old woodwork on the interior attest its age.

The Reid-Gregory House

Map no. 11-8   Photo no. 167

Notable

DATE OF CONSTRUCTION   Circa 1820

LOCATION   Highway 441, north at Harmony Road at edge of Eatonton city limits

ORIGINAL OWNER   Henry Reid

INTERIM OWNERS   Reese, Bradberry, Wells, Bell

PRESENT OWNER   J. M. Gregory, Sr.

The Reid-Gregory House was moved to its present location from Godfrey Road in Eatonton. It is possible that the porch was somewhat changed or enlarged at that time. The brick piers under wood columns are obviously twentieth century. The house retains its good clean lines, and with its pleasant porch, is all the more charming for being half-hidden from the road.

The Powell-Jordan-Key House

Map no. 8-9   Not illustrated.

Worthy of Mention

DATE OF CONSTRUCTION   1819

LOCATION   Green Street, Monticello

ORIGINAL OWNER   Dr. Norborne B. Powell

INTERIM OWNERS   Judge Edward Y. Hill (1838–1845), David Meriweather and widow (1845–1875), John R. Dyer and estate (1875–1888), Hannah S. Gould (1888–1889), Hunter Jordan (1889–1951)

PRESENT OWNER   Ernest D. Key

The Powell-Jordan-Key house was likely built as "the plain plantation type," with the upstairs three-rooms wide, but only one-room deep. It is now a large square house with a hipped roof, a type roof not generally used as early as the date of construction. The Victorian porch appears postbel-

166. *The Abercrombie-Skinner-Morris House,* Sparta
JL

167. *The Reid-Gregory House,* Putnam County
KK

168. *Woodland Terrace,* Sandersville
KK

lum. A number of distinguished citizens have lived in the house, including Dr. Powell, a physician who also served in the State Senate and introduced the bill which established Wesleyan Female College in Macon.

Woodland Terrace

Map 14-4   Photo no. 168

Notable

DATE OF CONSTRUCTION	Antebellum
LOCATION	270 North Harris Street, Sandersville
ORIGINAL OWNER	Nathan Haynes
INTERIM OWNERS	William Gainer Brown (before Civil War), descendants of William Gainer Brown
PRESENT OWNER	Estate of Robert Mitchell Brown

Though the rest of the house is changed, the porch and entrance must appear much as they did when General Sherman used this house for his headquarters November 26, 1864.

The house is being restored by Mrs. J. Phillips Adams, a descendant of W. G. Brown who purchased it before the Civil War. Mrs. Adams has some of the original furnishings, also mementos of the General's occupation.

The Scott-Smith House

Map no. 3-8   Photo no. 169

Too far deteriorated to evaluate in 1967. Destroyed in 1968.

DATE OF CONSTRUCTION	1806
LOCATION	Scottsboro, Baldwin County
ORIGINAL OWNER	General John Scott
INTERIM OWNERS	Colonel Farrish Carter, John H. Furman, Farrish Carter Furman, Mrs. F. C. (Emma LeConte) Furman, John R. L. Smith.
PRESENT OWNER	Descendants of John R. L. Smith. House has been owned by members of Farrish Carter family since 1806.

The Scott-Smith house, reportedly the oldest house still standing in Baldwin County in 1968, was built in two distinct parts and belongs to three different eras. The original house was basically the "plain plantation type," two stories high, the second story one-room deep, except that it had two balanced projecting wings. These wings, apparently as old as any part of the house, project toward the rear, but it is likely that this was originally the front, and that the first house presented a formal and balanced composition from that side. The wings are one-story high with great end chimneys, and are attached directly to face of the house. A pleasant court is thus formed, bounded by the main body of the house, and the two wings. The arrangement seems to have been unique for the area, though wings projecting to the front of the house were common farther north, particularly in Virginia, where the connection between the wings and the body of the house was usually less direct.

In 1820 Farrish Carter, the second owner and a man of immense wealth, remodeled the structure by adding what amounted to a complete and larger house on what is now the front southwest side. The old hall was extended, at larger scale, through the center of the addition, while a cross hall, possibly the size of an original porch, was built between the old part and the new, so that the remodeled house had cross axial halls. The newer part was built on a grander scale throughout, with higher and more fashionable ceilings, floor-length windows, and a front door so large that it was swung on pivots, castle style, instead of on hinges. The addition is said to have been in the Milledgeville-Federal style of other houses in the area built at the time. Evidently it was built on a larger scale than most, and there are Greek Revival details including the massive two vertical panel front doors which may represent a still later change. The main porch is said to have been the two-story type, so popular at the time. A second story porch was added to the old part, now become the rear, during one of the remodelings.

After the Civil War Mrs. Emma LeConte Furman became mistress of the house. She was a charming woman of amazing vitality and intellect. Her diary, written when she was seventeen, recounted her life at Columbia, South Carolina, when that city was bombed and burned.[7] Despite the vicissitudes of her life at that time, it is well written and is a reliable eye witness account of the tragedy.

Her energetic renovation of the house is more questionable. Feeling the need for outdoor exercise during inclement weather, she is credited with having replaced the colossal but narrow front porch with the present wide spreading Victorian one where she could walk on rainy days. The replacement is, or was, a delightful porch itself, and in many ways more suitable than its elegant predecessor. There were other changes within the house, some whimsical, but all with a definite Victorian charm. And whether Farrish Carter improved or impaired the original house, or whether Emma LeConte Furman improved or impaired the Farrish Carter house is an academic question. Years of neglect have left the old house in irreparable ruins.

169. *The Scott-Smith House,* Scottsboro, Baldwin County
JL & RH

170. *Garden Gate, The Gordon-Cline-O'Connor House*, Milledgeville
KK

171. *The Baxter-Carswell House*, Sparta
RH

The Gordon-Cline-O'Connor House

Map no. 4-29   Photo no. 170

No attempt to evaluate because of intangible qualities

DATE OF CONSTRUCTION	Circa 1820
LOCATION	311 West Greene Street, Milledgeville
ORIGINAL OWNER	—— Gordon
INTERIM OWNERS	—— Porter, —— Ward, Jeremiah Beall, Peter J. Cline
PRESENT OWNER	Cline-O'Connor

ARCHITECTURAL DATA

WALL Lattice brickwork, 5′ high one side of gate, 5′ 11″ other side

GATE Wood gate posts 11″ square, 5′ 9″ high one side, 6′ high other side; gate 3′ 11″ wide, 4′ to top of lowest picket, 5′ to top of center picket; pickets 1⅜″ by 1⅜″ at 3⅓″ on center; framing 2¼″ by 4″; bottom board 8″ wide (high); hinges are the pivot bolt type with strap leaf.

The Gordon-Cline-O'Connor house seems viable, changing, growing, and adapting to the times. Greatly damaged by fire at one time, portions of the house including the solid fluted Ionic columns with their hand-carved capitals are original. So, also, is the lattice brick fence which once surrounded the entire block. Within the house, furnishings made during various periods over the past century and a half mingle comfortably. Chairs upholstered in their original upholstery with motifs of the Early Republican era, and little the worse for more than a hundred years of wear, are casually and daily used. A concert grand piano that once belonged to General Stith Myrick, its carved wood dark and shining, adds early Victorian elegance. The dining room is panelled with the narrow beaded boards so popular toward the end of the last century. The panelling is stained dark, and the large, high-ceilinged room would be somber but for the tremendous windows, and the reflections from old silver and cut glass.

Built by a General Gordon, though not the one of Confederate fame, the house was rented as a residence for the Governor while the nearby Mansion was under construction. More recently it was the home of the late gifted writer, Miss Flannery O'Connor. Throughout the years, it has been home for distinguished and outstanding families.

The house is not one that can be judged architecturally. No doubt it was finer and more stately before the fire and the subsequent changes. It could hardly have been more heart-warming, however, for it is almost as though the successive occupants had bestowed some part of their personality to this hospitable and comfortable home.

The Baxter-Carswell House

	Map no. 6-14 Photo no. 171, 172
DATE OF CONSTRUCTION	Circa 1820
LOCATION	Corner Adams and Rabun Streets, Sparta
ORIGINAL OWNER	Believed to have been Andrew Baxter
AMONG INTERIM OWNERS	LaFayette Powell
PRESENT OWNER	Mrs. Marvin G. Pounds, Sr., occupied by the R. E. Carswells

Though built about 1820, the Baxter-Carswell house has been added to until it contains examples of several eras, all combining to form an extremely pleasant rambling house. The lattice enclosing the porch might have been added at any time from the time of its construction to the present. It is an ageless device, particularly suitable to the South where it suggests shade but is equally admirable as a screen.

It is interesting to know that similar wood lattice work is a favorite of such modern South American architects as Oscar Niemeyer, who uses it as an economical and attractive device that admits the circulation of air while providing shade and privacy.

The Harris-Rives Plantation

	Map no. 5-13 Photo no. 173
	Valuable
DATE OF CONSTRUCTION	Early 1800s
LOCATION	Sparta-Eatonton Highway 16, six miles from Sparta, Hancock County
ORIGINAL OWNER	Miles Harris
INTERIM OWNERS	——— Wiley, ——— Gardener, G. S. Rives, Jim Rives, ——— Rives
PRESENT OWNER	George Rives
	See drawing.

Though some of the original plantation buildings, and ruins of others still remain, the original house has long since been destroyed. From the drawing, it appears that it was a Georgian type, and more typical of early Virginia plantations than of the Oconee Area of Georgia. The present house itself, one of the oldest in the area, was moved to the site by Mr. George Rives, whose great-grandfather bought the plantation about 1870 for his son Jim Rives. This present house was built in the late 1700s or early 1800s by a Mr. Greene. The Harris-Rives Plantation is of particular interest not only because of the house which was moved there and because of

172. *Lattice Work,* Baxter-Carswell House
RH

173. *The Greene-Rives House, Harris-Rives Plantation,* Hancock County

the buildings and landscaping which remain from the Harris regime, but also because of the rare old drawing which gives such a precise idea of the plantation as it existed in pre-Civil War days.

The drawing illustrates interesting facets of plantation life. Not the least interesting to this architect was the due north-south orientation of the dwelling, with the axis of the driveway continued through the house and on to the rear, relating the interior of the house directly to the landscape. Also interesting from the architect's point of view is the note that the dwelling was enclosed with a picket fence painted white (as were the garden, the grass plot, and the "mellon" patch) and that the walks were gravel.

It is regrettable that no indication is given as to the planting of the rectangular plots in front of the dwelling. Since the grass plot to the side is specifically indicated, it is unlikely that these too were grass. There may have been formal gardens in front, as lesser plants are not indicated. Oak trees, both there and in the Negro lot, are mentioned in the notes.

The self-sustaining quality of the plantation and the variety of food grown are indicated by the farm buildings which include dovecotes, rabbit warrens, bacon (smoke) houses, the dairy, corn bins, and a house for storing peas; as well as a blacksmith shop, a carpenter shop, a cotton press, a cotton gin, and stables. Likewise indicated are the nursery, the school house, the carriage house, the Negro houses, and the overseer's house.

Of particular interest is the artificial fishpond with an island in it, and the mills which were nearly a mile distant, too far away to show on the drawing.

The Harris-Rives Plantation
Copied from drawing by John Waterman dated October 12, 1835; copy by Tim Hill (The original drawing belongs to George Rives, present owner of the plantation.)

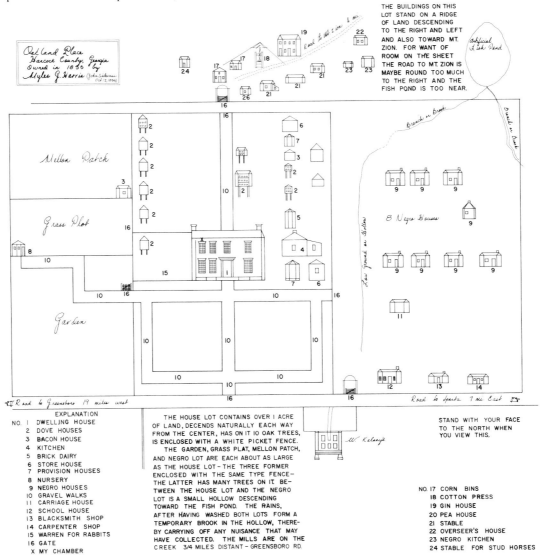

8. Victorian Architecture after 1865

The war brought a cessation of building activities, and in the grim and bitter years following, new homes, with few exceptions, were modest indeed. The gradual breakup of the plantation system tended to encourage the growth of villages, so that during this period a number of public buildings were constructed. Of these, the new courthouses were among the few that pretended to any architectural significance. The one at Sparta, particularly, is an imposing building. The courthouse, erected on one of the highest points in the city, with magnificent windows, exuberant Victorian detail, and a fantastic clock tower, is the outstanding example of Victoriana in the area.

Possibly because of finances, but also because poverty breeds a disdain for the old and a distorted love for things new, the war brought an abrupt end to the Greek Revival style, a style that had ended in sections other than the South fifteen or twenty years earlier. The very first houses built after the war were probably in the planning stage before the war started, and might be considered to belong to the earlier category.

Later houses tended to follow the styles current in other parts of the country. Unlike the prewar types which were planned primarily for suitability and frequently with cavalier disregard of current styles, the designs for postwar houses

187. *The Happ-Tarbutton House,* Sandersville. See page 118.
KK

174. *The Breedlove-Scott House,* Milledgeville
RH

175. *The Paschal-Sammons House,* Eatonton
KK

were usually adapted from plan books or magazines published in the north, and the regional quality that had been so much a part of the older houses gradually disappeared.

The Breedlove-Scott House

Map no. 4-30   Photo no. 174
Valuable

DATE OF CONSTRUCTION	Circa 1838, remodeled circa 1867
LOCATION	201 North Jefferson Street, Milledgeville
ORIGINAL OWNER	Breedlove
INTERIM OWNERS	——— McIntosh, Sam Walker (remodeled house), Barlow Fraley
PRESENT OWNER	Miss Katherine Scott

Cast iron verandas, which along with white columns, are synonymous with antebellum architecture, seem to have been bypassed in the Oconee Area. There were iron balconies and balcony railings, and the wonderful cast iron fence at Rockwell, but to the writer's knowledge the only nineteenth-century iron veranda is this one; and it is a combination of wood and iron, added when the antebellum house was remodeled shortly after the Civil War.

The house is painted gray, trimmed with green, and it is likely that these were the colors used when the porch was added. Since the early 1840s, designers such as Andrew Jackson Downing had deplored the use of white paint for houses, urging the use of muted colors. The filigree at the eaves of the porch, the wood brackets under the eaves of the house, the mansard roof, and the arch doors, are all features which had been introduced before the Civil War, but which were to gain added importance in the years following. The front door is handcrafted; twenty-eight different varieties of wood, all native to Georgia, are said to have been used in its fabrication.

The Paschal-Sammons House

Map no. 12-9   Photo nos. 175, 176
Valuable

DATE OF CONSTRUCTION	Antebellum, remodeled in 1860s
LOCATION	Maple Street, Eatonton
ORIGINAL OWNER	William R. Paschal
AMONG INTERIM OWNERS	U.S. Senator Lawson
PRESENT OWNER	M. M. Sammons
BUILDER	Greene Alford

The Paschal-Sammons house was built before the Civil War in the Greek Revival style, but the front was later remodeled in what was known as the "Italian Villa" style. The exact date of the remodeling is unknown. It is thought to have been done in the early 1860s; it may have been before the war. A photograph of the house taken in 1876 shows the tower and front just as it is today. It is interesting to study the north side and the back of the house, with its classic entablature and Greek Revival detail, and compare that part with the remodeled front and south side.

There is an iron fence at the front, with the most Victorian of gates, a long walk through a pleasantly overgrown and ancient garden, and finally the house, so delightfully Victorian that we cannot regret the loss of the older facade.

The Treadwell-Blanchard House

Map no. 6-15   Photo no. 177
Notable

DATE OF CONSTRUCTION	Thought to be about the time of the Civil War
LOCATION	Corner Broad and Rabun Streets, Sparta
ORIGINAL OWNER	Treadwell(?)
AMONG INTERIM OWNERS	Treadwell
PRESENT OWNER	Mrs. J. L. Blanchard

The date of construction of this cottage is unknown, but it is thought to have been built toward the end of, or right after the Civil War. Actually it is a pre-Civil War type, timelessly pleasing in appearance and so suitable to the area, that it is no wonder that the design has been repeated through the years and right up to the present.

The date of this house is undocumented. It is known to have been in existence since shortly after the Civil War, and, it is quite possible that it was built prior to that conflict.

176. *Gate,* Paschal-Sammons House
RH

177. *The Treadwell-Blanchard House,* Sparta
RH

178. *The Montgomery-Owens House,* Baldwin County
KK

The Montgomery-Owens House

Map no. 3-9   Photo no. 178
Notable

DATE OF CONSTRUCTION	Probably shortly after Civil War
LOCATION	Highway 441, six miles from Milledgeville, Baldwin County
ORIGINAL OWNER	Unknown
AMONG INTERIM OWNERS	Mrs. Ben Jones, Miss Marie Jones, W. H. Montgomery
PRESENT OWNER	W. H. Montgomery estate, occupants are Mr. and Mrs. J. L. Owens (Mrs. Owens is the daughter of W. H. Montgomery.)

The exact date of construction of this cottage is likewise unknown. It is known to have been in existence shortly after

the Civil War, and may have been built before that time. There are evidences that there have been additions and changes. The railing on the porch is pleasant, but more robust than was usual with such delicate columns, and it is probably a replacement. The informal tree shaded lawn, the sideporch, and the floor-to-ceiling windows are features which give this house a comfortable and inviting appearance.

The John Martin Baker House

Map no. 6-16   Photo nos. 179–181
Notable

DATE OF CONSTRUCTION	In the 1870s, additions circa 1897
LOCATION	East Hamilton Street, Sparta
ORIGINAL OWNER	John Martin Baker
PRESENT OWNERS	Children of John Martin Baker

The Baker house has been in possession of the same family since its construction in the early 1870s. The house is beautifully kept up, and most of its original furnishings are intact. The front part, which is the older part, is a typical Victorian cottage type of Gothic inspiration. Most of the second story and part of the first story in the rear were added in 1897. In disproof of a previous statement to the effect that most postwar architecture lacked regional character, the two-story porches with the outdoor steps are as distinctly southern as any antebellum house could be.

At one time Sparta was known for its big men, big in character, also big in stature. Such must have been the uncle for whom the porch chair, in which Miss Baker graciously consented to pose, was made.

Originally the long walk to the street was bordered with flower beds. The current cost of labor rendered their upkeep prohibitive, and the pleasant effect of the grass and trees used as substitutes mitigates their loss.

An older brother, of the generation which now occupies the house, died in childhood. Shortly before his death, he planted a wild fern by the corner of the porch. There the fern still grows, a fresh and tender memorial to a little boy who died almost four score years ago.

179. *The John Martin Baker House,* Sparta
JL

180. *Rear View,*The John Martin Baker House,
RH

181. *Miss Baker in Giant Porch Chair*
RH

The McCombs-Holloman House

Map no. 4-31   Photo no. 182

Valuable; with parlor furnishings, Valuable to Area

DATE OF CONSTRUCTION   Circa 1879

LOCATION   138 South Wilkinson Street, Milledgeville

ORIGINAL OWNER   Thomas Lawson McComb

INTERIM OWNERS   Mrs. William Trice Hines (née Antoinette McComb)

PRESENT OWNER   Mrs. Echols Holloman (née Frances Hines)

The McCombs-Hollomon house is another of the houses that is in just about perfect condition. It was built of brick with wood trim which was painted and sanded, i.e., sand was mixed with paint, giving the wood a stone-like texture. The color chosen was the then-fashionable "fawn color," and the same type and color paint has been used through the years. The roof, too, has always been painted with a special type paint, in this case to provide pure water for the cistern which is still in good working order and provides drinking water for the house. The old kitchen, built separately, is one of the few original features not used. The kitchen yard is paved with brick and screened from the street by a high brick wall. Beautifully landscaped, and completely private, it forms a delightful court for informal outdoor living.

The parlor with its gold frame mirrors and all its original furnishings in place is just as it was in the 1880s. This room could be described as a "museum piece," but it is too beautiful for that designation. Alone it could disprove the myth that the Victorian age was without taste.

182. *The McCombs-Hollomon House,* Milledgeville
RH

183. *The Cooper-Jenkins House,* Eatonton

184. *Front Lawn,* Cooper-Jenkins House
KK

The Cooper-Jenkins House

Map no. 12-10   Photo nos. 183–186

Valuable to Area

DATE OF CONSTRUCTION   Antebellum, remodeled 1885; moved about five hundred feet in 1909.

LOCATION   421 (end of) Madison Avenue, Eatonton

ORIGINAL OWNER   Cooper

INTERIM OWNERS   Various. Bought by Mr. and Mrs. William Frank Jenkins in 1883 and has been in same family since.

PRESENT OWNER   Mr. and Mrs. Franklin R. Jenkins

The Jenkins house was built in two distinct stages. The first part was Greek Revival. When the second part, Gothic in style, was added, it was placed directly in front of the origi-

185. *Parlor,* Cooper-Jenkins House
RH

186. *Parlor,* Cooper-Jenkins House
Drawing by Mrs. Jenkins

nal, the porch of which was used as a hall. From the front, the house is completely and delightfully Victorian Gothic. The deliberately off-center front doorway and the tower to one side are expressive of the new method of planning.

To approach the house is an experience in itself. The driveway is actually a continuation of Madison Avenue, and that end of the avenue is bordered by double rows (two rows on each side) of magnificent elm trees. At the end of this avenue are the gates to the grounds, and from the gates, across an open meadow the house appears, nestled in the surrounding trees and shrubs. The transition from the tree-lined avenue on through the massive gate into an immense open space is dramatic.

The drive is to one side of the grounds, and its axis is not to the front door, but toward heavy planting on that same side. It is the eventual curve of the driveway and the accent of the tower that direct the eye to the entrance. From the gate, the landscape unfolds in stages. First the meadow, open and free, then an immense round lawn defined by the full circle of the driveway, very much in the spirit of the forecourt of a seventeenth-century French chateau, and finally, the formal dooryard with brick paving and grass, soft like a carpet, this enclosed by a low balustraded wall.

The 1885 part of the house has especially fine plaster work with heavy moldings and center medallions in the ceiling. Like the Hines-Holloman house, this house boasts a parlor with its original furnishings. The rug is sun gold, with roses of rich and vivid red. The chairs and sofa are upholstered in the same Victorian red. Other colors are parchment, the dark brown of old walnut and mahogany, the gold of fine picture frames, the deep green of a verde-antique marble mantel. White lace curtains of the period hang at the windows. As with so many sophisticated color schemes, a verbal description might give the impression that the colors are bizarre. Instead, the room is rich and restful, and the colors completely harmonious.

The Happ-Tarbutton House

Map no. 14-5   Photo no. 187, p. 113

Notable

DATE OF CONSTRUCTION	Late 1880s
LOCATION	222 North Harris Street, Sandersville
ORIGINAL OWNER	Morris Happ
INTERIM OWNERS	Louis Cohen, his daughter Mrs. J. B. Lieberman
PRESENT OWNER	B. J. Tarbutton
ARCHITECTURAL DATA	See floor plan.

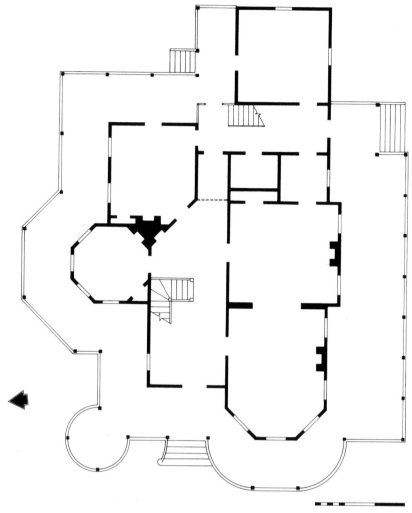

The Happ-Tarbutton House
Plan of first floor

No wonder the younger members of the profession are bewildered and intrigued by architecture like that of the Happ-Tarbutton house. Cupolas and turrets for the fun of it. Balconies and upstairs porches because they are romantic; oriel and bay windows just because somebody liked them; erratic porches whimsically tossed around three sides of the house; brackets, gingerbread, and ironwork for almost no reason at all. The original color? The writer doesn't know, but similar ones were painted butter yellow with white trim and bright green blinds, and the wood-shingled roof is a variegated pattern of different colors. Both owner and architect doubtless strove to make the house "pretty," a distasteful word to the early architects of the modern movement. Nevertheless, today's students are more intrigued than embarrassed by the word, and twentieth-century architecture may yet recover that sense of delight which all too often seems to have eluded architects of the recent past, and to have been so vital a part of Victorian architecture.

An interesting feature not shown on the floor plan is the oriel window on the second floor. These windows were popular during the era. They were used to deliberately break defined areas and to open up the corners, manipulating space in a manner which was to be adapted and carried much further by Frank Lloyd Wright.

The existing exterior steps are not original. Those shown on the floor plan are conjectural.

The burdens of the twentieth-century architect are formidable. His is the problem of housing every man equally and without loss of individuality, his the problem of ending urban blight, of halting water and air pollution, of slowing the destruction of our natural resources, of solving the transportation problems, and of revivifying the cities. Sociological requirements of the twentieth century are to be pushed forward via the alchemy of architecture. This is to be accomplished within the tenets of his profession, that is, form shall follow function, materials and structural methods shall be visually expressed, new techniques and structural systems shall be exploited at no risk to any person or to any person's pocketbook, economies of mass production are to be utilized without loss of desirable regional quality, spacial concepts shall interrelate with the total environment, and the organic unity of the universe shall be strengthened. Computer techniques promise to widen the architect's horizon.

188. *The Paris-Elkins House,* Sandersville
RH

189. *The J. H. Kelly House*, Monticello
RH

190. *The Beeson-Andrews House*, Milledgeville
KK

The Paris-Elkins House

Map no. 14-6   Photo no. 188

Notable

DATE OF CONSTRUCTION   Circa 1896

LOCATION   219 North Harris Street, Sandersville

ORIGINAL OWNER   Henry Paris

INTERIM OWNERS   G. J. Elkins

PRESENT OWNER   G. J. Elkins estate

By repeating the curve of the arches in the rounded portion of the porch, the designer of this Victorian house achieved an almost baroque effect. Originally such houses were usually painted in bright and vibrant colors. The shingles in the gable would probably have been stained in contrasting hues, and applied so as to form a pattern. Regardless of changes in color and in taste, the exuberantly arched porch remains a delightful feature.

The J. H. Kelly House

Map no. 8-10   Photo no. 189

Notable

DATE OF CONSTRUCTION   Late 1890s or early 1900s

LOCATION   506 College Street, Monticello

ORIGINAL OWNER   J. H. Kelly, Sr. House owned continuously by Kelly family.

Since almost exact duplicates of this house can be found in various parts of the country, it must be concluded that the basic plan was taken from a plan book or popular periodical. Nevertheless, the house with its many windows, projecting wings, and airy porches, seems not only well adapted to the South, but also to its individual site.

The plans of such houses are most interesting. Nonsymmetrical, with interiors seeming to burst into the exterior by way of bay windows and unexpected openings; and with room merging into room, these were the forerunners of the modern "open" plan.

The Beeson-Andrews House

Map no. 4-32   Photo no. 190

Notable

DATE OF CONSTRUCTION   Circa 1890

LOCATION   210 North Columbia Street, Milledgeville

ORIGINAL OWNER   Dr. Luther Beeson, onetime president of Georgia College at Milledgeville

PRESENT OWNERS   Mr. and Mrs. Louis H. Andrews

ARCHITECT   Said to have been from New Orleans

The graceful porch with baroque curves is a delightfully Victorian feature of a house whose simple lines and small paned windows might otherwise indicate that it predated that era. Contrasting colors accentuate its beauty.

The Brinson House

Map no. 10-1   Not illustrated
Worthy of Mention

DATE OF CONSTRUCTION	1879
LOCATION	300 South Marcus Street, Wrightsville
ORIGINAL OWNER	Dr. J. W. Brinson
INTERIM OWNER	Continuously in the Brinson family
PRESENT OWNERS	Mrs. Sara Brinson and children

Typical of scores of houses built in the postwar years of the nineteenth century, such cottages bring nostalgic memories to many older citizens. The plan with its central hall is not too different from the antebellum counterparts. Some of the differences were dictated by economy: smaller rooms, shallow porches, less sturdy construction, and narrow chimneys. Stylistic influence is apparent in extra gables, elaborately turned banisters and posts, and the scroll saw work. Like the old farmhouses, most of these Victorian cottages formerly had blinds and picket fences, and much of their charm was lost when these appurtenances were discarded. Similar to the McCrary house, no photograph is included.

The McCrary House

Map no. 10-2   Photo no. 191
Worthy of Mention

DATE OF CONSTRUCTION	Probably 1880s
LOCATION	212 West Court Street, Wrightsville
PRESENT OWNER	Mrs. L. A. McCrary

In appearance this house is almost identical with the preceding Brinson house. Minor differences here are that the extra gable has been omitted, and that the porch work is heavier and more ornate.

The Butterly-Jordan House

Map no. 10-3   Photo no. 192
Worthy of Mention

DATE OF CONSTRUCTION	1890s
LOCATION	202 Myrtle Street, Wrightsville
ORIGINAL OWNER	J. J. Butterly
INTERIM OWNER	C. D. Rountree
PRESENT OWNER	Roy Jordan
DESIGNER AND BUILDER	S. A. McWhorter

191. *The McCrary House*, Wrightsville
JL & RH

192. *The Butterly-Jordan House*, Wrightsville
JL

Another typical late Victorian house, this one has added interest because of the convenient porte-cochere, and the gazebo-like corner of the porch. The freedom with which this delightful porch was handled does not seem to derive from the compact square house plan.

The Graves Barn

Map no. 6-17   Photo nos. 193, 194, 195

Notable

DATE OF CONSTRUCTION   Circa 1899

LOCATION   Adams Street, Sparta

PRESENT OWNER   R. A. Graves

ARCHITECT   ——— Stone

The scroll saw work of this barn has achieved a perfection which indicates that a new art form is possible within the medium. The delicacy of the barge boards, the richness of the gable ventilator (suggestive of a Gothic wheel window), and the repetitive pattern of the ventilator over the double doors rebut our disdain for the scroll saw.

Nearby is a servant's house with scalloped boards along the eaves. The barn and house have long been a delight to passersby.

193. *The Graves Barn*, Sparta
KK

194. *Gable Ventilator*, Graves Barn
KK

195. *Door and Scroll-Saw Work*, Graves Barn
KK

9. The Classic Re-Revival

Since the early days of the Italian Renaissance, the architecture of ancient Greece and Rome has continuously influenced the architecture of western civilization. In North America colonial architecture reflected contemporary English Georgian architecture, which in turn was a reinterpretation of the ancient classic forms. Though there were stylistic differences, the early, middle, and late Georgian styles, all usually designated as Colonial in America, the Federal, and the Greek Revival have a common ancestor in the classic architecture of ancient Greece and Rome.

As previously mentioned, the Greek Revival era lasted in the South until the time of the Civil War. It was succeeded in postwar years by a variety of styles usually lumped together as Victorian and late Victorian. Nevertheless, the classic influence never fully died, and throughout those postwar years there were occasional buildings based on classic precedent. In the years immediately following the war, they were generally built by the conservative element, who clung to the old style with nostalgia. By the late 1880s and early 1890s, they were more likely to be built by returnees from Europe, and were more avant-garde than conservative.

The tentative beginning of the return to classicism received impetus with the Chicago Exposition of 1893, which, with its chaste white buildings, inspired by Renaissance and Roman architecture, and enhanced by lagoons and the marvelous new electric lights, bedazzled visitors from all sections of the country. In one clean sweep, the fanciful Victorian architecture was outmoded, and the tentative beginnings of modern architecture stalled. For several decades following, most buildings of consequence were firmly based on classic precedent.

Similar to those of the Exposition, the earlier buildings of this "re-revival" were usually based on Roman or Renaissance precedent, and were generally more ornate than those of the Greek Revival. In the South, particularly, the ornate classic forms were too often reproduced in cheap materials, economy having of necessity been the chief goal of builders since the Civil War. Classic forms have since remained popu-

197. *The Holt-Sullivan House,* Sandersville. See page 124.
RH

196. *The Stevens-Daniel House*, Baldwin County
KK

198. *The Sanford-Binion House*, Milledgeville
RH

lar. With the passage of time, the designs have been based more and more on the simpler forms of Colonial, Federal, or Greek Revival styles.

Many houses of an earlier era have, in the twentieth century, been remodeled into one of those classic types. In such cases, they are included in this section, since their present form reflects this re-revival of classic architecture.

The Stevens-Daniel House

	Map no. 3-10 Photo no. 196
DATE OF CONSTRUCTION	Circa 1900
LOCATION	Baldwin County
ORIGINAL OWNER	John Henry Stevens
PRESENT OWNER	Albert K. Daniel

The large sheets of glass in the single-paned windows, and the curved extension linking the porticoes of the Stevens-Daniel house are typical of the late nineteenth and early twentieth-century classic revival, features which differentiate the architecture of this era from that of the antebellum Greek Revival. The fine oak door with small Victorian-type panels of both glass and wood indicate the change even more emphatically. Within, the nonsymmetrical arrangement of the rooms, the heavy oak stairway, and the oak panelling is altogether Victorian Gothic, with hardly a trace of classic influence. The present owner has some of the original golden oak furniture, extremely handsome, and possibly made specifically for the panelled room. To those accustomed to thinking of golden oak as a derogatory term, a trip to this room will be revealing. The panelling and woodwork is warm and rich, and the furnishings luxurious and enticingly comfortable, characteristics not usually associated with the golden oak era.

The Holt-Sullivan House

	Map no. 14-7 Photo no. 197, p. 123
DATE OF CONSTRUCTION	Circa 1907
LOCATION	239 North Harris Street, Sandersville
ORIGINAL OWNER	Lewis Holt
INTERIM OWNERS	None
PRESENT OWNER	Miss Louise Sullivan
ARCHITECT	Unknown; said to have been from Dublin, Georgia.
CONTRACTOR	Jesse Tompkins

The curve of the two-story portico of this classic revival house is reflected in the concave curve of the balcony, thereby defining a vibrant space, and giving the house a baroque character rarely if ever found in the older Greek Revival architecture. This baroque quality is skillfully countered by the horizontal lines of the one-story porches and the porte-cochere. Exquisite chandeliers and ceilings with hand-painted designs are features of the formal rooms.

The Sanford-Binion House

	Map no. 4-33 Photo no. 198
DATE OF CONSTRUCTION	Circa 1825, rebuilt circa 1900
LOCATION	330 South Clark Street, Milledgeville
ORIGINAL OWNER	General W. A. Sanford
INTERIM OWNER	Dr. T. O. Powell
PRESENT OWNER	Mrs. Richard Binion (daughter of Dr. Powell)

The original house, built about 1825, was remodeled extensively even before the Civil War. The four-columned portico was enlarged until there were fourteen columns and until it extended around three sides of the house, Greek Revival style.

The house was rebuilt, using the same fourteen columns, about the turn of the century. The powerful and simple lines are doubtless a carry-over from the Greek Revival period of the house, the general vogue being for more ornate architecture at the time it was rebuilt.

The J. D. Persons House

	Map no. 8-11 Photo no. 199
DATE OF CONSTRUCTION	Early 1900s
LOCATION	College Street, Monticello
ORIGINAL OWNER	J. D. Persons
PRESENT OWNER	J. D. Persons

An unusual example, the Persons house has a classic curved portico brought to story-and-a-half height. The academically correct detail indicates that the house was designed by an architect trained in the Beaux-Arts tradition. Such features as the dormer and bay windows, and the curved porch indicate that the free forms of late Victorian architecture left its imprint on the succeeding styles. There is a marvelous play of reflected light within the portico.

The Edmondson-Neligan House

	Map no. 11-9 Photo no. 200
DATE OF CONSTRUCTION	Circa 1810, additions 1840, remodeled early 1900s
LOCATION	Highway 441, Eatonton to Milledgeville, Putnam County

199. *The J. D. Persons House*, Monticello
RH

200. *The Edmondson-Nelligan House*, Putnam County
KK

201. *The Knit-Wit House,* Monticello
RH

202. *The Malone-Warren House,* Monticello
JL

ORIGINAL OWNER	Mrs. Polly Edmondson
INTERIM OWNERS	Clyde Carpenter, Mrs. J. B. Farris
PRESENT OWNER	Dr. Patrick J. Neligan

An old photograph shows that the original porch consisted of upper and lower stories with four (eight in all) square columns to each story. The columns were slender as would be expected on a house of that date. The first story windows corresponded with those of the second story. The tile roof, the triple arched windows, and the tall round columns are all fairly typical of early twentieth-century classic architecture, and doubtless date from that time. The present owners plan to restore the antebellum features of the exterior.

Originally two staircases served the upstairs rooms, one stairway for the boys' section, the other one for the girls', the latter with access only by way of the parents' bedroom.

The Knit-Wit House

Map no. 8-12   Photo no. 201

DATE OF CONSTRUCTION	Antebellum; moved 1865; porch remodeled early twentieth century.
LOCATION	1271 Forsyth Street, Monticello
ORIGINAL OWNER	Unknown
INTERIM OWNERS	Lawrence Wood Robert, J. L. Benton, Sr., Mrs. J. L. Benton, Sr.
PRESENT OWNER	Mrs. W. H. Jordan (daughter of Mrs. J. L. Benton, Sr.)

Originally a plantation house similar to the Jordan-Bellew and the Jordan-Fitzpatrick houses, the Benton house was moved to its present site shortly after the Civil War. During the early years of the twentieth century it was badly damaged by fire. The present porch, deeper than the original, and with round fluted Ionic columns and classic entablature instead of the original square Italianate columns with bracketed entablature dates from that time. The new entablature contrasts pleasantly with the older cornice of the house proper.

The large front room on the right is used by Mrs. Benton to display the vast array of knitting yarns which she retails in her home; thus the name the Knit-Wit House.

The Malone-Warren House

Map no. 8-13   Photo no. 202

DATE OF CONSTRUCTION	1916
LOCATION	39 Forsyth Street, Monticello
ORIGINAL OWNER	John S. Malone

PRESENT OWNERS   Mr. and Mrs. Ben Warren (Mrs. Warren
is the daughter of John S. Malone.)

ARCHITECT   Henry H. Jordan

The Ionic columns of the stately portico rest on independent piers, and gain importance thereby. This was not an uncommon practice during the antebellum era, though again the semicircular porch on the side, very popular during the early years of the present century, would have been unusual in the days of the earlier Greek Revival.

In front, pine trees planted between the sidewalk and the street are likewise unusual, and appear to be completely successful as street trees.

The Dr. E. W. Allen, Sr., Residence

Map no. 4-34   Not illustrated.

LOCATION   State Hospital Grounds, Milledgeville

PRESENT OWNER   State Hospital

This traditional white house with green blinds, brick walk, and tree-shaded lawn has a pleasant charm due in part to its colonial-inspired design, and in part to its easy acceptance of the new. Anything but institutional in character, it is one of the staff houses at the Milledgeville State Hospital, and for a number of years has been the residence of Dr. and Mrs. E. W. Allen, Sr.

The Carter-Evans House

Map no. 14-3   Photo no. 203

Notable

DATE OF CONSTRUCTION   Circa 1850

LOCATION   603 South Harris Street, Sandersville

ORIGINAL OWNER   William W. Carter

INTERIM OWNERS   Jeff A. Irwin, Sr., Dr. Nathaniel Lozier, George W. Gilmore

PRESENT OWNER   Julian H. (Dock) Evans

The house faces wsw, oblique to the present highway.

Obviously disregarding rules in parts, this house too owes much to the principles of Greek Revival architecture. The front porch was originally the full width of the house, but changed to its present form about 1940. In November of 1864, it was used as headquarters by Confederate General Joseph Wheeler.

Ferncrest

Map no. 14-8   Photo no. 204

DATE OF CONSTRUCTION   Foundation is very old; a later antebellum house burned in 1870s; present

203. *The Carter-Evans House,* Sandersville
KK

204. *Ferncrest,* Sandersville
RH

house circa 1890, remodeled 1938, additions 1954 and 1967

LOCATION   Sandersville

PRESENT OWNER   Dr. Thomas W. Gilmore

The house faces 13 degrees west of south.

The foundations of this house are likely to be the oldest of any house in the area. As mentioned in the section "Early Settlers" there is substantial evidence that the Spaniards were operating silver mines in North Georgia during the seventeenth century. Tradition has it that parts of the foundation date back to Spanish times, having been reused in the antebellum house which was erected on the site. The antebellum house was burned in the 1870s, but the foundation was again reused for its replacement. This third house with many additions is the one that stands today, the old foundations having determined the proportions of the impressive hall and flanking rooms. The house was remodeled extensively in 1938, and received further additions in 1954, but the size of these rooms has never been altered.

The added wings are symmetrically placed, and the house has a portico reminiscent of the Brothers Adam; nevertheless, it is not pedantic. The walls of the wings are of hand-split shingles, and the overall design has been freely handled without undue reliance on precedent.

The grounds are impressive. Piers of almost militant power mark the entrance to the grounds and to a long straight tree-bordered drive. The drive goes through lush pastures, and finally loops in a great circle in front of the house, seeming to cut through the masses of azaleas, boxwoods, shrubs, and trees of the front lawn. Farm buildings to each side as well as the Hereford cattle in the pasture indicate that this is a working plantation, and that the great house is the center of farm operations which are as vital to the community as a modern industrial plant.

The Murray-Wilson House

Map no. 12-11   Photo no. 205

DATE OF CONSTRUCTION   1939

LOCATION   South Washington Street, Eatonton

ORIGINAL OWNER   Mrs. William Murray

PRESENT OWNERS   Mr. and Mrs. Harvey L. Wilson

ARCHITECTS   Dennis and Dennis, Macon

The continuing viability of the Classic Revival, particularly in the south, is evidenced by this charming example of the 1930s.

205. *The Murray-Wilson House*, Eatonton
JL & RH

Oak Lodge Plantation

	Map no. 13-12 Photo no. 206
DATE OF CONSTRUCTION	Circa 1873; remodeled 1928 and 1940.
LOCATION	One-fourth mile west of Tennille on Georgia Route 68, Washington County
ORIGINAL OWNER	John Thomas Cook, 1873–1910
PRESENT OWNER	Thomas Cook Wylly since 1910
ORIGINAL ARCHITECT	James Barwick of Jefferson County
ARCHITECT FOR 1928 REMODELING	George Beck of Indianapolis, Indiana
ARCHITECTS FOR 1940 REMODELING	Dennis and Dennis of Macon

Though appearing to be a bit of the antebellum South miraculously preserved, the Oak Lodge Plantation house was not built until 1873, and then in a different style. It was remodeled in 1928, and after being badly damaged in a storm, again remodeled in 1940. It was at that time that the columns were added.

Before Thomas Cook built the original part of the house, the land belonged to Cicero Gibson, and was known as the Tarbutton Place.

Magnolia Hall

	Map no. 14-9 Photo no. 207
DATE OF CONSTRUCTION	Circa 1878; remodeled 1898, remodeled 1955
LOCATION	235 North Harris Street, Sandersville
ORIGINAL OWNERS	—— Bryant and William W. Walkins
INTERIM OWNER	Jeff A. Irwin
PRESENT OWNER	Miss Louise Irwin (daughter of Jeff Irwin)
ARCHITECT FOR 1898 REMODELING	Mr. Gude
ARCHITECT FOR 1955 REMODELING	W. Elliott Dunwoody, Jr.

Magnolia Hall was originally a four-room cottage named Cedar Hall, and that name still remains etched in the transom over the front door. Shortly after the house was built, it was rented to the Horace Adams family, and after that to the Virgil Joiners. In 1888 Jeff D. Irwin, father of the present owner, rented the house. In 1897 he purchased it, and remodeled it completely the following year, adding the second story and a larger Victorian porch.

In 1955 his daughter, Louise, again remodeled the house, this time to its present Georgian colonial style. Within, the best of each of the three periods has been retained. The floors are the original wide pine boards, and run unpieced

206. *Oak Lodge Plantation*, Washington County
KK

207. *Magnolia Hall*, Sandersville
RH

the full length of the rooms. Ceilings are fourteen feet high, and the wainscot in the hall is curly pine of the late Victorian period. Furnishings, most of them heirlooms, date from the eighteenth century to the present, and are beautiful individually and together.

Its type is likely to remain popular for a long time in the South, where it easily fulfills Vitruvius's dictum of comfort, commodity, and delight.

The Hines-Bone House

	Map no. 4-36 Photo no. 208
DATE OF CONSTRUCTION	1955
LOCATION	529 West Hancock Street, Milledgeville
ORIGINAL OWNER	Mrs. T. M. Hines
PRESENT OWNERS	Mr. and Mrs. Frank E. Bone
ARCHITECTS	Bodin and Sambertson, Atlanta

The handsome and classic house was once illustrated in *Fortune* magazine as one of the best of its type in the country.

Windy Acres

	Map no. 4-37 Photo no. 209
DATE OF CONSTRUCTION	1958
LOCATION	1721 Cedarwood Road, Milledgeville
ORIGINAL OWNERS	Mr. and Mrs. Robert L. Griffith
PRESENT OWNERS	Mr. and Mrs. Robert L. Griffith
ARCHITECTS	Bothwell and Nash, Atlanta

This mid-twentieth-century example of the revival of Classic Revival architecture is further evidence of the continuing vitality of that style.

208. *The Hines-Bone House,* Milledgeville
     KK

209. *Windy Acres,* Milledgeville
     JL

10. Toward a New Architecture

Structures such as television towers and the new water tank at Milledgeville have begun to spring up throughout the area. Completely different from older forms, they have become a part of the landscape and have an undeniable beauty of their own. Like airplanes and bridges, they are designed primarily according to engineering principles, and it is these principles which seem to resolve their esthetic success.

The new schools are a case in point. Varying special requirements such as long spans for gymnasiums and more than normal light and ventilation, combined with modest budgets demanded a new approach to their design. By basing his exterior design on the exterior and interior functional requirements, and by taking advantage of the latest building and engineering techniques, the modern architect no longer relies on precedent, but constantly derives new forms to meet changing needs and conditions. The Wilkinson County High School (23), built in 1954, is a good example of such architecture.

Modern architecture is not dependent on new materials, however, nor did it spring into being overnight. Houses in the area dating back to the eighteenth century have features which exemplify modern architectural theory, and examples of some of the older houses which embody such features are included in this section.

The Little Red House on the Square

Map no. 6-18   Photo no. 210

DATE OF CONSTRUCTION   Original part 1797
LOCATION   Facing the square, Sparta
ORIGINAL OWNER   Major Charles Abercrombie
AMONG INTERIM OWNERS   DuBose family, Hugh White
PRESENT OWNERS   Mr. and Mrs. George Dickens

The best of modern architecture has its roots deep in the past. The charm of the Little Red House on the Square derives in part from the unselfconscious way in which rooms were added as they were needed, in the simple frank expression of its structure, and in the interrelation of yard, porch, and interior space. These are qualities which are considered basic to good modern architecture, and are according to precepts laid down by early architects of the modern movement. The rooms added as the need arose exemplify the axiom that "form should follow function"; the straightforward structural expression that "truth is beauty." The interrelation of the enclosed yard, the porch, and the interior space is completely modern in spirit. It is, of course, also completely in the spirit of eighteenth- and early nineteenth-century indigenous architecture. The writer has deliberately placed this house in the modern category to emphasize the fact that the best of modern architecture is closely related to the indigenous architecture of the past.

The Walker-Moore House

Map no. 6-19   Photo no. 211

DATE OF CONSTRUCTION   Early twentieth century
LOCATION   108 Rabun Street, Sparta
ORIGINAL OWNER   John D. Walker
PRESENT OWNER   Mrs. G. B. Moore, Sr.

210. *The Little Red House on the Square,* Sparta
RH

211. *The Walker-Moore House,* Sparta
KK

There is a quality about this house which is reminiscent of the work of the brothers Greene and Greene whose early twentieth-century California houses are now recognized as modern masterpieces.

The relation of lawn to terrace, of terrace and of drive to the porches, and of the porches to the interior of the house is magnificently worked out so that one type space flows into the next. The almost exaggerated expression of structure with exposed rafter ends and extremely heavy brackets under the roof was new to the area, but the vigor of the unorthodox columns might be matched in some of the Greek Revival houses.

212. *Sun Porch, The Cohen-Benton House*, Monticello
JL

213. *Old Tavern*, Wrightsville
JL

The Cohen-Benton House

Map no. 8-14   Photo no. 212

DATE OF CONSTRUCTION	1910
LOCATION	4 Church Street, Monticello
ORIGINAL OWNER	Sam Cohen
INTERIM OWNER	L. O. Benton (purchased house in 1914)
PRESENT OWNER	L. O. Benton Estate

In principal, the modern use of glass or opaque panels between vertical structural members of wood or metal is at least as old as the medieval half-timber house. It reappeared in conservatories and sun parlors like the lovely example from the Cohen-Benton house, and in more recent times the metal and glass curtain wall utilizing this same basic principal has become standard for skyscrapers and office buildings.

Old Tavern

Map no. 10-5   Photo no. 213

DATE OF CONSTRUCTION	Early twentieth century
LOCATION	Elm Street, at State Street, Wrightsville

This interesting tavern has several features that are based on principles which are common to good architecture of all ages. Among them is the integration of landscape features such as the retaining wall with the porch railing and with the body of the house. The straightforward expression of structure indicated by the unbroken line of the brickwork along the sidewalk, the logical flat arches over openings occurring in the brick wall of the first story, the simple wood posts, and the practical lattice work railing are all features which could be found in good modern architecture where conditions are similar.

The George T. Walker House

Map no. 14-10   Photo no. 214

DATE OF CONSTRUCTION   1966

LOCATION   623 Evergreen Drive, Sandersville

ORIGINAL OWNER   George T. Walker

PRESENT OWNER   George T. Walker

CONTRACTOR   Marvin Avant Construction Company

The interior-exterior relationship so vital to this type of architecture is enhanced by the integration of the garden wall with the wall of the house, and is further accentuated by the roof hovering over the wall with the underside of the roof continuing into the interior; also by the interpenetration of the exposed beams. All of these work together for unity of interior and exterior space.

The G. Lee Dickens, Jr., House

Map no. 4-39   Photo no. 215

DATE OF CONSTRUCTION   1963

LOCATION   1726 Columbine Road, Milledgeville

ORIGINAL OWNERS   Mr. and Mrs. G. L. Dickens, Jr.

PRESENT OWNERS   Mr. and Mrs. G. L. Dickens, Jr.

ARCHITECT   Adapted from plans by Irving E. Palmquist, of Detroit, Michigan

Directly related to the site by the roof lines which seem to repeat the slope of the land, the Dickens house achieves distinction by its harmony with its surroundings, and by its studied simplicity.

The Emory S. Cook, Jr., House

Map no. 4-40   Photo no. 216

DATE OF CONSTRUCTION   Unknown

LOCATION   1800 Tanglewood Road, Milledgeville

ORIGINAL OWNER   Emory S. Cook, Jr.

PRESENT OWNER   Emory S. Cook, Jr.

ARCHITECT   Adapted from plans by Palmquist and Pullman.

Post and beam construction permitted a radically new approach not only to the floor plan but to ceiling height and to roof design as exemplified here.

214. *The George T. Walker House,* Sandersville
JL & KP

215. *The G. Lee Dickens, Jr., House,* Milledgeville
KK

216. *The Emory S. Cook, Jr., House,* Milledgeville
RH

East Forty

Map no. 3-11   Photo no. 217

DATE OF CONSTRUCTION   1964

LOCATION   Sandersville Road two miles east of Milledgeville, Baldwin County

ORIGINAL OWNERS   Mr. and Mrs. John Elwin Johnson

PRESENT OWNERS   Mr. and Mrs. John Elwin Johnson

ARCHITECT   John Elwin Johnson

The simple forms and clean sharp lines of the John E. Johnson house proclaim its modern design as surely as do the cantilevered concrete slab and the exposed steel posts. The open gable porch seems to reach up and out to bring the landscape into the house.

The Peoples Bank

Map no. 12-12   Photo nos. 218, 219

DATE OF CONSTRUCTION   1965

LOCATION   Jefferson Avenue, Eatonton

ORIGINAL OWNER   Peoples Bank

PRESENT OWNER   Peoples Bank

ARCHITECT   Carlton P. Fountain, Atlanta

This new bank building marks a new direction in modern architecture, the re-revival of classic symmetry and proportion. Having reacted violently against the restrictions of classic canons, the modern architect recognizes that they do have validity, that they are not necessarily restrictive, and that they can be a source of inspiration. As in many modern buildings, much of the power of this building results from its marvelous indoor-outdoor relationship. This is most apparent from the interior which has the feel of a garden rather than of a room, and a garden that is one with the surrounding walks and lawns. To appreciate this building, one must go inside it and enjoy the sensation of being simultaneously indoors and outdoors.

217. *East Forty,* Baldwin County
     KK

218. *The Peoples Bank*, Eatonton
     RH

219. *Interior,* Peoples Bank

11. Baldwin County

As the Oconee Area might be said to be a microcosm of the state of Georgia, so Baldwin County could be said to be a microcosm of the Oconee Area.

Located in the geographic center of the state, it is on the fall line, and includes areas typical of both the upper and lower parts of the area. The Oconee River, so important in time past as a means of transportation, and even more important today as a source of power, is the great natural feature of the county. Its waters flow from Lake Sinclair in the upper part of the county, and from there past Milledgeville whence the river is navigable to the sea.

The land was purchased from the Creek Indians in 1802, and the county organized in 1803. Milledgeville, the county seat, was marked off and made the state capital in 1804, although the first session of the legislature was not held there until 1807. The photograph of the gateway (220) was taken before the beautifully aged and lichen-covered stucco was scraped off, replaced, and painted to match the walls of the old State House, walls which were necessarily repaired after the fire which almost destroyed that building in 1941. In 1868 the capital was moved to Atlanta, but some state institutions including the State Hospital remained in the county.

220. *Gateway,* The Old Capitol, **Milledgeville**
 Built circa 1867. Designed by Col. B. W. Froebel.
 Map no. 4-53
 Photo taken about 1936 by Eberhart Studios

Other state institutions such as the State Farm and the Georgia Training School for Boys were located there after the capital was moved. Though small industries were developed from the early days of the county, and one of the larger industries today, Stevens Pottery, was started in 1861, the principle industrial growth of the area has occurred more recently.

From early days when the urban gentry maintained plantations in the country, and when planters in turn maintained town houses as well as plantation homes, the history of Milledgeville has been the history of Baldwin County, and vice versa.

Today, Milledgeville, like Baldwin County, is a mixture of the new and the old. For the moment, it still has much of the charm and beauty it possessed in antebellum days. Fine old residential sections, as yet unspoiled by commercial intrusion, lie within a few blocks of the center of the city. These downtown residential sections with their hospitable porches, their trees and small lawns, are as delightful as they are rare. They constitute a major asset of the city. Much of the architecture dates back to the Federal era and it is due to the unique quality as well as to the unusual number of such buildings that the old Confederate town of Milledgeville has been called "The Federal City."

Another asset derives from the wisdom of the original city planners, who, two years after the land was purchased from the Indians, and while the whole area was still a forest wilderness, had the foresight to set aside four twenty-acre squares for public use. The gridiron plan of the city was varied so that areas assigned for public use were larger than average, each one being the size of four typical blocks. The orientation is about 25 degrees off the north-south axis.

The combined area set aside for public use comprised 15 percent of the total area, exclusive of that given over to streets. The squares were for specific uses, most of which have changed over the years. The principal square was for the capitol building and for churches. Except for the space allocated to the churches, this has become the campus of the Georgia Military College. The square originally called Penitentiary Square is the campus of the Womans College of Georgia. The old Governor's Mansion which was on Government Square, is now the official home of the president of that college. The fourth square was for a cemetery, which remains a green and pleasant place within the city.

By a chain of circumstances, some of them distressing at the time, Milledgeville has a wealth of antebellum buildings. Though occupied by Sherman's army, Milledgeville and the surrounding area were spared the wholesale burning of houses and buildings which elsewhere marked the scorched earth policy of that army's march to the sea.

Soon after the war, Milledgeville lost its position as state capital to Atlanta. This blow to an already despoiled economy left the area in a woeful financial condition that lasted well into the twentieth century. As a result, there was little new construction during that time, and the old houses and buildings which were spared by Sherman's army, were likewise spared the usual destruction wrought in the name of progress.

With the advent of large new industries, the near explosive growth of colleges, and the ever expanding and improving development of all the state-supported institutions in the area, rapid and continued growth of the city is inevitable. With Milledgeville the vital question is not will it grow, but how will it grow, and will it be able to preserve that quality of delight which it now possesses.

There are some encouraging signs. In an area now just outside the city limits but which will surely be included within the city limits in the future, Edward J. Grassman is restoring the old mansion called Lockerly (116) and planting extensive gardens to be known as the Lockerly Arboretum Foundation. This project will ensure a degree of beauty and tranquility to that section of Milledgeville and will be enjoyed by generations to come.

Another favorable aspect is that the community is now aware that its squares, its trees, and its fine old buildings are a rare and irreplaceable heritage. Planned tours of the historic houses and buildings have developed renewed appreciation for the timeless beauty of the older sections of the city.

Nevertheless, Milledgeville is in danger of losing both the old residential sections and the open space of her squares. These were saved partly because of poverty and a waning population; they are now in danger of being lost by prosperity and an exploding population. The residential sections, so beautiful and convenient, are likewise inviting for commercial buildings, particularly as property values in the present commercial section increase. A good—or rather horrible—example of what will happen unless adequate steps are now taken to prevent it, can be seen in Athens, Georgia. Twenty years ago Athens, too, was renowned for the beauty of its older residential sections. Today, like broken and gaping teeth squat little office buildings have replaced many of the houses; hamburger and fried chicken stands blaze with lights and garish decorations, spreading noises and smells throughout the areas. A number of the old houses still remain, but the owners of most have deserted them, or are planning to do so, for the quiet of the suburbs.

If the old residential sections of Milledgeville are to be saved, immediate steps are necessary. Among the first of these should be a traffic study. Heavy automotive traffic is incompatible with pleasant living areas, not only because of the concomitant filling stations and commercial enterprises but also because of the smells, noises, and actual danger from traffic itself. And traffic is going to be a problem in Milledgeville. Through traffic will have to be routed around residential areas, if those areas are to be saved. There will also have to be zoning laws, strong laws followed by constant vigilance on the part of dedicated citizens to see that the ordinances are neither broken nor weakened. In other places it has not been too difficult to get the necessary ordinances passed; but after the first flush of enthusiasm, expediency has usually reigned, minor concessions have been made, and cancer-like, have pervaded and ultimately destroyed the area that was to be protected.

The old squares of Milledgeville, pleasant with trees and grass and open space, features which become increasingly desirable as a city grows, are threatened from another direction. As land values increase, there is increasing temptation to build on the remaining open area. It is to be hoped that the city can and will adopt a policy to prohibit further building there, even for such worthy institutions as the colleges located thereon. The squares are not large enough to accommodate all the necessary expansion and the inevitable purchase of additional land for that purpose should be done before the cost of adjacent land becomes prohibitive.

The downtown section of Milledgeville is blessed with trees and grass and fine buildings. It also has its unsightly aspects, eyesores to which the local citizen has become accustomed, but which strike the visitor forcibly. The clutter of signs in the business district is more apparent than the buildings, and unsightly wires and poles detract from every section of the city. Many cities have ordinances against signs projecting from buildings. There have also been instances where the necessary traffic and warning signs have been combined or unified to prevent sign clutters. Wires can and should be run underground. Behind the garish signs, the telephone poles, and the wires, Milledgeville is too beautiful a city to remain so besmirched. One hopes that strong civic action will be taken to protect the fine buildings, old and new.

As yet the downtown area is not seriously threatened by outlying shopping centers, but in a few years it will be. Already a few establishments have moved out and plans should be started now to provide facilities downtown that are as conducive to shopping as are those in the suburban centers.

221. *Spire, The Baldwin County Courthouse,* Milledgeville
Built circa 1880. Remodeled 1930.
Map no. 4-41
RH

222. *Milledgeville City Hall,* Milledgeville
Built 1907-1908. John Swain, Builder.
Map no. 4-42
KK

This means easy parking, spacious sidewalks, covered access to most of the shops and offices, and open space for displays and special attractions. Eventually such features will have to be provided in all the larger cities if the economy of their downtown areas is to progress. The sooner the plans are made and put into effect, the more reasonable will be the cost, and the greater the returns. It is hoped that unlike those at the shopping centers, the parking areas (open, underground, or multi-story) will be designed to be attractive or at least unobtrusive, and that the canopies or covered sidewalks will be designed to lend an overall unity to the city blocks and at the same time to defer to the rich architecture of the better buildings.

When Milledgeville was laid out, 15 percent of the land not devoted to streets was given over to the squares which form so vital a part of the city today. With new growth, and expanding city limits, provision for parks and open spaces should likewise be made for those areas. Such areas will be dependent on the city for many services; it could hardly be termed unreasonable if the city in turn required developers to set aside a specific percentage of each subdivision for parks. Most subdivided areas have rugged or low places difficult to develop for homes, but with possibilities for imaginative development into parks, parks which would increase the value of the remaining property and help prevent future slums.

The writer knows of no other community, not even among the ones that are being planned from scratch, that has the potential for so combining the delights of both village and city life, of both tradition and progress. It will be interesting to see whether the citizens of Milledgeville exploit this potential, preserving and enhancing their heritage, or

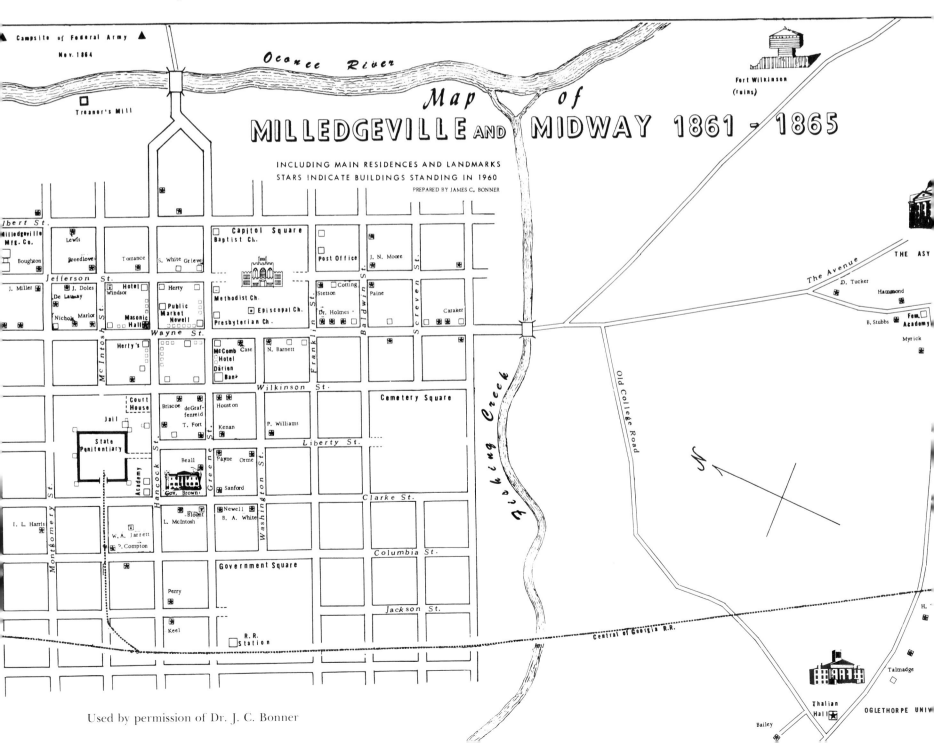

whether they permit it to grow into a typical drab and crowded industrial city in the name of progress.

Photographs 220 through 224 present examples of Baldwin County architecture designed for public use. The poet, Sidney Lanier, roomed in Thalian Hall (223) when he was a student at old Oglethorpe University. The photograph of the gateway (220) was taken before the beautifully aged and lichen-covered stucco was scraped off, replaced, and painted to match the walls of the old State House, walls which were necessarily repaired after the fire which almost destroyed that building in 1941.

BALDWIN COUNTY

HISTORY	Created by Legislative Acts of May 11, 1803. Named for Senator Abraham Baldwin, member of Continental Congress and author of the bill to establish in Georgia the first state university in America.
COUNTY SEAT	Milledgeville. Established 1804. For more than sixty years the capital of Georgia. Named for the Honorable John Milledge, patriot of the Revolution, governor of the state, member of Congress, and later member of the U.S. Senate. Elevation 335. Population 11,601 (1970).
COUNTY POPULATION	34,240 (1970)
AREA	164,480 acres
PRECIPITATION	Average annual, 45 inches. Monthly averages range from 5⅓ inches in July to 2¼ inches in October.
TEMPERATURE	Average annual, 63.3 degrees. Monthly mean temperatures range from 80.1 degrees in July to 45.9 degrees in January. Freeze-free period averages about 235 days extending from around March 20 to November 10.
RAILROADS	Georgia Railroad, Central of Georgia
U.S. HIGHWAYS	441
STATE HIGHWAYS	22, 24, 29, 49, 112, 212, 243
AIR SERVICE	Commercial—Macon, 31 miles sw; landing strip—4500′ paved at Milledgeville.
ARCHITECTURE	Ranges from early nineteenth-century indigenous to contemporary. Particularly noted for architecture of the Federal period; likewise unusually fine examples of Greek Revival architecture.

223. *Thalian Hall* (formerly an Oglethorpe University Dormitory), Milledgeville
Built 1859. Joseph Lane, Builder.
Notable
Map no. 4-43
JL

224. *Victorian Building, State Hospital,* Milledgeville
Map no. 4-45
KK

12. Hancock County

Gold is found in Hancock County, and semiprecious stones as well. More important to the economy are deposits of kaolin and great quantities of granite, especially the rare and beautiful pink granite. There are lime sinks too, with prehistoric fossils, and shells from the time this land was under the sea. The soil is, in general, fertile, producing good crops, and trees and grass in abundance.

Pre-Columbian Indians had extensive and densely populated settlements here; they built mounds and canals, and remains of some of these still exist. These were an agricultural people, with a culture different from that of the later nomadic Indians who fought and traded with the white settlers. The latter Indians were still a menace when the county was formed in 1794, formed from parts of Washington and Greene counties, though originally the whole area had been a part of Washington County which was opened to settlement in 1784.

By the middle of the nineteenth century Hancock County was a model agricultural community, and an 1860 visitor dubbed it a "Modern Mecca" describing vividly "its white mansions, gardens, and orchards."[1] There were also vineyards, and the Devereux Wine of Hancock County was esteemed even in epicurean New Orleans.

The Hancock Planters Club, founded in 1837, encouraged experimentation, and such practices as terracing, diversified farming, crop rotation, and soil conservation were customary here long before the Civil War. One of the members of the club, Dr. William Terrell, endowed a chair of agricultural chemistry at the University of Georgia, then called Franklin College, in 1854. From this beginning the present School of Agriculture grew.

There was considerable industry in the area, mostly of a rural type. Many plantations were practically self-sustaining, and the spinning and weaving, the soap-making and the distilling of whiskey, would in the aggregate represent a big hunk of industry. There were also blacksmith shops, both those run in conjunction with the larger plantations, and independent shops. Numerous surviving examples of hand-crafted hardware attest the quality of the products of the local forges. Sawmills and gristmills were vital to the economy. Granite quarries were in operation before the Civil War, as was Montour Cotton Mills, and doubtless other fairly large industries.

Small academies, as much a part of the social as of the educational fabric of the South, flourished throughout the county. Besides those at Sparta, there were academies at Rockby, at Mt. Zion, at Jewell, at Powellton, and at Linton, the latter boasting a race track, and on occasion, there were gala displays of horsemanship and chivalry.

The most impressive commercial building in the area must surely have been the Edwards House, later renamed the Drummer's Home and today the LaFayette Hotel (225). This imposing building replaced the old Eagle Tavern, which burned during the 1830s and which dated back to the eighteenth century; here LaFayette was entertained during his visit to Georgia in 1825. The Edwards House, appropriately enough for the principal building of a town named Sparta, was built in what was known as the "Greek Style," which in this case meant that the whole of the front boasted a magnificent two-story portico. The portico is raised a full story off the ground, and has great square columns of Greek Doric inspiration. The massive wooden entablature terminates abruptly and somewhat awkwardly against the masonry walls of the building, accentuating a difficulty which plagued designers of the period, the difficulty of properly relating an architectural form which had crystallized some two thousand years earlier to a contemporary structure. Such solecisms, painful to the pedantic critics of a later classic revival, now charm by their very artlessness. In general the buildings of the area are unusual in that the Greek architectural forms have been modified to conform to local building methods, or the indigenous architectural forms have been subordinated to classic prototypes. At Mount Zion Presbyterian (now Methodist) Church (17), not far from Sparta, indigenous and classic architectural forms have been synthesized into one harmonious structure which seems both Greek and Hancock County, Georgia.

Most of the surviving public buildings of that era are plain, and are admirable for their fine brickwork, their good proportions, and their simplicity of design. In some cases these good qualities have been lost during various renovations.

228. *The Hancock County Courthouse,* Sparta. See page 144.
  Built 1881-1883. Parkins and Bruce, Architects.
  Of National Importance
  Map no. 6-20
  KK

The Civil War brought an abrupt end to the thriving economy of the area, and to the building industry. It is interesting to note that cities such as Atlanta that were burned to the ground were forced to rebuild and forge a new economy, while the economy of many that were spared died of attrition. At this distance in time it is hard to understand the seeming inertia into which the whole county fell for more than half a century following that tragedy. As late as 1937 a Federal Writers Project[2] recorded of Hancock County: "One of the older counties of Georgia, as attested by the number of old houses on its numerous unpaved roads. Most of them are in a state of disrepair, and are inhabited by poor tenants, white or Negro."[2] The old system had thrived partly because of its slave labor, but it seems strange that a new agricultural system of mutual advantage to both races was not worked out.

It is interesting to note that an independent Negro community, Springfield, did develop in the county. According to the Federal Writers Project forty of the seventy-five farm families in the community owned their own small farms of from fifty to one hundred and fifty acres each, and the Negro land holdings there amounted to twelve thousand to fifteen thousand acres. Expensive farm equipment was owned and operated jointly by the farmers of the community, and both marketing and buying were done on a collective basis, the latter through a community-owned store. In 1931 under the direction of the sons of Camilla and Zack Hubert, a project named in their honor the Camilla-Zack Country Life Center was originated, and carried out by Negroes of the community. The project centered about a sturdy and picturesque log cabin (226), equipped with modern conveniences. In this building were held the meetings of the various clubs maintained by and for the community; here also social events and parties were held.

Springfield, generally called the Log Cabin Community, thrived during the depression days of the 1930s. Attractive houses with conveniences modern for the time, but built of logs and deliberately quaint to be in keeping with the log construction of the Camilla-Zack Center, were typical of the dwellings. Like the minimal tenant houses in other sections, these once-attractive homes are mostly deserted today, and falling into decay.[3] Something about the area reminds one of the poems "The Deserted Village," or Gray's "Elegy in a Country Churchyard." It would be interesting to know why the project so successful in depression years, failed in more prosperous times. The failure of small farms has not been confined to this community. Throughout the Oconee Area, the past decade has witnessed a wholesale closing down of small farm operations.

226. *The Camilla-Zack Community Center,* Hancock County
Built 1932
Map no. 5-16

In general the tenant farmer system prevailed in the county from the end of the Civil War until recent years, prevailed with meager returns to both landlord and tenant. The plantation industries died a lingering death. Spinning, weaving, and soap-making became symbols either of extreme poverty or of leisure that belonged to a time that was past. Mail-order hardware replaced the skillful products of the forge, and a blacksmith became a man who shod horses. Store-bought flour and grits accounted for the disappearance of the old rusty mill. The making of wine and whiskey became illegal. There were some faltering steps toward the newer type industries. The textile mill near Jewell, and Montour Mills at Sparta survived the Civil War, and grew in the years following.

The village of Jewell still exists. With its expansive open green (227) defined by a few widely spaced buildings, it appears idyllic, like a stage setting or a bit of the nineteenth century forgotten into the twentieth. The central building is a small two-story frame schoolhouse (21), vintage 1880, consisting of a classroom downstairs with a meeting hall over the latter reached by winding steps. Though no longer used, the building is kept painted, and the benches, the blackboard, the platform, and even the old stove pipes are still in place. Other buildings include several houses, one or two of which appear to be antebellum. There are two churches, a handsome brick warehouse with brick pilasters and corbelled brick trim, and an ancient commissary that also served as a post office, this last fast failing into decay. The textile mill, which was the mainstay of the community, is not visible from the site. Except for the commissary, and the roof of the warehouse, part of which has caved in, all the buildings appear to be kept painted and in repair, and the grounds well cared for.

227. *The Village Green,* Jewell, Hancock County
Map no. 5-14
RH

225. *The LaFayette Hotel*, Sparta
Built 1840 (other sources say 1854-1856)
Valuable to Area
Map no. 6-21
KK

The school building, tall and narrow, has a suddenness about it, as though it had just popped up from the ground. It is flanked on one side by the old brick Baptist Church, on the other side by a large frame house, delightfully Victorian. The total composition is, for some reason, memorable; having been there once, one does not forget the place. It is also a unique record of an industry which survived, and at times flourished, during the hard years following the Civil War.

The outstanding building of the postwar era was the Hancock County Courthouse (228), built at Sparta in the 1880s. It is a masterpiece of Victorian architecture magnificently rising from the hill upon which the town is located. To approach it via Highway 15 from Eatonton or Greensboro is an experience. The highway curves, crests a hill, then heads in a straight line toward the flamboyant and stately structure. Among the houses facing this stretch of highway are the Greek Revival Springer-Holten mansion (112) and the Italianate Terrell-Stone house (51) of the Federal period. Behind newer ones which are built nearer the highway, stand the crumbling ruins of the historic Old Dominion (44).

There is an open square in front of the courthouse; here the highway bisects, or rather terminates at a right angle street. There is a Confederate monument in the center of the square, and axial walks which admirably relate the highway to the architecture of the courthouse, and to the town itself. The remainder of the square has been planted mostly in grass, its simplicity providing the perfect foil for the ornate courthouse. The only improvement to the square that the writer could suggest would be the elimination of parking in front of the courthouse and the planting of tall growing trees on either side (east and west sides only) of the square, these planted not on the plaza proper, but in the space between the sidewalk and the street. High growing trees in that location would not clutter the square nor obscure the courthouse, but should dramatize the axial effect of the highway, and the magnificence of the building, which, incidentally, should be sprinklered for fire protection. It is too fine an example to risk loss by fire.

It has not been long that such Victorian architecture was derided; and almost cause for embarrassment to academic esthetes. Today, a new and less inhibited generation appreciates its exuberant fantasy, relaxes and enjoys its foibles.

Not many cities have so interesting a public building; almost none have a grand entrance with such a building as the focal point. That section of the highway, from the city limits to the courthouse should certainly be set aside as a "beautified highway." Properly zoned, properly planted and maintained, this approach to Sparta could become one of the showplaces of Georgia.

One other legacy of the postwar era which should not go unmentioned, is the weekly newspaper with the intriguing name of the *Ishmaelite*. The paper is still being published and is a vital force in the community.

In spite of some progressive forces, postwar years in Hancock County were in general years of poverty, and the first half of the twentieth century showed little improvement. County population was less in 1970 than in 1860. Cotton acreage has considerably declined with more and more farmland converted to woodland. This last may be to the good, but there is the question whether crops other than pine trees might not, as in the past, be more profitable and furnish more jobs.

Dairying and the raising of livestock are still an important part of the economy, in fact, an increasingly important part, as are poultry and poultry by-products. The lively agricultural studies and experiments are a thing of the past. So, too, are the famous grapes, the vintage wines, and the thoroughbred horses. Some spark seems to have gone out. Hancock is still a predominately agricultural county, but it is no longer a leader in that field.

Its citizens are aware that the county has not been living up to its heritage. In 1965 local leaders, with the aid and encouragement of individuals and of state and area agencies such as the Institute of Community and Area Development and the Oconee Area Planning and Development Commission, launched a movement to revitalize the economy of the county. A new look was taken at the county's assets and liabilities, and a broad program outlined, encompassing all phases of its economy. With enthusiasm reminiscent of antebellum days, the leaders plan to "give everything a good try so long as it promises to help Sparta and Hancock County."

The town of Sparta is pleasant, with many fine old buildings (225, 229, 230). Though there are overhead wires, unsightly signs, and some of the clutter common to most twentieth-century towns, they do not seem as obtrusive as in most, and with the revived interest in the appearance of the town, it is to be expected that corrective measures will be taken and efforts made to make the business section a place of beauty.

The beauty of the fine old houses, both in the town and out in the county, has been described earlier. Fortunately Hancock County citizens are well aware of the value of these houses and their surroundings, and take pride in keeping them up in true antebellum style. It is gratifying to note that

229. *The Dickens Law Building,* Sparta
Antebellum
Notable
Map no. 6-23
KK

the observation previously quoted from the Federal Writers Project of 1937 to the effect that most of the old houses were in a state of disrepair no longer applies. Even houses such as Glen Mary (84) which are located in outlying areas of the county are being restored, and it is to be hoped that such examples will encourage further the restoration of those that remain neglected but which are still structurally sound and potentially pleasant for living.

A tour of homes, the majority of which were old homes restored, was held in conjunction with the "Forward Sparta–Hancock County Renaissance Festival" in October 1965. It is planned for such tours to be held at regular intervals. Successful restorations, when so displayed, are contagious, and tours of them can do much to save Hancock County's heritage of fine architecture.

As in most areas of the South, leaders of Hancock County are vitally interested in getting industries to locate there. In 1962 the Hancock Redevelopment Corporation was organized specifically to promote industrial development. Local industries include a furniture manufacturing corporation, a garment company, several lumber mills, and many sawmills and pulpwood yards.

Granite has been quarried in Hancock County since before the Civil War. Much of the granite quarried today is for gravel, and most of the granite marketed is gray. The writer, an architect, was surprised to learn of the deposits of pink granite in the county, and of the use of this pink granite in the new U.S. House of Representatives buildings in Washington.

Hancock County is rich in natural and historic resources, and it is hoped that the enthusiastic support given the Forward Sparta–Hancock Renaissance Festival will be sustained until there is indeed a Hancock County Renaissance.

HANCOCK COUNTY

HISTORY	Created by Legislative Act of December 1793 from parts of Greene and Washington counties. Named for the Revolutionary patriot and signer of the Declaration of Independence, John Hancock.
COUNTY SEAT	Sparta. Established 1795, incorporated 1805. Named for the ancient Greek city. Elevation 560. Population 2,172 (1970).
COUNTY POPULATION	9,019 (1970)
AREA	305,920 acres
PRECIPITATION	Average annual, 44 inches. No month averages as much as 5 inches or as little as 2 inches. March is normally the wettest month and October the driest.
TEMPERATURE	Average annual, 64 degrees. Monthly mean temperatures range from 80 degrees in July to 47 degrees in December and January. Freeze-free period averages 235-240 days extending from around March 20 to near mid-November.
RAILROADS	Georgia Railroad
U.S. HIGHWAYS	None
STATE HIGHWAYS	15, 16, 22, 77, 278
AIR SERVICE	Commercial—Macon, 56 miles sw; Augusta, 70 miles east.
ARCHITECTURE	Prehistoric Indian mounds and moats. More modern architecture ranges from late eighteenth century to contemporary. Outstanding examples of the Greek Revival period predominate though there are splendid examples of indigenous, Federal, Early Republican, and early and late Victorian architecture. The late Victorian (1880s) courthouse is renowned.

230. *The Watkins-Fraley Building*, Sparta
Antebellum
Valuable
Map no. 6-22
KK

13. Jasper County

Jasper County was originally part of Baldwin County and when created in 1807 was named for the patriot, John Randolph of Virginia. Later there was a sharp political dispute between Randolph and Thomas Jefferson. The citizens of Randolph County, strong Jeffersonians, were offended at Randolph's position, and changed the name of their county to Jasper to honor the Revolutionary hero, Sergeant Jasper, who more than once risked his life to save his country's flag from the British, and was killed in such an attempt during the Siege of Savannah. The feeling against Randolph was evidently not lasting, as another Georgia county was subsequently named for the fiery old aristocrat.

Monticello, the county seat, was named after Jefferson's estate of that name. The fact that many of the first settlers came from Virginia may account for the use of the Virginia names.

A yellowed newspaper clipping in the files of the University of Georgia Library gives an interesting account of Jasper County's early history. The clipping is not dated but is titled "Unwritten Chapters in Georgia History: The Early Days in Jasper"; its author was George G. Smith of Vineville. The paper appears to have been published in Atlanta.

Some particularly interesting excerpts are "Records of Jasper County have been carefully preserved. The first minutes were kept on a few quires of foolscap paper, bound in a casing of buckskin, and the buckskin has a patched place on it which shows where the bullet had entered the deer. . . . As in Jones, much whiskey was made, and it was freely used, and there was no little dissipation. The county records show that there was a great deal of fighting and gambling. . . . It was a universal thing to have brandy on the sideboard, and when no one was considered at all out of the way that took his dram, and when fruit, especially peaches, was so abundant and stills so common, there was but little effort to do more than put down drunkenness and disorder. The people, if not moral, were very orthodox in their opinions. The Baptists built the first church in the county. The Methodists came into it before it was severed from Baldwin County and preached all over it. . . . The Presbyterians came soon afterward."[1]

The writer made it plain that the Jasper County citizens of his own day were a more virtuous group. It is likely that the article was written about the turn of the century when the hard times still continuing from post-Civil War days com-

bined with a nationwide temperance movement, put an end to such high living. The effect of the temperance movement was greater in the South than is generally realized. Records of the early Presbyterian Church indicate that it was not unusual for a minister's salary to be partly paid in produce, including whiskey.[2] Tradition has it that those pious Presbyterians saved the best of their whiskey for the preacher, in keeping with old Testament law that a sacrificial offering was to be good, and without blemish.

Another bit of information from the same source, was that in the very early days, the wealth of the county was in cattle, and since the cattle roamed at will over the grass-covered hills and in the cane brakes, the stock marks were recorded. Evidently there was open range and branding of cattle in Jasper County long before there was a cowboy in the West. It is interesting to note that livestock, again an important part of the economy of the county, was its source of wealth before it was superseded by cotton. Peaches, which have to some extent replaced cotton in recent years, are like-

231. *The Jasper County Courthouse,* Monticello
Built 1907. Lockwood Brothers, Architects.
Map no. 8-16

232. *Pine Trees along Forsyth Street,* Monticello
RH

wise mentioned as having been plentiful, and when converted to brandy were probably an additional source of revenue for the county's farmers. In fact the agricultural output of the county today parallels that of those very early days in many ways. More and more cropland is being converted back into woodland, and forest products are again an important aspect of the economy. The most striking recent change in the farm economy has been the increase in dairy products. Increase in poultry products has also been considerable. Though we have little such data regarding the early settlers, we know that most of them raised cattle and poultry, which were vital to the prosperity of the county.

Another forward step that hails backward in time has been the creation of national forests and wildlife refuges and management areas, about 20 percent of the area of the county now being in Oconee National Forest or one of the National Wildlife areas. These combined with privately owned forest, and with rivers, lakes, and fields, provide Jasper County with hunting and fishing, with good camping sites, and with opportunities for swimming, boating, and water skiing.

There are certain irritants for the tourist. If he happens to be in this peach country during the peak of the season and orders them from a restaurant menu, he will be served a dish of insipid canned peaches, possibly from California. The melons and cantaloupes seen in the fields are seldom available in the restaurants. Delicious wild blackberries which waste along the roadsides can be had for the picking, but are not to be casually purchased. There are compensations. Fried chicken is likely to be true southern fried chicken, fried in a frying pan, and not the greasy substitute boiled in deep fat. Small catfish are a surprising delicacy to the stranger who associates all catfish with rank scavengers of the sea. A new name should be invented for the small freshwater type. There are numerous lakes and ponds in the area, and a shrimp-processing plant in Monticello. Some day local freshwater crayfish may replace the imported shrimp.

In addition to natural resources already mentioned, Jasper County has deposits of feldspar, and the feldspar mines yield by-products of mica and quartz. With the feldspar deposits of Jasper County, Georgia has most of the materials needed for pottery, an industry that is just beginning to grow in Georgia. Georgia could also supply most of the materials used in the ceramics studios and classes now so popular throughout the nation. The few industries in the county are similar to those in surrounding areas and are generally connected with feldspar mining, wood, textile, or agricultural operations.

233. *Lay-By Time, Public Square,* Monticello
RH

The many pre-Civil War academies have long since been replaced by public schools, but it should be mentioned that the Monticello Female Institute was founded in 1825 and was among the first in the state for women.

It should also be noted that though the population of the county has long been declining the total income of the county has continued to rise. The small town of Monticello supports four banks. The business section of Monticello is built around the courthouse and square (231). There are no parking meters, and five-hour parking is available and permissible in the center of town. The old store fronts are harmonious, and though most of them could use some paint or new canopies, few are unsightly, and none garish. Through occasional openings, green foliage can be glimpsed behind the buildings. Electric wires are mostly underground, and even the signs over the stores seem less blatant than usual in small towns. The older residential sections are pleasant, and along a part of Forsyth Street, pine trees, rarely considered as street trees, flourish between the street and the sidewalk (232).

White and Negro citizens loaf, chat, and rest on the benches of the tree-shaded square (233). There is the customary Confederate monument on the square, this one of truly outstanding design. It consists of an obelisk flanked by statues of two Confederate soldiers, one an officer complete with Van Dyke beard and saber, the other of a young private (234). Both are fitting representatives of an army that included old men and beardless youths, grandfathers, fathers, and adolescent sons. The sculptor seems to be unknown, but he infused the statue of the private with life and youth.

Citizens of Monticello and of Jasper County have been accused of being uninterested in change and progress. In such a city and such a county, the lack of enthusiasm for change is understandable, but without change there is no life, and some change is necessary if only to preserve the best of the old. Jasper County is faced with the difficult problem of changing to remain vital and to maintain and develop its delightful qualities, while resisting change for the mere sake of change, even when presented in the name of progress.

234. *Statue of Confederate Soldier Boy*, Monticello
Monument unveiled April 10, 1910
Sculptor unknown. McNeal Marble Company, Contractor.
Map no. 8-15
JL & KP

235. *The Shady Dale Post Office*, Jasper County
Map no. 7-10
JL & KP

JASPER COUNTY

HISTORY
Created as Randolph County by Legislative Acts of December 10, 1807, from Baldwin County. Name changed December 10, 1812, to Jasper County in honor of the Carolinian, Sergeant Jasper, who fell mortally wounded at the Siege of Savannah in the Revolution, while trying to rescue his country's flag from the British.

COUNTY SEAT
Monticello. Established 1808, incorporated by Legislative Act December 15, 1810.[3] Named for the estate of Thomas Jefferson. Elevation 680. Population 2,132 (1970).

COUNTY POPULATION
5,760 (1970)

AREA
238,720 acres

PRECIPITATION
Average annual, 47 inches. March, with an average of just under 6 inches, is normally the wettest month, and October, with less than 2½ inches, usually the driest.

TEMPERATURE
Average annual, 63.5 degrees. Monthly mean temperatures range from 80 degrees in July to 47 degrees in December and January. Freeze-free period averages about 235 days.

RAILROADS
Central of Georgia

U.S. HIGHWAYS
None

STATE HIGHWAYS
11, 16, 83, 142, 212, 213, 221, 229, 300

AIR SERVICE
Commercial—Macon, 36 miles south.

ARCHITECTURE
Ranges from very early nineteenth century to contemporary. Most of the outstanding architecture was produced during the antebellum period, the Italianate style predominating. A unique building (235) is located in the Shady Dale community. Built for a bank in the early 1900s, it is now used for a post office. Carefully designed in the Classic Re-revival Style, it contrasts blithely with its rural surrounding.

236. *The Johnson County Courthouse*, Wrightsville
     Built 1895. Remodeled 1940 by W.P.A.
     Golucke and Stewart, Architects
     Notable
     Map no. 10-6
     RH

14. Johnson County

Johnson County is the newest in the area, having been created in 1858 from parts of Laurens, Washington, and Emanuel counties. It was named for Hershel V. Johnson, jurist, governor, and United States senator, as well as Confederate state senator. He was the unsuccessful candidate for vice-president of the United States on the Douglas ticket in 1860 against Lincoln. A staunch unionist, he is said to have made his most fervent speech at the Secession Convention when he tried, and almost succeeded, in persuading the legislature to vote against joining the Confederate states. He evidently accepted defeat of his policy, for he remained loyal to the state, serving in the legislature after Georgia joined the Confederacy.

The county seat, Wrightsville, was named for John B. Wright, a pioneer of the area, whose home (40) is described in Chapter 3. Wright was twice a legislator, and introduced the law whereby property inherited by a woman remains hers even after marriage, a radical idea for those times. Wright had several daughters and consideration of their inheritance may have influenced him to push for such a law.

The site selected for Wrightsville was on land deeded by William Hicks, a stipulation of the deed being that five blocks were to be set aside, one for the courthouse (236), one for the school, and three blocks for churches. There was a further stipulation that whichever of the three churches (Baptist, Methodist, and Presbyterian) started construction first would have its choice of the three blocks. The Methodists won, and when that building was replaced in 1899, knee-high stumps were found under the original building, the builders evidently having left them in their haste to get construction started. One of the larger churches today is the Christian Church (237), a denomination so small when Wrightsville was founded that it was not allotted a space for its building.

The practice of setting aside open land for public use was always followed in opening up new towns, such land invariably becoming one of the major assets of the developed city. It should be required in the expanding areas of existing towns, which too often have pleasant parks in the older areas and a dismal lack of open space in the newer ones. Existing towns such as Wrightsville would do well to examine their building codes and see to it that provision is made for parks in all areas of expansion, including suburban areas. The time seems distant when towns such as Wrightsville will need to worry about open spaces, but growth of towns and cities in other areas indicates that the same conditions will inevitably come even here. Probably almost unnoticed by local residents, striking changes have already taken place. A 1930 report[1] states that "the county seat is rather inaccessible as a town being on no paved highway." Since that time, not only paved highways but several industries have moved to Wrightsville, including two plants for the manufacture of men's trousers, an electric scoreboard manufacturing plant, a plant which produces travelling kennels, and a corporation which manufactures prefabricated houses. These are in addition to the older manufacturers, which include lumber companies and beef and pork packing plants.

In Johnson County cotton is still an important crop, though less than one-third as much acreage is devoted to cotton as in its peak years. It is interesting to note that in 1960, more than nine thousand bales of cotton were produced on less than thirteen thousand acres, compared to less than nine thousand bales on more than thirty-eight thousand acres in 1919, the year of peak acreage. It must be admitted, however, that 1919 was an unusually bad crop year, as more than

237. *The Christian Church,* Wrightsville
    Built 1938
    Map no. 10-12
    JL & RH

238. *Field and Sky, Soybean Field,* Johnson County
JL & KP

fourteen thousand bales were harvested from slightly fewer acres in 1909. The number of bales per acre has doubled over the last six decades. In addition to woodland, the land not being used for cotton is now in use for livestock, poultry, soybeans (238), and horticultural specialities, which have made marked gains since 1939. Other crops such as pecans, sweet potatoes, corn, and sorghum continue to be produced.

Oak trees abound in the area, and it is a shame that no scientist has done for the acorn what George Washington Carver did for the peanut. It is said that the Indians relished the bitter nuts and made a nutritious kind of acorn meal by drying and pounding them.[2] When allowed to roam, hogs fatten on them, and the zesty flavor of wild turkey meat is supposed to derive in part from the turkey's diet, predomi-

nately of acorns. There should be practical uses for the wasted acorns of Johnson County, though it must be mentioned that several types of acorns are poisonous.

The topography of the countryside is generally flat, with gray soil that glistens white in the sun and contrasts with dark forests where pine, oak, and broad-leaved evergreens predominate. Mistletoe abounds in the deciduous trees, and the evergreens include holly and other red-berried trees and shrubs. It is typical of Georgia that even at the farmers' markets the evergreens and Christmas trees for sale are likely to be shipped from afar, and dried out in the process. In Athens, Georgia, the writer tried in vain to find a longleaf pine, which makes the most beautiful of Christmas trees, or one of the fragrant native cedar trees. It is doubtful that a larger variety or more beautiful holiday greens could be found anywhere than in Johnson County. Nor is any section more favorable to the rapid growth of pine trees.

Since the county was formed just before the Civil War, and Wrightsville not incorporated until 1866, most of the architecture of the area is postbellum, though there are scattered examples of antebellum houses throughout the county, among them the Hicks-Herrington house (155) near Wrightsville and the aforementioned John B. Wright plantation.

The majority of public buildings were built in the late nineteenth or early twentieth century, and most of the architecture is Victorian, a style that is just beginning to be appreciated. Good examples, including the Methodist Church and older parts of the Baptist Church, abound in the area. Many of the storefronts in Wrightsville boast intricately patterned brickwork (239) displaying the skilled craftsmanship of late nineteenth- and early twentieth-century masons.

A hotel built during the early years of this century and illustrated in the section titled "Toward a New Architecture" exemplifies interesting principles of design which have been incorporated in much of the most advanced modern architecture. The new County Health Center (240), likewise built in Wrightsville, is an unusually well-designed building. Simple and with good proportions, it is in harmony with the older buildings and at the same time is completely modern in its restrained elegance.

In 1958 the centennial of Johnson County was celebrated at Wrightsville with pageantry and enthusiasm. Carriages, shays, buggies, and wagons became the fashionable mode of transportation. Male citizens sported beards, and the women flounced petticoats and hoopskirts. There was a parade, the governor spoke, and at night a street dance was held. Several citizens managed to forget that Johnson County was the first in the state to pass a prohibition law.

A ride from Wrightsville to the village of Kite is rewarding. Long stretches of the highway are bordered by trees which were planted along the roadside. Sandy fields, baked and white in summer, stretch to the horizon or are interrupted by patches of piney woods. There is a pond along the way, with water lilies whose delicate beauty emerges like a miracle out of the black water, water so black that it reflects in deeper values the sky and the clouds, yet water so clear that pebbles can be seen glistening on the sandy bottom. And, always in summer, there are bothersome gnats which have a particular affection for the nonnative. Kite itself is an unusual town. Stores once forsaken have been taken over as residences, the canopied fronts transformed into pleasant

239. *Fine Old Masonry,* Wrightsville
Map no. 10-14
JL

sidewalk porches. In summer thriving pot plants add coolness and color to these improvised porches. The relation
here of dwelling, sidewalk, and street suggests a south European village, unexpectedly set down in Middle Georgia.

JOHNSON COUNTY

HISTORY	Created by Legislative Act of December 11, 1858, from parts of Laurens, Washington, and Emanuel counties. Named for Hershel V. Johnson, jurist, governor, U.S. senator, and Confederate senator.
COUNTY SEAT	Wrightsville. Incorporated February 23, 1866, and named for John B. Wright, a leading pioneer resident. Elevation 320. Population 2,106 (1970).
COUNTY POPULATION	7,727 (1970)
AREA	200,320 acres
PRECIPITATION	Average annual, 44 inches. Monthly averages range from just under 5 inches in July to just over 2 inches in October.
TEMPERATURE	Average annual, 66 degrees. Monthly mean temperatures range from 81 degrees in July and August to 50 degrees in December and January. Freeze-free period averages about 240 days with the average dates of the last spring and the first fall freezes falling around mid-March and the second week of November.
RAILROADS	Wrightsville and Tennille Railroad, which is connected to Central of Georgia at Tennille and to Seaboard Coast Line at Dublin.
U.S. HIGHWAYS	319, 221, 80
STATE HIGHWAYS	15, 57, 78, 171
AIR SERVICE	Commercial—Macon, 54 miles west; landing strips—3000' paved at Dublin; 2300' turf in Johnson County (closed by FAA).
ARCHITECTURE	Predominately postbellum, though there are good examples of earlier periods throughout the county. Most noticeable are the Victorian buildings of the 1870s, 1880s, and 1890s.

240. *The Johnson County Health Center,* Wrightsville
     Built 1959. Bernard A. Webb, Jr., Architect.
     Map no. 10-7
     JL & RH

15. Putnam County

The riddle of the great "Rock Eagle" mounds in Putnam County continues unanswered. Modern archeologists have not been able to assess their age, the assigned dates varying from shortly before Columbus's time to centuries before the great pyramids were built. It is generally assumed that they were erected about the time of Christ and centuries earlier than the earth mounds in nearby counties, though a similar effigy in miniature was carved in the dais of the great council chamber of one of the earth mounds near Macon.

It is agreed that some religious significance was attached to the representations, but nothing is known of that religion, not even whether the bird represented was an eagle or a vulture. Whatever the species, the effigies were built on a scale that could only be appreciated from above. The tall tower erected in recent years at Rock Eagle Park enables the visitor to discern the shape of the one there, but it is only from a helicopter that man is truly able to appreciate the power of these ancient art forms, the oldest stone monuments of consequence in all North America. So it is that the true history of architecture in North America begins in Putnam County, Georgia.

Even allowing for changes in climatic conditions, it is understandable why this should have been the Eden of North America. It is pleasant country, high enough to avoid summer humidity yet rarely extremely cold in winter. The land is generally rolling, fertile, and well watered. The abundance of fish and game undoubtedly attracted early peoples, even as it does the sportsmen today, who have the additional lure of Lake Sinclair for boating, skiing, and swimming.

The modern architecture of the Georgia Power Company power plant contrasts dramatically with the waters of Lake Sinclair and the surrounding woods, fields, and hills. It also suggests the wide range of the county's assets, from forests and lakes to abundant supplies of electric power, and from prehistoric to modern architecture.

As with other counties of the area, Putnam's halcyon days were before the Civil War. The true picture of those days once seemed preserved in the Uncle Remus stories of native-born Joel Chandler Harris, stories retold in the dialect of the antebellum Negro. The soft dialect, however, has succumbed to education and television, and the music of the telling is lost on a generation that has never heard those gentle voices. There is an "Uncle Remus" museum (241) in Eatonton with mementos of antebellum days, mementos including cotton

bolls and stalks which prove as strange and interesting to many young southerners as to the tourists from the North.

The disappearance of the cotton fields is not likely to be regretted. Green pastures have replaced many of these, and the transition from cotton farming to dairying and cattle raising has brought new prosperity to the area.

Like other counties in the area, Putnam County has lost population since the Civil War. Though largely self-sustaining as far as necessities were concerned, its prewar prosperity was dependent on cotton farming. Cotton farming in turn was dependent upon vast labor supplies, labor furnished in antebellum days by the slave system. Today, in many areas cotton again means prosperity, but only when it is raised on a scale favorable to machine cultivating and picking. The small gristmills and home and farm industries of pre-Civil War days have been superseded by a smaller number of larger industries.

Most of the commercial and industrial activity of the

241. *The Uncle Remus Museum,* Eatonton
Antebellum cabin moved to present site
Map no. 12-19
RH

county is centered at Eatonton, the county seat named for General William Eaton, hero of a long-forgotten American intervention in Tripoli. The courthouse square (242) is flanked by a few houses and many store buildings, most of the latter built in the nineteenth century and providing a nostalgic contrast to the high water tank that dominates the area. Though the bottom stories of most of these buildings have been remodeled, the second stories and the roof lines still display the fine scale, delightful patterns worked in

brick, and the interesting roof lines of the mid-nineteenth century (243, 244). The pedimented windows provide a pleasant rhythm, and existing hinges indicate that these windows once boasted blinds. If the bottom stories could be brought back into some sort of harmony with the upper stories, and if a good unified overall color scheme could be adopted by all, the square would be well on its way to becoming a place of beauty. The new Peoples Bank has set a superb example for future commercial architecture, being at once

242. *The Putnam County Courthouse,* Eatonton
    Built 1905. J. W. Golucke and Company.
    Map no. 12-13
    KK

modern, outstanding, and in harmony with the best of the old architecture. Both the bank and the square could, however, profit from improved landscaping.

An interesting building from the Classic Re-revival period likewise faces the courthouse square in Eatonton (245). Built as a combination bank and office building in 1904, the style is sometimes called Beaux-Arts architecture when, as would be the case here, the perfection of classic proportions and detail indicated that the architect might have studied at the Ecole des Beaux Arts in Paris.

To the outsider, Eatonton's glory abides in the beauty of her tree-lined streets. Here, antebellum mansions, ornate Victorian houses and churches, and comfortable front-porch-type houses of the twentieth century combine to form the most serene of village scenes. The farsighted citizens who

243. *The Old Temperance Building,* Eatonton
     Built 1820 as Masonic Hall. Remodeled
        1848 for "Sons of Temperance."
    Valuable
    Map no. 12-16
    JL

244. *Nineteenth-Century Store Buildings and*
     Twentieth-Century Water Tank, Eatonton
    Valuable
    Map no. 12-14
    KK

long ago planted trees along the streets and sidewalks left to Eatonton a heritage of beauty. It is interesting to note the different kinds of trees: ancient and picturesque cedar trees (*juniperus virginiana*) combined with deciduous trees along sections of Jefferson Street (246); water oaks and a variety of types along Wayne Avenue; and the magnificient double rows of elm trees at the end of Madison Street (247). Most of the trees are very old, some are dying. It is hoped that provisions will be made to replace such trees, also to resume the practice of planting trees along those streets which are now without them. It would be good if developers of new areas would follow the example set by the early builders who first planted the trees.

In this connection it is to be noted that the Planning Commission of Eatonton has been particularly farsighted, and has already prepared a master plan and ordinance regulating the subdivision of land in the city. Eatonton's future as a fine residential area and a retreat from the disadvantages of overcrowded cities depends upon such farsighted planning combined with the maintenance of her idyllic heritage.

245. *Bank Building of the Classic Re-revival,* Eatonton
Built in early twentieth century
Map no. 12-17
JL

PUTNAM COUNTY

HISTORY	Founded 1807; created from Baldwin County. Named for Revolutionary General Israel Putnam of Connecticut.
COUNTY SEAT	Eatonton. Founded 1809 and named for General William Eaton, hero of the Tripolitan War. Elevation 575. Population 4,125 (1970).
COUNTY POPULATION	8,394 (1970)
AREA	218,240 acres
PRECIPITATION	Average annual, 46 inches.
TEMPERATURE	Average annual, 63.5 degrees. Monthly mean temperatures range from 80 degrees in July to 47 degrees in January.
RAILROADS	Central of Georgia
U.S. HIGHWAYS	129, 441
STATE HIGHWAYS	17, 142, 212, 300
AIR SERVICE	Commercial—Macon, 42 miles SW; landing strip—4500′ paved at Milledgeville.
ARCHITECTURE	Prehistoric Indian mounds and monuments. Later architecture dates from very early nineteenth century to contemporary. Outstanding examples of Greek Revival architecture.

246. *Cedar and Other Street Trees, Jefferson Avenue,* Eatonton
    RH

247. *Elm Trees, Madison Street,* Eatonton
    RH

16. Washington County

Washington is the oldest of the counties in the Oconee Area and originally included the counties of Greene, Hancock, Johnson, and Montgomery, and part of Oglethorpe and of Laurens counties. It is true Deep South country, and long straight rows of cotton still spread out over the flat land, though the amount of land planted in cotton is less than 15 percent of the amount planted during peak years. Cattle raising and dairying have increased during the past decade, and lush pasture land has taken the place of many cotton fields.

Washington County is rich in kaolin, and the kaolin mines present a fantastic scene. Here the verdure ends, and the landscape assumes strange shapes and brilliant colors, as of earthworks thrown up in a violent upheaval. It is spectacularly beautiful, reminiscent of the deserts of the West, but grossly wasteful of potentially fruitful land (248). Kaolin mining, processing, and related industries form the backbone of Washington County's industrial development, which, however, includes wood processing and textile plants as well as a number of smaller industries.

Sandersville, the county seat, was laid out in 1796 at the crossing of important old Indian trails. Despite hardships and the threat of Indian raids in early days, the town prospered and by 1850 boasted more than one thousand homes. The town has, however, experienced its share of disasters. Two major fires, one in 1855 and another in 1888, destroyed much of the commercial area. During the Civil War Sherman's army burned all the public buildings except the old Masonic hall, which accidentally burned in 1921. At that time, the Masonic hall housed some seven thousand volumes of books which had been collected as the nucleus of a public library under the auspices of the Transylvania Club, a ladies organization founded as a literary society in 1908 which has been actively promoting the cultural aspects of Sandersville and Washington County ever since.

Undismayed by the loss of the books, the club pushed forward, and two days later the library was reopened in the home of the librarian. Today the library occupies a charming brick building painted white and opening onto a walled garden at the rear (249). It is still owned and run by the Transylvania Club. This club has likewise been instrumental in having Queensware plates manufactured by the Wedgewood Company in England to commemorate scenes, events, and personages of Georgia.

248. *Lake in Abandoned Kaolin Mine*, Washington County
Map no. 13-4
KK

249. *The Public Library*, Sandersville
Built shortly after Civil War for R. L. Warthen Law Office.
Remodeled 1931 for library. Remodeling plans by Miss Louise Irwin.
Map no. 14-11
KK

Like other towns of the area, the business section has grown up around the courthouse square. The courthouse itself is a fine example of good Victorian architecture, non-symmetrical, and admirably suited to the site (250). It is run down and has a prosaic addition dating from the 1930s, but the original design is powerful enough to take these in stride. There was also a delightfully Victorian bandstand on the grounds which has been converted into an office for the Chamber of Commerce without losing too much of its playful character.

The square itself is unusually large, and interesting in that the courthouse is not in the center but to one side, leaving room for a useable and inviting park. Much of the area has been given over to parking.[1] The pros and cons, beauty versus practicality, could be argued endlessly, but the obvious intrusion on the park could be alleviated to some extent if the parking area were redesigned so that trees could be planted there. This would not be a major undertaking and would relieve the hot bareness of the area that immediately repels the visitor.

The buildings around the square and up the side streets are mostly attractive, and despite the disastrous fires of the past the masonry walls of some of them appear quite old, with interesting brickwork and an occasional iron balcony (251) or arched doorway of real beauty. As is true of most old commercial sections, the lower parts of the buildings have too frequently been remodeled without regard to the original architecture, and garish and unsightly signs spread across the fronts. If this condition could be corrected to some degree, trees planted in the downtown parking area, and a coordinated color scheme worked out for all the buildings, the business district of Sandersville could be one of outstanding beauty. Hayne Street, particularly, with its row of buildings displaying almost identical arched windows and doors (252), could be truly impressive if the separate shops were unified by being painted one color, and the arches and graceful fanlights accentuated in a contrasting one.

The county has many smaller towns, most of them interesting. In the village of Warthen in an open field across from the old Warthen house, Jefferson Davis with a small group of refugees spent a night while trying to escape capture by Federal troops. The Warthen family urged him to stay in their house, but he preferred to camp out for fear of implicating his would-be host, who, despite the scarcity of food at the time, managed to scrape up a "tray of good southern cooking" for the president.

Still standing in Warthen is a small jail where Aaron Burr is said to have been held for a night (253). It is built of logs

250. *Spire, The Washington County Courthouse,* Sandersville
Built 1870. Remodeled 1899.
Greene Brantley and J. W. Renfroe, Builders
L. F. Goodrich, Architect for remodeling.
Valuable to Area
Map no. 14-12
JL & KP

and has wooden bars in the one window, if that opening could be called a window. The building in only 10′ by 12½′, and the door only 5′ high. It looks more like a child's playhouse than a jail that once held a famous political prisoner.

A county village, which has changed little in the past century or more, has the intriguing name of Riddleville. There are a few old houses and a general store at the crossroads. Here in the summer, the "customers" gather to sit and talk, and sometimes go inside to make a purchase. Occasionally an unfamiliar car stops, conversation likewise stops, and the self-conscious visitor feels himself a stranger in a place that was long ago and vaguely remembered.

The thriving town of Tennille is the second largest in the county and in sharp contrast with the picturesque and sleepy villages throughout the area. Most of the larger county industries are located in the Sandersville-Tennille area. Here, too, are lime sinks from which lime for the masonry of the older buildings was obtained, and unexplored and unexploited caverns which are so frequently found in limestone country.

The county enjoyed two peak periods of prosperity. The first, of course, was the long and almost continuous period of prosperity before the Civil War. The second occurred just before and just after World War I and culminated in the early twenties when cotton reached the price of forty cents a pound. Evidence of these two prosperous eras abounds in the area. In Sandersville, houses of both eras rise proudly along North Harris Street, known locally as "Silk Stocking Street."

In Davisboro large brick warehouses as well as a row of picturesque but mostly vacant store buildings, recall the days when cotton meant prosperity. The roofs of the store buildings project over the sidewalk and are supported by rustic

251. *Cast Iron Balcony over Store*, Sandersville
Nineteenth Century
Valuable
Map no. 14-15
JL & RH

252. *Stores with Fanlights*, Sandersville
Built circa 1888
Valuable
Map no. 14-14
KK

wooden posts, like a long porch on a comfortable country house, yet prophetic of the canopies of modern shopping centers.

About eight and one-half miles from the Sandersville city limits, leading from Highway 24 to Davisboro, is Washington Farms with a half-mile-long drive bordered with crape myrtle trees, a glorious sight in late summer.

The whole county abounds in picturesque places and homes. There is the Jordan Mill Pond on Swamp Creek, its dark waters reflecting trees and sky with added richness. Nearby is the Hines-Jordan house, built in the 1850s by Joseph Hines to impress his sophisticated Savannah bride. The once-elegant house is deserted and forlorn. Many of the plantation houses have been thus forsaken. Others have been continuously maintained, while still others, like the Jordan-Pierson house (35), have been restored by appreciative new owners.

In Sandersville, particularly, owners are taking new interest and pride in their heritage of fine homes. A tour of homes was sponsored by the women of Grace Episcopal Church in 1966, and it is gratifying to know that twentieth-century as well as antebellum houses and postbellum houses were included, indicative of the broad range of architecture in the area.

WASHINGTON COUNTY

HISTORY	Created by Legislative Act of February 25, 1784, on land ceded for the county by treaty with the Creek Indians, who later repudiated the treaty. Named for George Washington.
COUNTY SEAT	Sandersville. Laid out in 1796 and incorporated in 1812. Named for a Mr. Sanders who donated the land. Elevation 465. Population 5,546 (1970).
COUNTY POPULATION	17,480 (1970)
AREA	431,360 acres
PRECIPITATION	Average annual, 44 inches. Monthly averages range from 4½ inches in March and July to an average of around 2½ inches in November.
TEMPERATURE	Average annual, 65 degrees. Monthly mean temperatures range from 81 degrees in July and August to 49 degrees in December and January. Freeze-free period averages approximately 240 days extending from mid-March to mid-November.
RAILROADS	Central of Georgia, Sandersville Railroad, Wrightsville and Tennille Railroad
U.S. HIGHWAYS	None
STATE HIGHWAYS	15, 24, 57, 68, 88, 102, 231, 242, 248, 272
AIR SERVICE	Commercial—Macon, 60 miles SW, Augusta, 75 miles NE; landing strip—3000′ at Sandersville
ARCHITECTURE	Ranges from late eighteenth century to contemporary. Most of the periods between are well represented. In general, the remaining antebellum houses are noteworthy for their restraint and simplicity.

253. *The Aaron Burr Jail,* Warthen, Washington County
Built circa 1783
Valuable to Area
Map no. 13-14
JL & RH

17. Wilkinson County

254. *Public Well*, Irwinton
     Built before 1800
     Map no. 16-3
     RH

255. *The Union Church*, Irwinton
     Built 1856. Patrick Ward, Builder
     Valuable to Area
     Map no. 16-2
     KK

In most of the counties of the Oconee Area, as indeed throughout the state, the county seat is the most populous city, and in general the business of the county revolves around that city. In Wilkinson County, two towns, Gordon, with a population of over two thousand, and Toomsboro, with a population of less than eight hundred, are larger than the county seat of Irwinton.

Irwinton is a pleasant village, charming by its very smallness. There is a courthouse square, but most of the stores and offices are built on a street just to the north of this, while the newspaper offices are another block away. The square itself is planted in grass, with large shrubs grouped at the base of the courthouse. This architect would like to see more trees planted on the square, and throughout the downtown area, and possibly some of the shrubbery removed. Ivy, the Boston or English variety, would do much to transform the bare walls of some of the buildings and to give the appearance of coolness on hot days. The old well house (254) still stands on the square and, either because of its simple, good lines or because of its nostalgic appeal, endears itself to the visitor.

It is of interest to note that there are unexplored Indian mounds in the county and that there was once an Indian trading post where the courthouse now stands. Also, that when a part of Sherman's army encamped in Irwinton, breastworks were thrown up at strategic points, and in most cases traces of these redoubts can still be seen. The house in which General W. F. Smith of that army made his headquarters still stands (159).

At the fork of Highways 29 and 57 stands old Union Church, one of the landmarks of this area (255). Chartered by the state legislature in 1854 and built in 1856, the church was used jointly by the Baptists, Methodists, and Presbyterians, hence its name, Union Church. The walls are of handmade brick, and inside there is a slave gallery. Most of the furnishings are still intact. For many years it stood unused, but a movement is now underway to restore the building. A unique feature is the Greek-style portico with three columns, an arrangement studiously avoided by classic architects, primarily because it focuses attention on the central column instead of spaces between the columns or on the building as a whole. That this is the case is apparent by a glance at the photograph, an effect exaggerated by the abrupt hillock on which the church stands. The centrality is augmented by the pediment, which continues the upward visual movement to the peak of the spire. It should be noted that the spire is crowned by a weathervane; Baptists, Methodists, and Presbyterians of that day avoiding the architectural use of the cross as savoring of popery. The use of the three columns of the portico encourages speculation: Did they represent the three denominations of Union Church, or the Trinity, or were they used because the spacing seemed proper, particularly for a church with two doors? Whatever the reasons for the three columns, Union Church is a fascinating building, and the Oconee Area owes a debt of gratitude to those who are working to save this historic church.

The soil of Wilkinson County is rich in kaolin, and Gordon, the largest town in the county, is dominated by a kaolin plant (256). This plant, with its immense warehouses, tanks, conveyors, and exhausts has a kind of powerful beauty that sometimes results from a straightforward expression of industrial use.

Gordon itself is an old town, and the contrast between the old and the new is probably most apparent from the cemetery (257) which was located long ago on land given by the Solomon family, land which is now near the present site of the kaolin plant. Here ancient monuments and graves, ornate iron fences and crumbling brick walls, stand almost adjacent to the modern industrial plant. The contrast is heightened by the gnarled and twisted cedar trees, weeping with long Spanish moss, the whole scene muted with the gray patina of kaolin dust. Bits of the past appear, disappear, and reappear in the industrial town of Gordon.

At Toomsboro, the sleepy present seems to have descended on a once-bustling town. At first glance, it appears a ghost town, straight from a western movie, and with a name too apt. The vacant store buildings and the handsome railroad station are from another era, though the oldest of all, Hall's General Store, is still being operated (258).

There was a time when wagons filled with cotton lined the roads leading to the gin, and when hundreds of bales of cotton were shipped from the old town. During ginning season the whole countryside would be congregated there. Bankers, plantation owners, and Negroes, old and young—all excited at the prospect of finally cashing in on the year's work. There was the year long remembered when cotton brought forty cents a pound. There was a later year when it was less than ten. Harvest time came, the crop might be good, but pockets no longer jingled. The stores closed, most of the people left. For those who remained, things eventually picked up. A veneer plant now operates in Toomsboro. The freight cars may not carry as much cotton as formerly, but there are flat-

256. *The Freeport Kaolin Company*, Gordon, Wilkinson County
Map no. 15-2
JL & KP

257. *The Solomon Street Cemetery*, Gordon, Wilkinson County
Land for cemetery given in 1858 by David Solomon.
Map no. 15-16
RH

cars piled high with lumber. Livestock brings in more cash than did cotton at forty cents a pound. Hall's Store continues, almost but not quite unchanged. A gasoline pump has been added, the Coca-Cola sign is this year's model, and new advertisements have been tacked on the wall, replacing older ones. Its unpainted walls, tin-covered canopy, its forthright architecture remain the same. The changes seem to signify its changelessness.

The old McIntyre home at the village of McIntyre was reputedly saved from destruction in 1864 because Sarah McIntyre displayed a Masonic signal when Federal troops sought to burn it. Numerous houses and buildings throughout the area were claimed to have been thus saved, and it is true that Masonic buildings were spared in towns where all other public buildings were destroyed. There is some room for doubt that the McIntyre house would have been burned, signals or no signals, as few houses in the Oconee Area were demolished. Certain it is though that neither Sarah McIntyre nor the men of Sherman's army dreamed that the peculiar white clay of the area comprised a treasure more valuable than the pretty white house or even the fluffy white cotton that grew there.

Another interesting village in Wilkinson County is Allentown. Tranquil and pleasant, with old trees and houses of varying styles, its outstanding building is the Allentown Methodist Church (259). Though built in 1956, it is Colonial in style, but was designed with a degree of skill and sensitivity that is rare in any period.

WILKINSON COUNTY

HISTORY	Created by Legislative Acts of May 11, 1803, and June 26, 1806, out of land acquired from the Creek Indians in cessions of June 16, 1802, and November 14, 1805. Named for Major General James Wilkinson, an officer of the Revolutionary War.
COUNTY SEAT	Irwinton. First incorporated December 4, 1816, and was reincorporated in 1854. Named for Georgia Governor David Irwin. Elevation 465. Population 757 (1970).
COUNTY POPULATION	9,393 (1970)
AREA	293,123 acres
PRECIPITATION	Average annual, 45 inches. Monthly averages range from 5 inches in July to just under 2 inches in October.
TEMPERATURE	Average annual, 65 degrees. Monthly mean temperatures range from 81 degrees in July and August to 49 degrees in December and January. Freeze-free period averages about 245 days extending from mid-March to mid-November.
RAILROADS	Central of Georgia
U.S. HIGHWAYS	441
STATE HIGHWAYS	18, 29, 57, 96, 112, 243
AIR SERVICE	Commercial—Macon, 30 miles west of Irwinton.
ARCHITECTURE	Ranges from early nineteenth century to contemporary. Indigenous houses and buildings of the county are particularly interesting.

258. *Hall's General Store,* Toomsboro, Wilkinson County
     Built before the Civil War as a whiskey store; later converted to a
         general grocery store with club room on second story
     Valuable to Area
     Map no. 15-18
     JL & RH

259. *The Allentown Methodist Church,* Allentown, Wilkinson County
     Built 1956. W. Elliott Dunwoody, Jr., Architect
     Map no. 15-21
     JL & KP

Maps

COUNTIES AND COUNTY SEATS

The maps on the following pages are keyed by the double map numbers found in the text description of each house. The first number is the map number and the second is the house number as it appears on the map. Below each map is a legend listing the houses and other structures which are shown on the map, some of which may not be illustrated in the book. Those not illustrated are followed with a boldface **NI**. Those which are illustrated are followed by two numbers: the first in boldface is the picture number; the second number is the page number on which that picture with its description may be found.

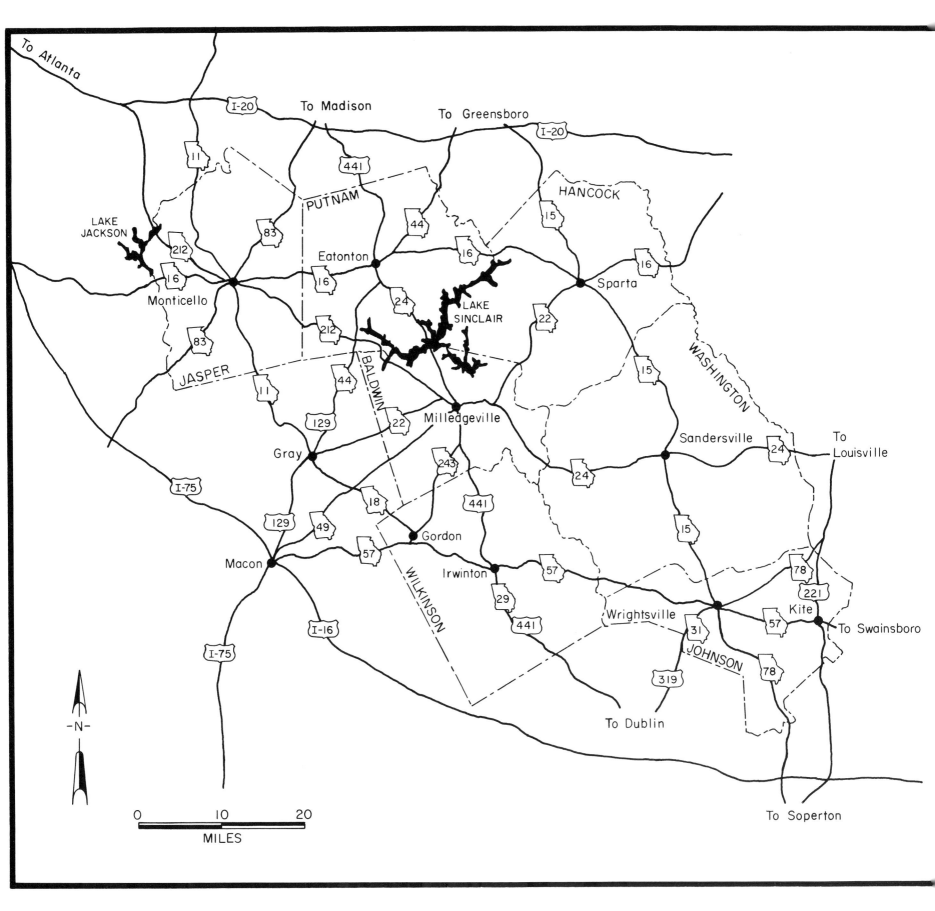

THE OCONEE AREA: PRINCIPAL HIGHWAYS

MAP NO. 1

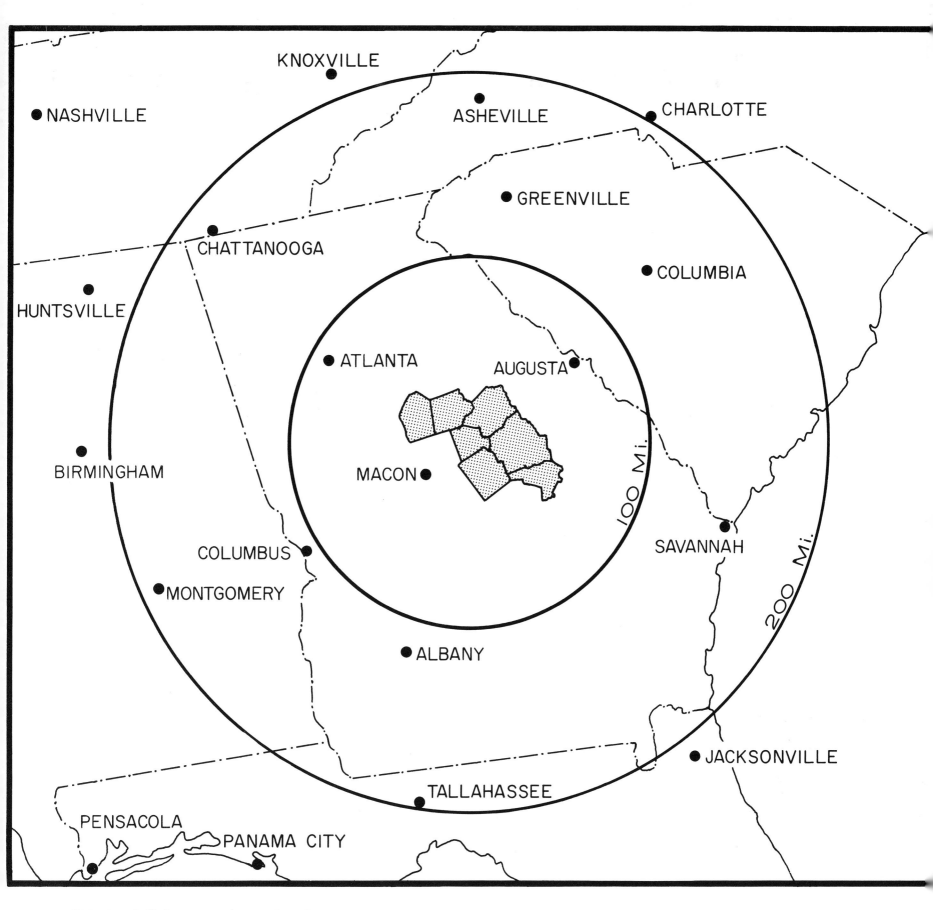

THE OCONEE AREA: GENERAL LOCATION

MAP NO. 2

BALDWIN COUNTY

MAP NO. 3

1. Georgia Power Company Plant   **NI**
2. Lake Sinclair Dam   **NI**
3. Mount Nebo (destroyed c. 1940)
   57   40
4. Boykin Hall   **65**   44
5. Westover   **70**   47
6. The Smith-Baugh House   **77**   54
7. The McKinley House   **139**   95
8. The Scott-Smith House (destroyed
   1969)   **169**   109
9. The Montgomery-Owens House
   178   115
10. The Stevens-Daniel House   **196**
    124
11. East Forty   **217**   134
12. The Elijah Clark House   **NI**

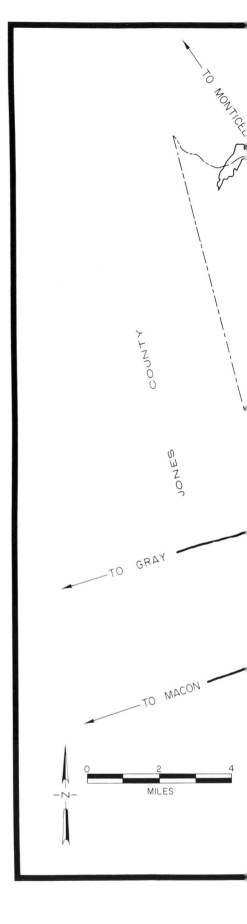

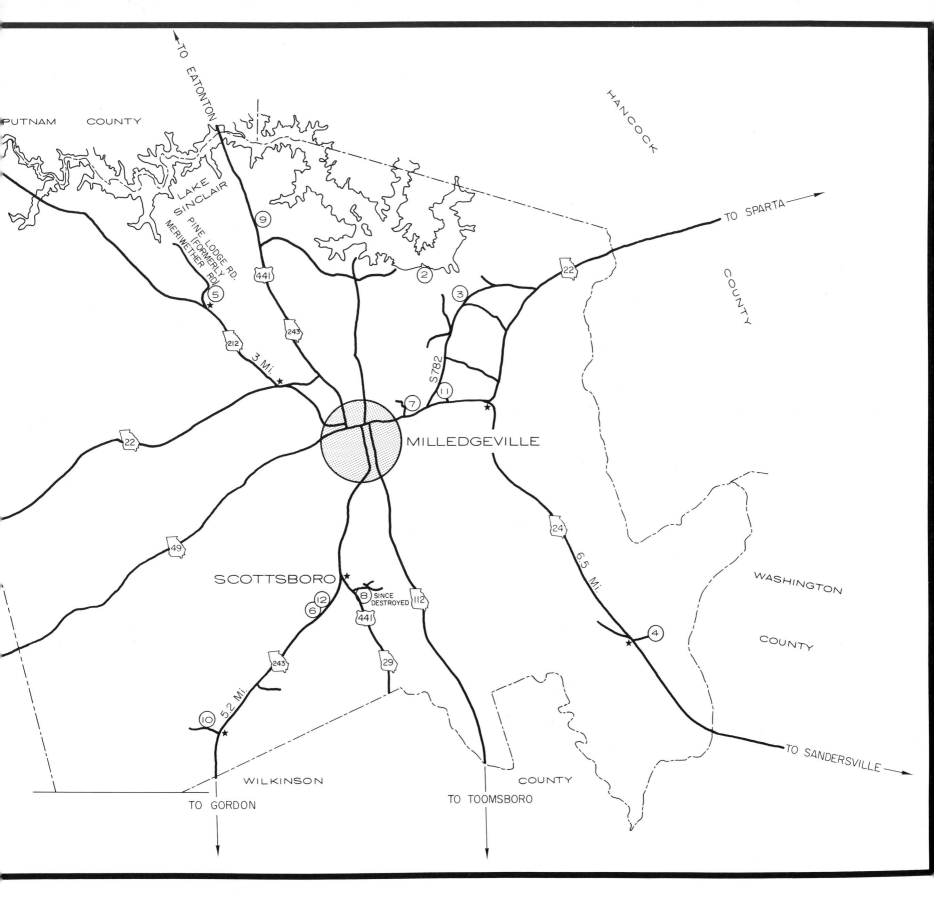

MILLEDGEVILLE

MAP NO. 4

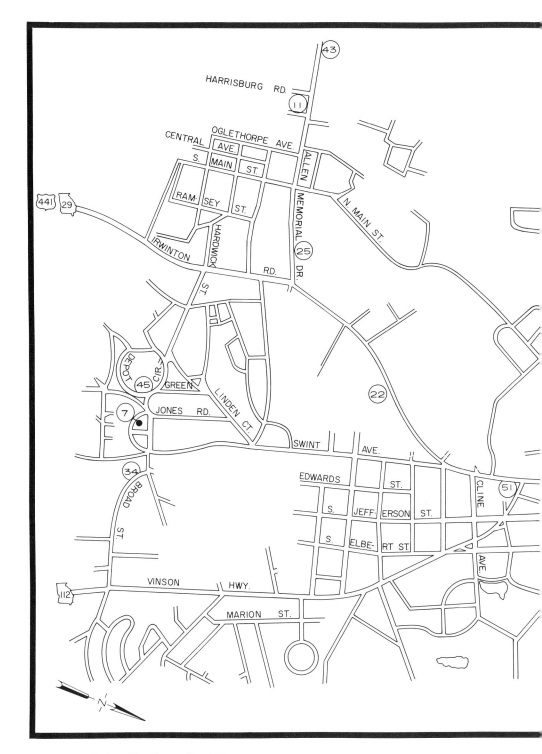

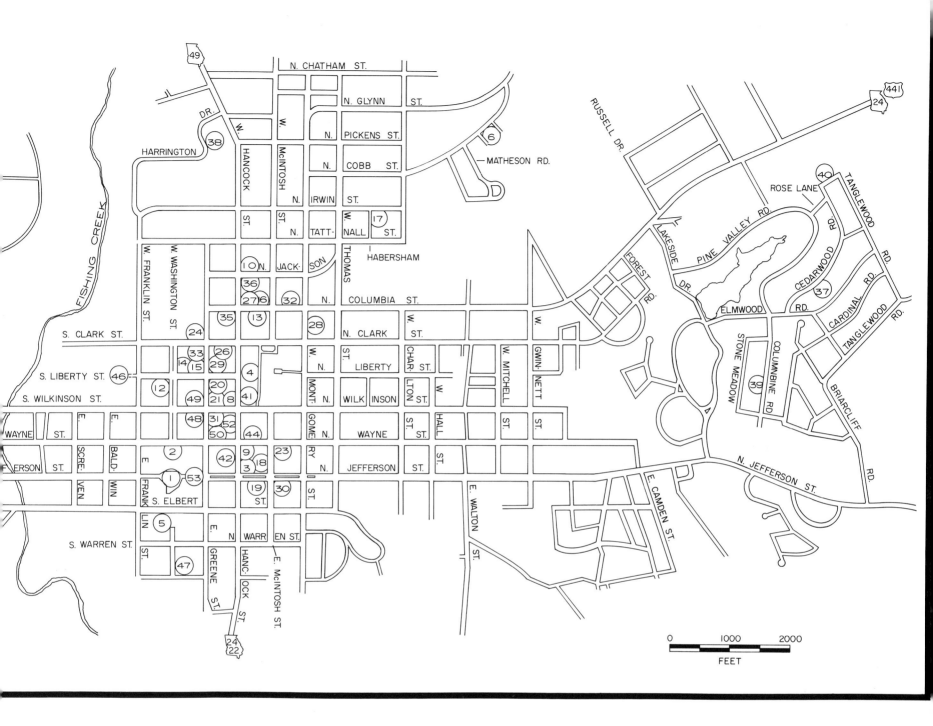

FISHING CREEK

N. CHATHAM ST.

N. GLYNN ST.

HARRINGTON DR. ⑭38

N. PICKENS ST.

N. COBB ST.

N. IRWIN ST.

W. NALL ST. ⑰17

HABERSHAM

N. JACK-SON

N. COLUMBIA ST.

N. CLARK ST.

LIBERTY ST.

WILKINSON

WAYNE

JEFFERSON

S. ELBERT

S. WARREN ST.

E. McINTOSH ST.

MATHESON RD.

RUSSELL DR.

ROSE LANE ⑭40

TANGLEWOOD RD.

CEDARWOOD RD.

⑭37

CARDINAL RD.

TANGLEWOOD RD.

BRIARCLIFF RD.

PINE VALLEY RD.

LAKESIDE DR.

FOREST RD.

ELMWOOD RD.

STONE MEADOW

COLUMBINE RD. ⑭39

N. JEFFERSON ST.

E. CAMDEN ST.

E. WALTON ST.

49

6

24 441

0   1000   2000

FEET

175

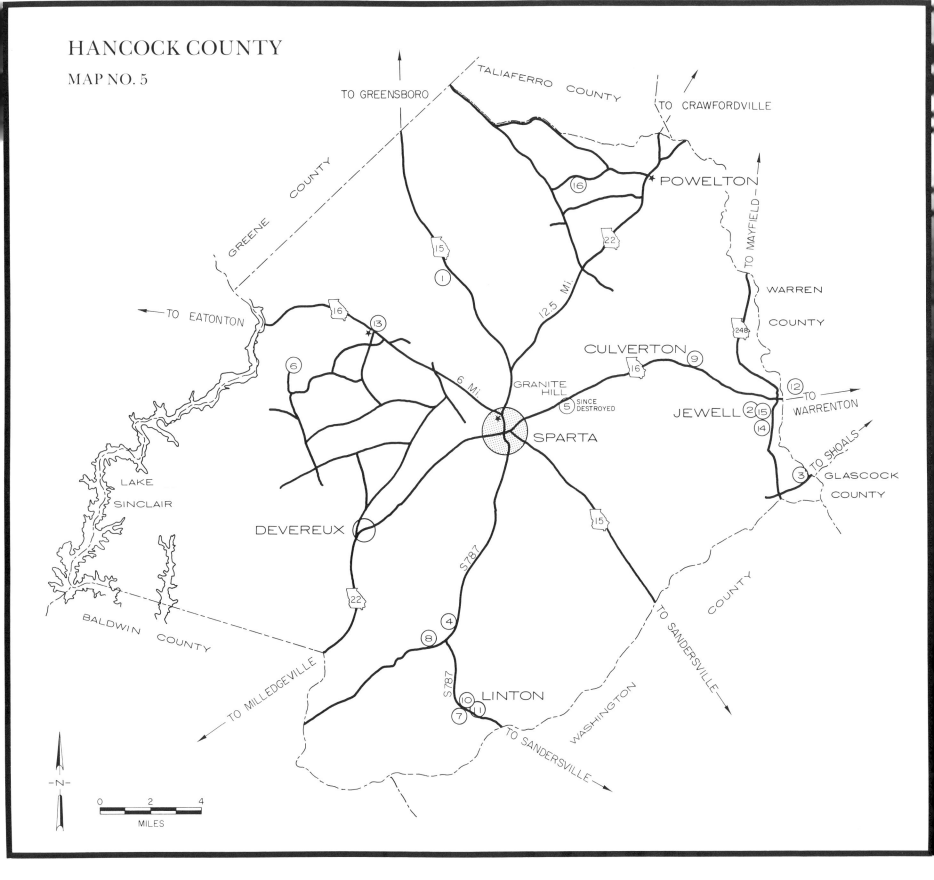

HANCOCK COUNTY

MAP NO. 5

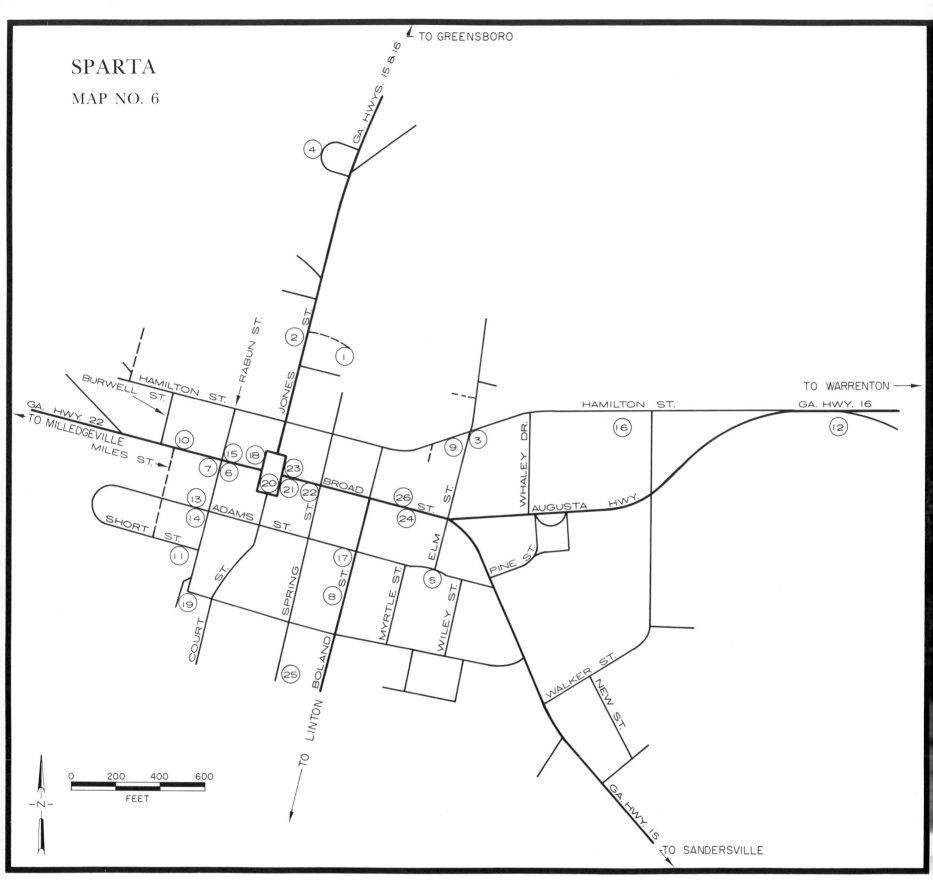

SPARTA
MAP NO. 6

TO GREENSBORO

GA. HWYS. 15 & 16

TO WARRENTON

GA. HWY. 22
TO MILLEDGEVILLE

HAMILTON ST.
GA. HWY. 16

RABUN ST.

JONES ST.

BURWELL ST.

HAMILTON ST.

MILES ST.

WHALEY DR.

AUGUSTA HWY.

BROAD ST.

ADAMS ST.

SHORT ST.

SPRING ST.

BOLAND ST.

COURT ST.

MYRTLE ST.

ELM ST.

WILEY ST.

PINE ST.

WALKER ST.

NEW ST.

GA. HWY. 15
TO SANDERSVILLE

TO LINTON

0   200   400   600
FEET

-N-

177

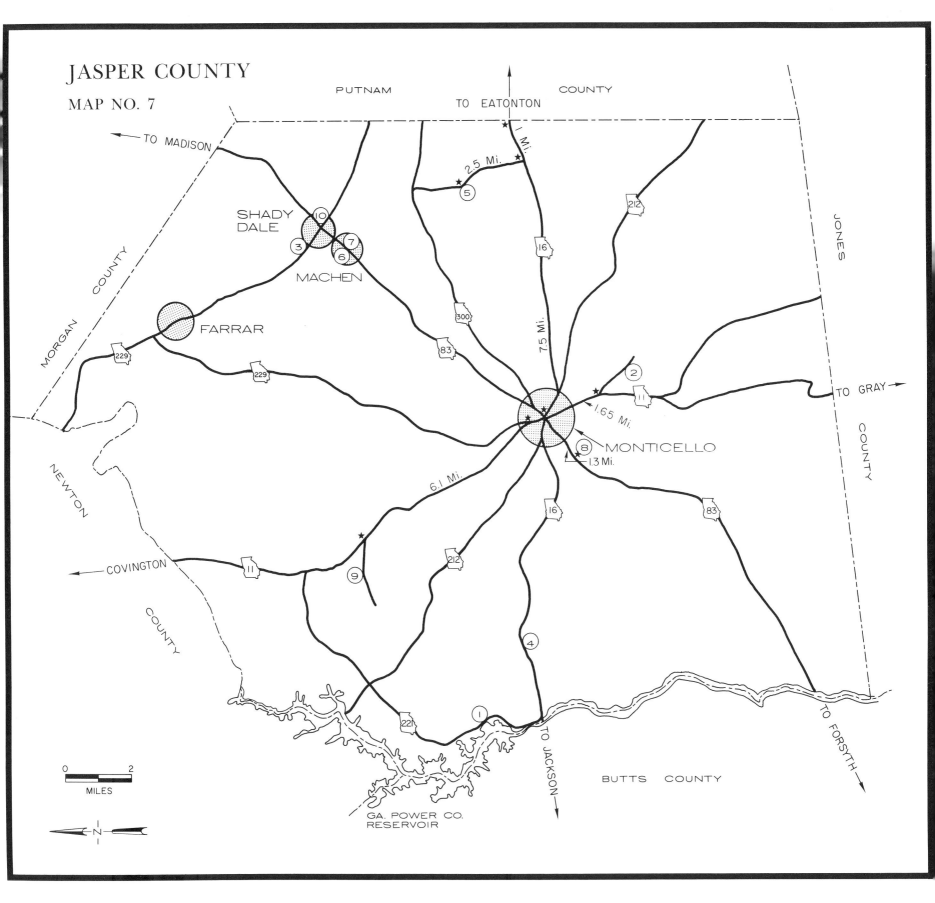

JASPER COUNTY

MAP NO. 7

PUTNAM   COUNTY

TO EATONTON

← TO MADISON

1 Mi.

2.5 Mi.

212

SHADY
DALE

10

3   7

6

MACHEN

16

FARRAR

300

229

83

7.5 Mi.

229

2

11

83

1.65 Mi.

8 → MONTICELLO

1.3 Mi.

MORGAN   COUNTY

JONES   COUNTY

TO GRAY →

NEWTON

6.1 Mi.

16

83

212

← COVINGTON

11

9

4

221

1

TO JACKSON

TO FORSYTH →

BUTTS   COUNTY

GA. POWER CO.
RESERVOIR

0   2
MILES

← N →

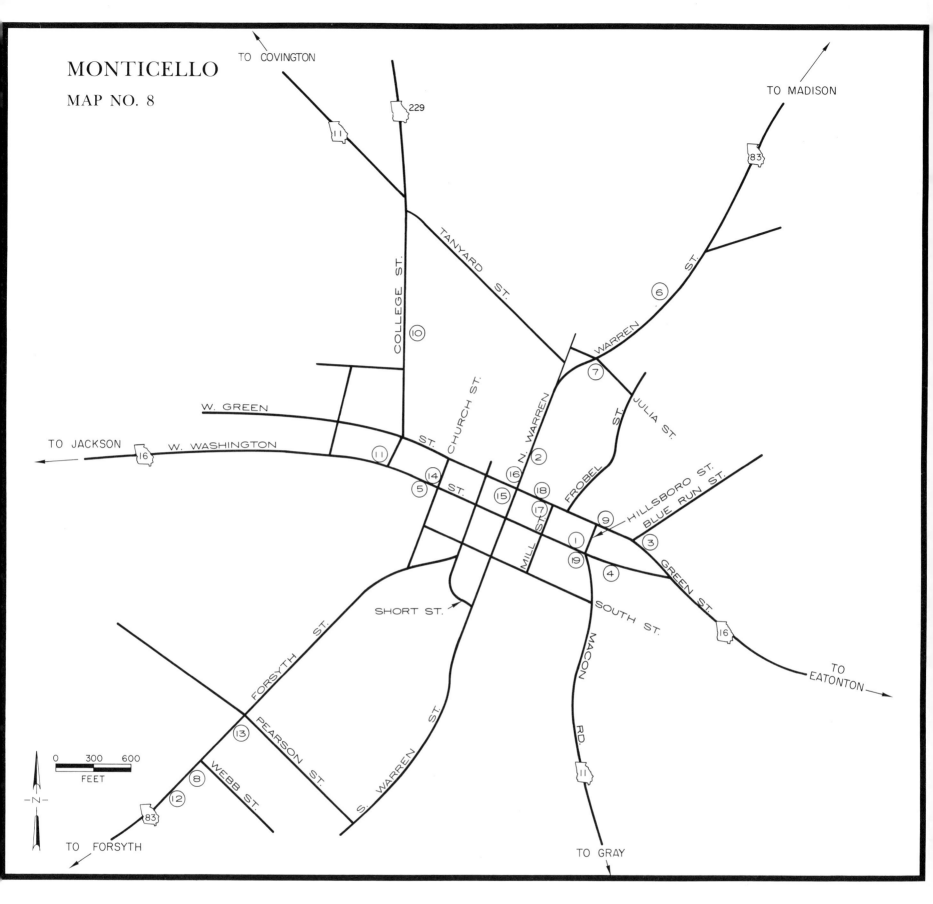

MONTICELLO

MAP NO. 8

TO COVINGTON

TO MADISON

229

11

83

TANYARD ST.

COLLEGE ST.

6

WARREN ST.

10

7

CHURCH ST.

W. GREEN

JULIA ST.

FROBEL ST.

TO JACKSON

W. WASHINGTON

16

11

ST.

14

N. WARREN

2

16

5

ST.

15

18

MILL ST.

17

HILLSBORO ST.

9

BLUE RUN ST.

1

3

19

GREEN ST.

4

16

SHORT ST.

FORSYTH ST.

SOUTH ST.

TO EATONTON

MACON RD.

S. WARREN ST.

PEARSON ST.

13

0 300 600
FEET

—N—

8

WEBB ST.

11

12

83

TO GRAY

TO FORSYTH

1. The Dickerson-Miller House 26
2. The Hitchcock-Walker House **73** 50
3. The Reese-Sorensen House **106** 73
4. The Eli Glover House **NI**
5. The Hurd-Edwards House **143** 97
6. The Jordan-Bellew House **150** 100

7. Monticello Female Academy (destroyed 1970) **153** 101
8. The Ballard House **162** 105
9. The Powell-Jordan-Key House **NI**
10. The J. H. Kelly House **189** 120
11. The J. D. Persons House **199** 125
12. The Knit-Wit House **201** 126
13. The Malone-Warren House **202** 126

14. The Cohen-Benton House **212** 132
15. Statue of Confederate Soldier Boy **234** 156
16. The Jasper County Court House **231** 153
17. The Farmers National Bank Building **NI**
18. The Bank of Monticello **NI**
19. The Monticello Presbyterian Church **NI**

JOHNSON COUNTY

MAP NO. 9

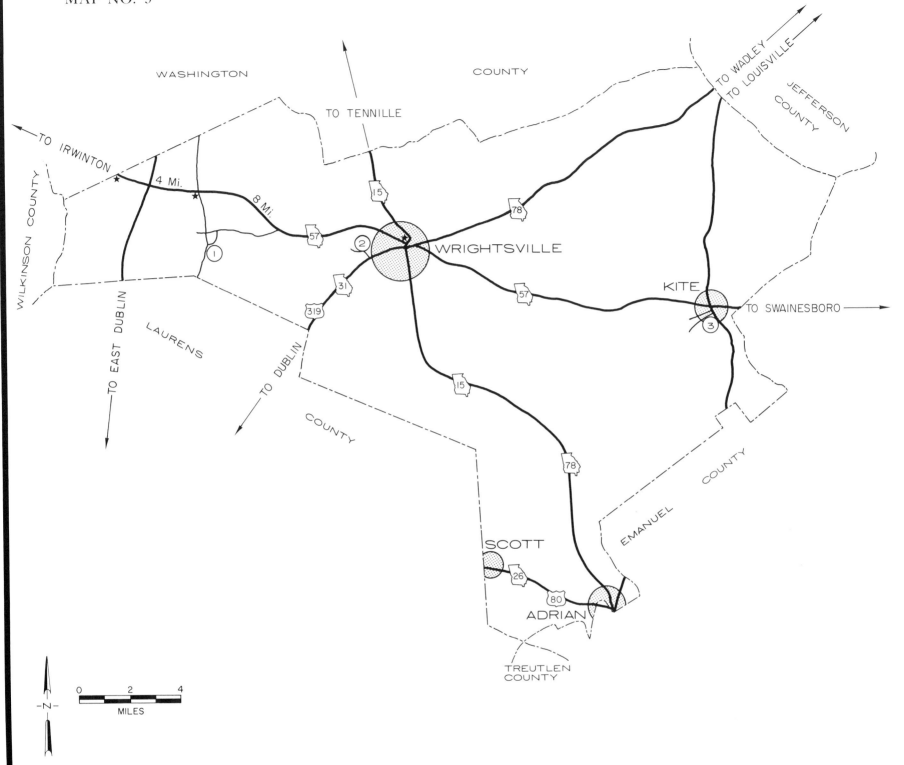

1. The Wright-Phillips House   28
2. The Hicks-Herrington House   **155**
   102
3. The Village of Kite   **NI**

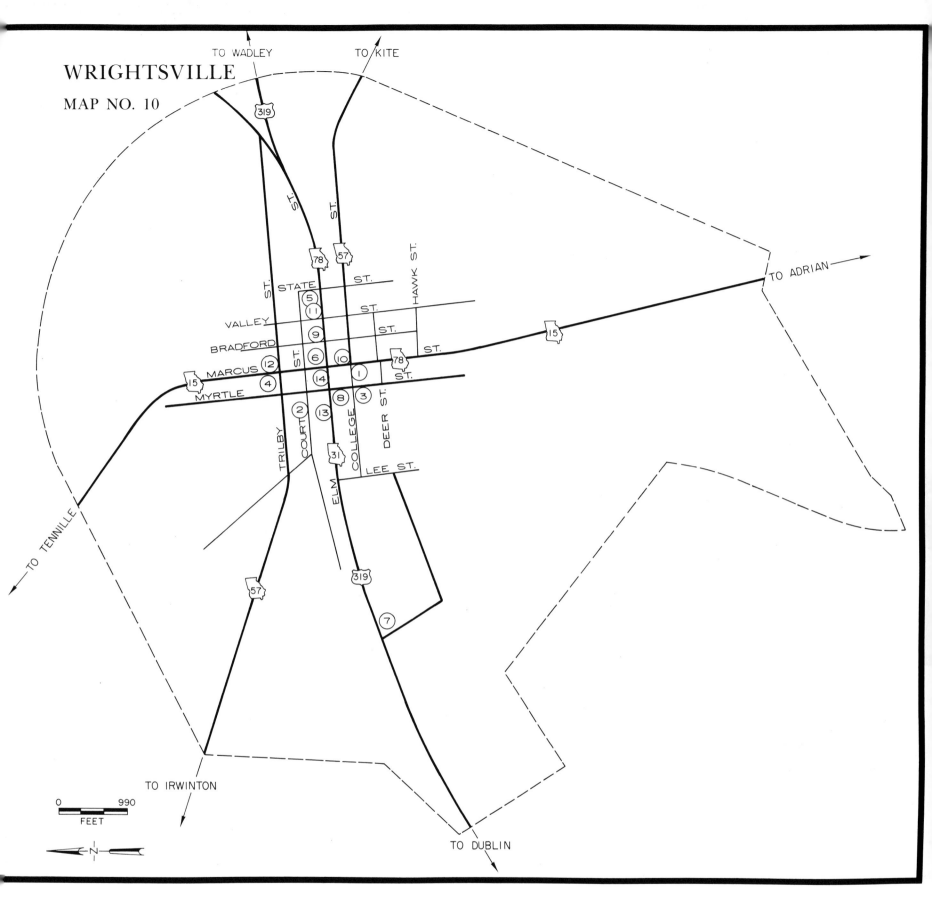

WRIGHTSVILLE

MAP NO. 10

TO WADLEY

TO KITE

TO ADRIAN

TO TENNILLE

TO IRWINTON

TO DUBLIN

0   990
FEET

N

1. The Brinson House **NI**
2. The McCrary House **191** 121
3. The Butterly-Jordan House **192**
   121
4. The Claxton House **NI**
5. Old Tavern **213** 132
6. The Johnson County Court House
   236 160
7. The Johnson County Health Center
   240 164

8. The Exchange Bank **NI**
9. The Bank of Wrightsville **NI**
10. U.S. Post Office **NI**
11. The Brown Memorial Baptist
    Church **NI**
12. The Christian Church **237** 161
13. The Methodist Church **NI**
14. Fine Old Masonry over Store
    Buildings **239** 163

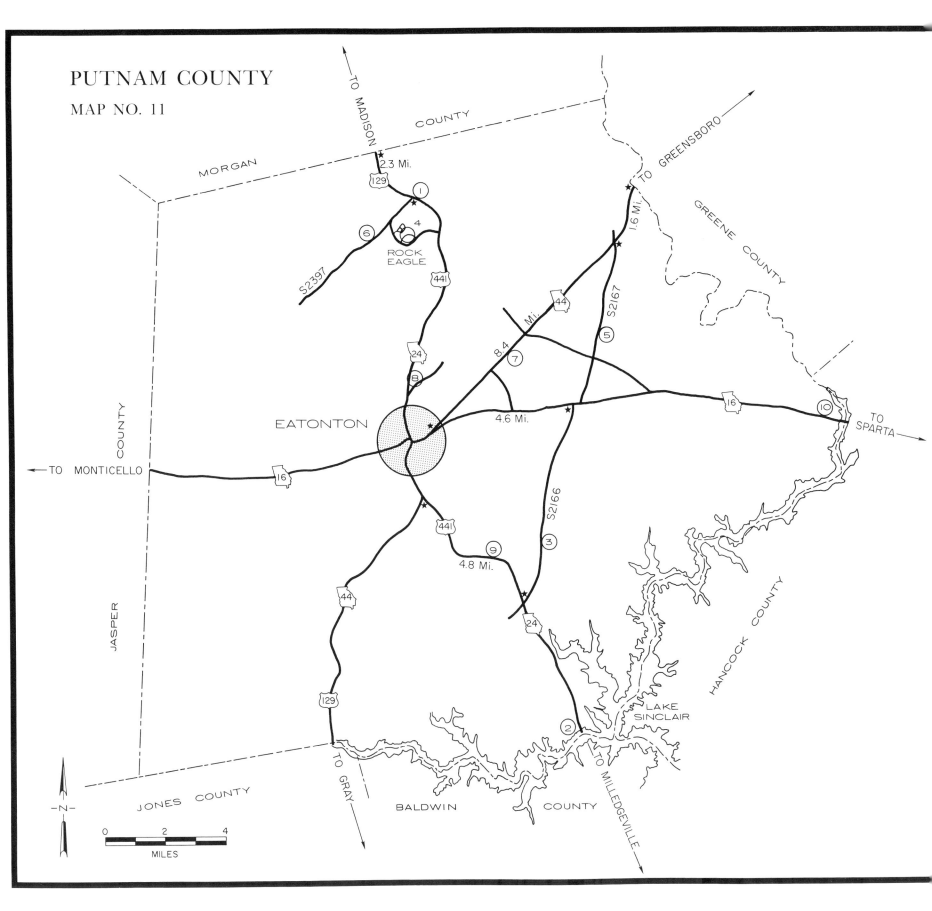

PUTNAM COUNTY

MAP NO. 11

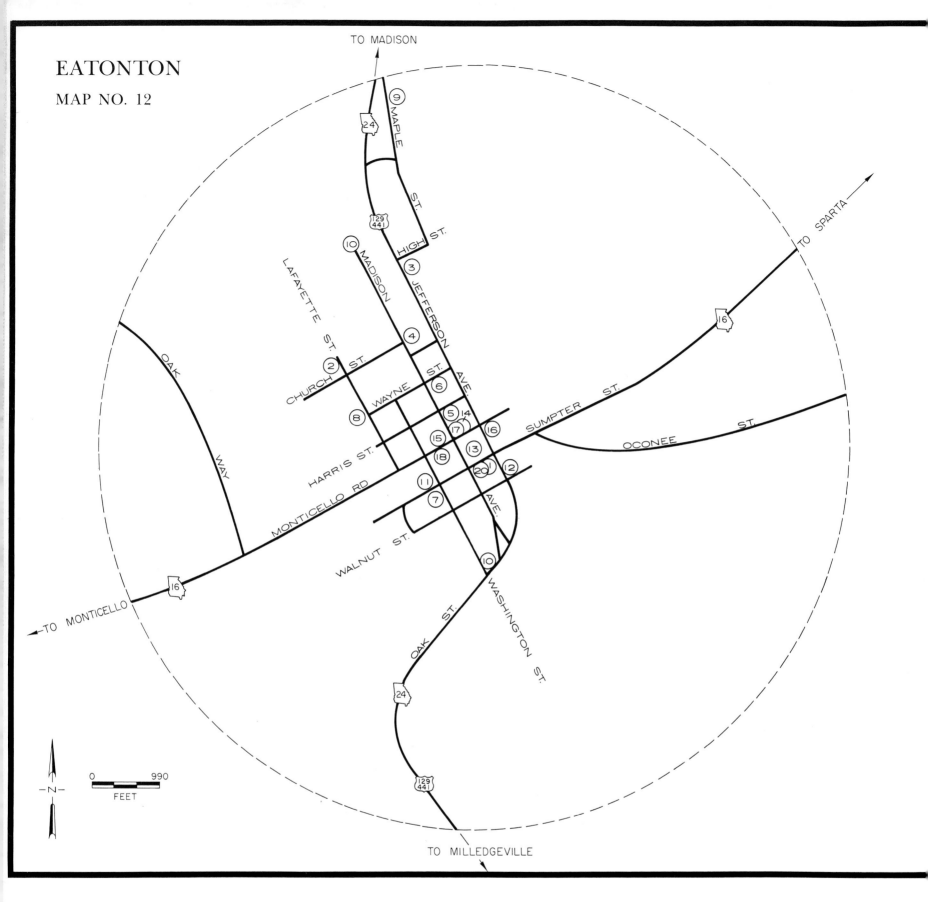

EATONTON

MAP NO. 12

TO MADISON

TO SPARTA

TO MONTICELLO

TO MILLEDGEVILLE

—N—

0   990
FEET

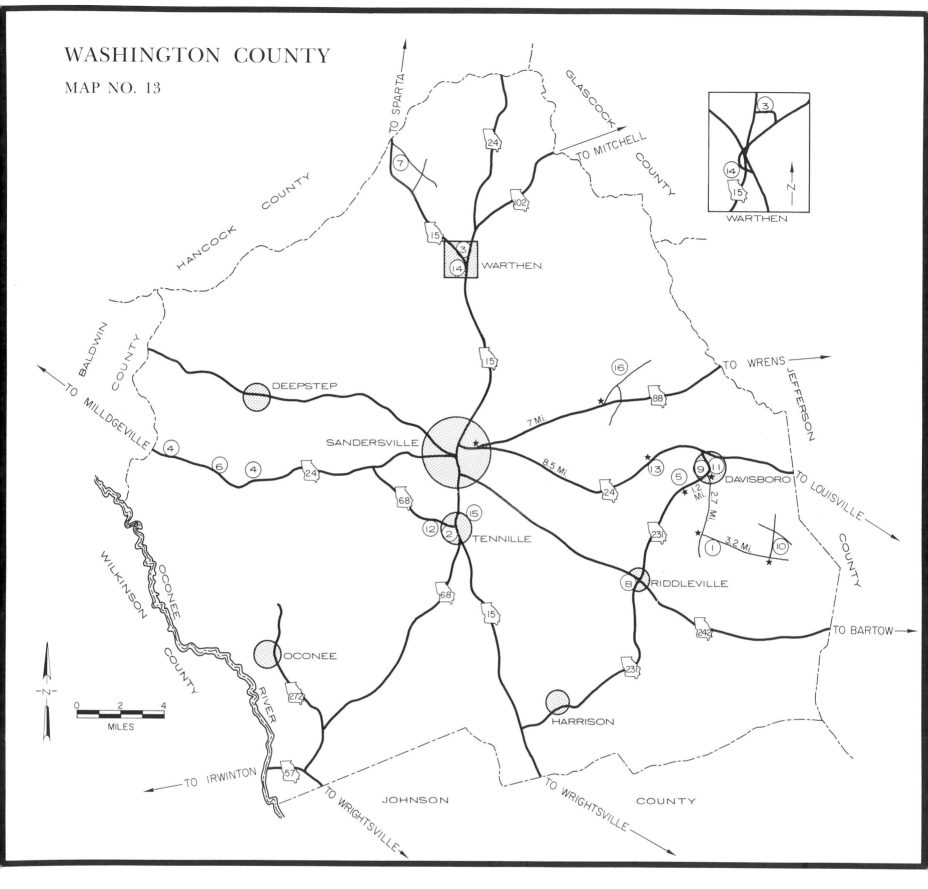

WASHINGTON COUNTY

MAP NO. 13

WARTHEN

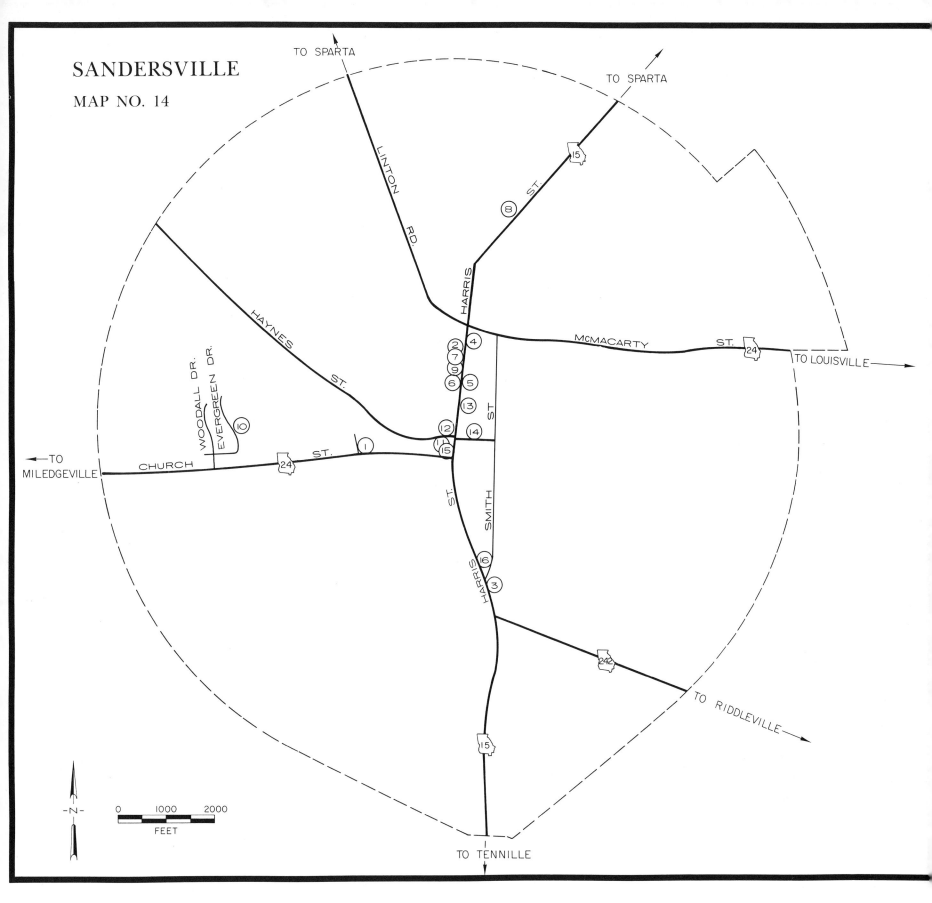

SANDERSVILLE

MAP NO. 14

TO SPARTA

TO SPARTA

15

8

LINTON RD.

HARRIS ST.

McMACARTY ST.

24

TO LOUISVILLE

HAYNES ST.

WOODALL DR.

EVERGREEN DR.

10

2 4

7

9

6 5

13

12 14

1

15

CHURCH ST.

24

TO MILEDGEVILLE

ST.

SMITH

HARRIS ST.

16

3

242

TO RIDDLEVILLE

15

-N-

0   1000   2000

FEET

TO TENNILLE

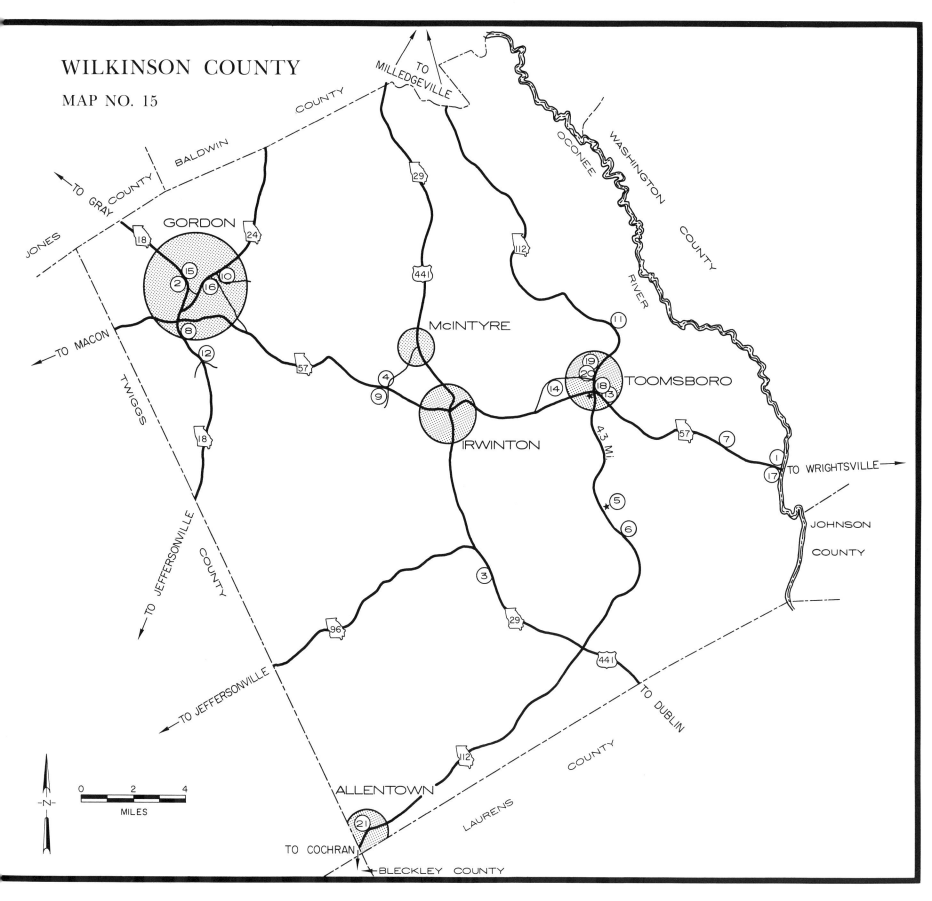

WILKINSON COUNTY

MAP NO. 15

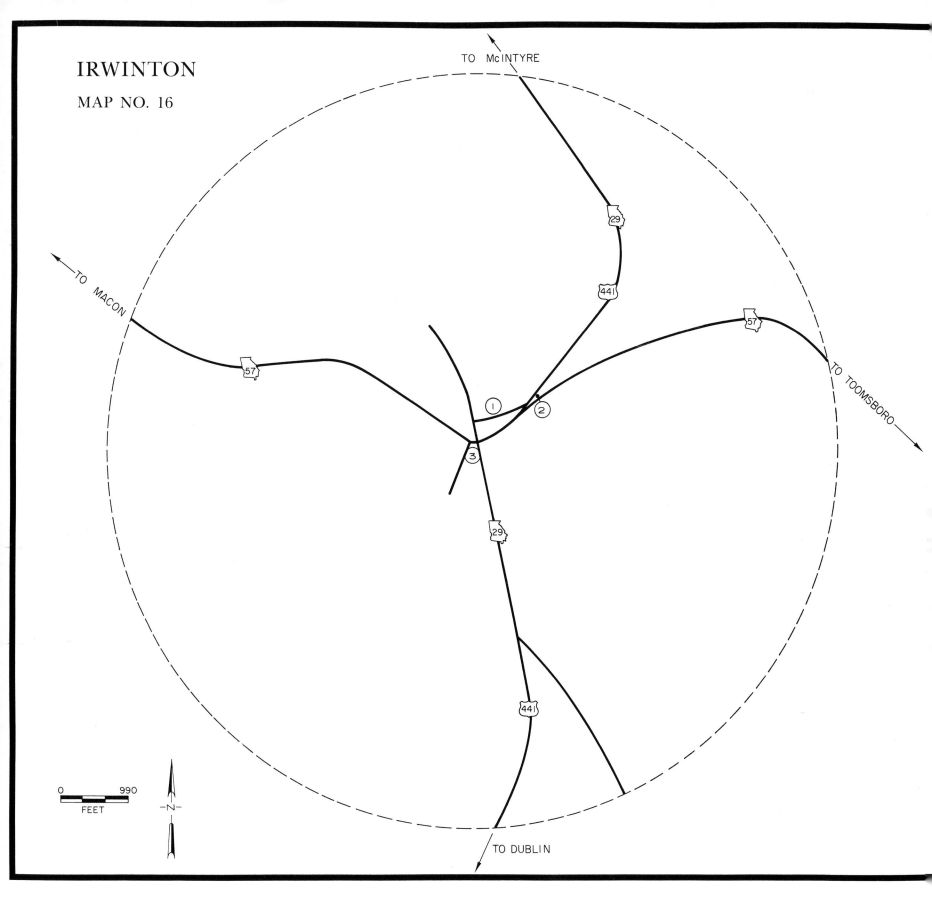

IRWINTON

MAP NO. 16

TO McINTYRE

TO MACON

29
441
57

57
TO TOOMSBORO

① ②

③

29

441

TO DUBLIN

0   990
FEET

-N-

1. The Fisher-Carswell House   **159**
   103
2. The Union Church   **255**   180
3. The Wilkinson County Court
   House   **NI**
3. The Public Well   **254**   180

Notes

Chapter 1.

1. Much of the information in this section was obtained from *A Regional Survey of the Oconee Area* (March 1966) by Howard Schretter under the auspices of the Institute of Community and Area Development, University of Georgia, Athens, Ga.

2. George White, *Historical Collections of Georgia* (New York: Pudney and Russell, 1854), pp. 266, 492, 588.

3. Anna Maria Green Cook, *History of Baldwin County, Georgia* (Anderson, S.C.: Keys-Hearn, 1925), p. 48.

4. 1970 Census of Population, Population Division, Bureau of the Census, U.S. Department of Commerce.

Chapter 2.

1. *The Travels of William Bartram,* ed. Francis Harper (New Haven: Yale University Press, 1958), p. 232. See also pp. 25, 35, 206, 330–32.

2. New York: D. Appleton.

3. George M. Sloan, "The Rock Eagle Effigy," *Current Lines,* Tri-County Electric Membership Corporation (December 1962). Copy in University of Georgia Library, Georgia Room, vertical file labeled "Rock Eagle."

4. Transcript, University of Georgia Library (probably U.S. Historical Records Survey), Georgia Room, vertical files.

5. A. L. Kelly, "Eatonton Effigy Mounds and Related Stone Structures in Putnam County, Georgia," *Georgia Mineral News Letter* 7, no. 2 (Summer 1954): 82–86.

6. Jones, *Antiquities of the Southern Indians,* p. 37.

Chapter 3.

1. Anna Maria Green Cook, *History of Baldwin County, Georgia* (Anderson, S.C.: Keys-Hearn, 1925), pp. 47–48.

2. C. C. Jones, Jr. (New York, 1873), pp. 48–52.

Chapter 4.

1. University of North Carolina Press, 1957.

2. Page 124.

3. Pages 118, 124.

4. New York: Holt, Rinehart and Winston, 1952, pp. 67–68.

5. University of North Carolina Press, 1957, p. 130.

Chapter 6.

1. University of North Carolina Press, 1957, pp. 126–27.

2. Peter Benchley, "Life's Tempo in Nantucket," *National Geographic* 137 (June 1970): 834.

Chapter 7.

1. Harnett T. Kane, *Plantation Parade* (New York: William Morrow, 1945), pp. 59, 133, 191, 221, 229.

2. Andrew J. Downing, *The Architecture of Country Houses* (New York: D. Appleton, 1851), pp. 188–206.

3. Loutrel W. Briggs, *Charleston Gardens* (Columbia: University of South Carolina Press, 1951), p. 59.

4. Donald Wyman, *Shrubs and Vines for American Gardens* (New York: Macmillan, 1968), p. 305.

5. New York: D. Appleton, 1851, pp. 304–11.

6. "Proud Old Homes of Sparta," *Georgia Magazine* 4, no. 3 (October-November 1965): 20.

7. *When the World Ended: The Diary of Emma LeConte,* ed. Earl Schenck Miers (New York: Oxford University Press, 1957).

Chapter 12

1. J. C. Bonner, "A Georgia County's Historical Assets," *Emory University Quarterly* 9 (1953): 24–30.

2. Velma Bell, "Side Tour to Sparta," Federal Writers Project (1937), University of Georgia Library files.

3. The deserted houses have been torn down since 1967.

Chapter 13

1. George C. Smith, "Unwritten Chapters in Georgia History . . .," n.d., University of Georgia Library, Georgia Room, vertical file labeled "Jasper County."

2. Rev. George D. D. Howe, *History of the Presbyterian Church in South Carolina* (1883; reprint ed., Synod of South Carolina Presbyterian Church in the United States, 1966), 1: 392.

3. Ruby F. Thomas, *Historic Spots and Places in Georgia* (Atlanta: Georgia Bicentennial Commission, 1935). According to the 1921 code of the city of Monticello, Georgia, Monticello was incorporated in 1901. Other sources give the date 1872.

Chapter 14

1. "Johnson County," University of Georgia Library files.

2. From the *Georgia Historical Quarterly* 55 (Spring 1971), 132, an excerpt from *Benjamin Hawkins' Journey across Georgia in 1796,* edited by Marion R. Hemperley is of interest: "I saw on the path as I came here some [Hillabee Indian] women picking up red oak acorns, for the purpose of making oil. They gather the acorns, dry them on reed mats, hull them, beat them fine in a mortar, mix them up in water and let them stand for an evening. The oil rises to the top, and they skim it off with a feather. This oil is used for food; one bushel of acorns makes about a pint of oil."

Chapter 16

1. Since the text was written, the remainder of the old square has been mutilated for parking.

Selected Bibliography

Articles from vertical files, Georgia Room, University of Georgia Library: Georgia counties (Baldwin, Hancock, Jasper, Johnson, Putman, Washington, and Wilkinson); Georgia cities (Eatonton, Milledgeville); Rock Eagle.

Bartram, William. *The Travels of William Bartram.* Edited by Francis Harper. New Haven: Yale University Press, 1958.

Beck, Lewis H. *Historic Gardens of Georgia.* Griffin, Georgia: Southern States Printing, 1942.

Beeson, Leola Selman. *History: Stories of Milledgeville and Baldwin County.* Macon, Georgia: J. W. Burke, 1943.

Benjamin, Asher. *The American Builder's Companion.* 6th ed. Boston: R. P. and C. Williams, 1827. Reprinted, New York: Dover Publications, 1968.

————. *The Builder's Guide; or, Complete System of Architecture.* Boston: B. B. Mussey, 1854. Copy in the University of Georgia Library.

Bonner, James. C. *The Georgia Story.* Oklahoma City: Harlow Publishing, 1961.

————. *A History of Georgia Agriculture, 1732-1860.* Athens: University of Georgia Press, 1964.

————. "Sherman at Milledgeville in 1864." *Journal of Southern History* 22, no. 3 (August 1956): 273-291.

Bremer, Frederika. *The Homes of the New World: Impressions of America.* London: Arthur Hall, Virtue, 1853. 3-volume set belonging to John Linley.

Briggs, Loutrel W. *Charleston Gardens.* Columbia: University of South Carolina Press, 1951.

Buist, Robert. *American Flower Garden Directory.* Philadelphia: Carey and Hart, 1845. Copy belonging to John Linley.

Bullock, John. *The American Cottage Builder.* New York: Stringer Townsend, 1854. Copy belonging to John Linley.

Cook, Anna Maria Green. *History of Baldwin County, Georgia.* Anderson, South Carolina: Keys-Hearn, 1925. Georgia Room, University of Georgia Library.

————. *Journal of a Milledgeville Girl, 1861–1867.* Edited by James C. Bonner. Athens: University of Georgia Press, 1964.

Downing, Andrew Jackson. *A. J. Downing's "Cottage Residences, Rural Architecture, and Landscape Gardening."* Introduction by Michael Hugo-Brunt Watkins. Glen, New York: Library of Victorian Culture, 1967.

————. *The Architecture of Country Houses.* New York: Appleton, 1851. Copy belonging to John Linley.

Hamlin, Talbot. *Greek Revival Architecture in America.* London: Oxford University Press, 1944.

Hemperly, Marion R., ed. "Benjamin Hawkins' Trip across Georgia in 1796." *The Georgia Historical Quarterly* 55, no. 1 (Spring 1971): 114-137.

Howe, George. *History of the Presbyterian Church in South Carolina,* vol. 2. Columbia: W. J. Duffie, 1883. Reprinted, Synod of South Carolina Presbyterian Church in the United States, 1966.

Jones, Charles C., Jr. *Antiquities of the Southern Indians, Particularly of the Georgia Tribes.* New York: Appleton, 1873. Georgia Room, University of Georgia Library.

Kane, Harnett T. *Plantation Parade.* New York: William Morrow, 1945.

Milledgeville and Baldwin County Civil War Centenniel, Milledgeville, Georgia. Souvenir Program. Sponsored by Milledgeville and Baldwin County Chamber of Commerce, 1961. Vertical file labelled "Milledgeville," Georgia Room, University of Georgia Library.

Moore, Virginia H. "Beautiful Georgia Homes and Gardens: Proud Old Homes of Sparta." *Georgia Magazine* 4, no. 3 (October-November 1965): 18-21, 32.

————. "Historic Sparta and Hancock County." *Georgia Magazine* 4, no. 3 (October-November 1965): 16-17.

Nichols, Frederick Doveton. *The Early Architecture of Georgia.* Chapel Hill: University of North Carolina Press, 1957.

Nicholson, Peter. *The Carpenter's New Guide.* 9th ed. Philadelphia: John Grigg, 1827. Copy belonging to John Linley.

————. *The Carpenter's New Guide.* 16th rev. ed. Philadelphia: Lippincott, 1856. Copy belonging to John Linley.

Oconee Area Planning and Development Commission, Milledgeville, Georgia.
Economic Profile of Gordon-Irwinton, Georgia, 1966.
Economic Profile of Milledgeville, Georgia, 1966.
Economic Profile of Monticello, Georgia, 1966.
Economic Profile of Tennille, Georgia, 1966.
Economic Profile of Wrightsville, Georgia, 1966.
Initial Overall Economic Development Program for the Oconee Economic Development District, 1967.

Perkerson, Medora Field. *White Columns in Georgia.* New York: Rinehart, 1952.

Rainwater, Hattie C., ed., and Rainwater, Hattie C., comp. *Garden History of Georgia, 1733-1933.* Atlanta: The Peachtree Garden Club, 1933.

The Restoration of Colonial Williamsburg in Virginia. Reprinted from the *Architectural Record* (December 1935). New York: F. W. Dodge, 1935.

Satterfield, Virginia, and Betty Ferguson. *A Guide Book for Milledgeville.* Bulletin of Georgia State College for Wom-

Smith, J. Frazer. *White Pillars.* New York: William Helburn, 1941.

Stoney, Samuel Gaillard. *Plantations of the Carolina Low Country.* Edited by Albert Simons and Samuel Lapham, Jr. Charleston: Carolina Art Association, 1938.

Todd, Sereno Edwards. *Todd's Country Homes.* Philadelphia: Bradley, 1876. Copy belonging to John Linley.

Vaux, Calvert. *Villas and Cottages.* New York: Harper and Brothers, 1857. Copy belonging to John Linley.

Waterman, Thomas Tileston. *The Early Architecture of North Carolina.* Chapel Hill: University of North Carolina Press, 1947.

Woodward, George E. *Woodward's National Architect.* New York: George E. Woodward, 1869. Copy belonging to John Linley.

en, Milledgeville, Georgia, 1949. Vertical file labelled "Milledgeville," Georgia Room, University of Georgia Library.

Schretter, Howard. *A Regional Survey of the Oconee Area.* Prepared for the Oconee Area Planning and Development Commission, 1966.

Sesqui-Centennial of Milledgeville and Baldwin County, Georgia, 1803–1953. Milledgeville, Georgia. Souvenir Program published by the Old Capitol Historical Society. Vertical file labelled "Souvenir Program," Georgia Room, University of Georgia Library.

Shaw, Edward. *Civil Architecture; or, A Complete and Practical System of Building.* Boston: March, Capen and Lyon, 1836. Copy available in the University of Georgia Library.

Sloan, Samuel. *The Model Architect,* vol. 1. Philadelphia: E. S. Jones, 1852. Copy belonging to John Linley.

Index

Owners and Former Owners of Houses Featured*

*Incomplete. All owners not known.

Italic page numbers indicate location of pictures.